Psychologizing

A Personal, Practice-Based Approach to Psychology

Patrick M. Whitehead
Darton State College

ROWMAN & LITTLEFIELD
Lanham • Boulder • New York • London

Associate Editor: Molly White
Marketing Manager: Karin Cholak
Cover Designer: Chloe Batch

Credits and acknowledgments for material borrowed from other sources, and reproduced with permission, appear on the appropriate page within the text.

Published by Rowman & Littlefield
A wholly owned subsidiary of
The Rowman & Littlefield Publishing Group, Inc.
4501 Forbes Boulevard, Suite 200, Lanham, Maryland 20706
https://rowman.com

Unit A, Whitacre Mews, 26-34 Stannary Street, London SE11 4AB,
United Kingdom

British Library Cataloguing in Publication Information Available

Library of Congress Cataloging-in-Publication Data
Names: Whitehead, Patrick M., 1986–
Title: Psychologizing : a personal, practice-based approach to psychology / Patrick M.
    Whitehead, Darton State College.
Description: Lanham : Rowman & Littlefield, 2016. | Includes bibliographical references
    and index.
Identifiers: LCCN 2016033668 (print) | LCCN 2016034054 (ebook) | ISBN
    9781442268722 (hardcover : alk. paper) | ISBN 9781442268739 (pbk. : alk. paper) |
    ISBN 9781442268746 (electronic)
Subjects: LCSH: Psychology—Study and teaching.
Classification: LCC BF77 .W465 2016 (print) | LCC BF77 (ebook) | DDC 150—dc23
LC record available at https://lccn.loc.gov/2016033668

Printed in the United States of America

To Christopher M. Aanstoos

Contents

Preface

Presumably, the idea behind an introductory course is to provide students a firm footing in the breadth of the indicated academic discipline (which is, in this case, psychology). Also, it is assumed that students come into the course with a very rudimentary grasp of said discipline, if any. Furthermore, it is assumed that those who come into the course with some prior knowledge are mistaken (Vaughan 1977). This is to say that these students may also be lumped into the previous category of ignorance. In an "Introduction to [insert academic discipline here]" class, it is the duty of the professor to fill the empty receptacles (the students) who fill her classroom each day with unerring [insert adjective form of academic discipline here] facts. After forty-two days of receptacle filling, the students, now overflowing with inerrant [insert adjective form of academic discipline here] knowledge, get to regurgitate the abstracted gems onto a Scantron Sheet, provided they are competent enough to do so. The student-completed Scantrons are compared with the correct one, and the students are judged on their understanding. Students who pass are free to build upon their now-authorized [insert adjective form of academic discipline here] base; students who fail must survive another forty-two class periods of receptacle filling because it apparently didn't "take" the first time.

This is *not* how this book treats the introductory curriculum it covers. The sample "introduction to . . ." course described above is intended to be a caricature of a college class and not to represent any actual course (or the textbooks accompanying it). If what I described above in any way resembles experiences of learning that you have had in the past, I am deeply sorry for this. With the exception of ease, I fail to find any merit in this style of learning. My convictions about learning may be expressed by an exemplary educator, Eduard Lindeman, from 1926:

> It represents a process by which the [student] learns to become aware of and to evaluate his experience. To do this he cannot begin by studying "subjects" in the hope that some day this information will be useful. On the contrary, he begins by giving attention to situations in which he finds himself, to problems which include obstacles to his self-fulfillment. . . . In this process the teacher finds a new function. She is no longer the oracle who speaks from the platform of authority, but rather the guide, the pointer-outer who also participates in learning in proportion to the vitality and relevancy of her facts and experiences. In short, my conception of student education is this: a cooperative venture in nonauthoritarian, informal learning, the chief purpose of which is to discover the meaning of experience; a quest of the mind which digs down to the roots of the preconceptions which formulate our conduct; a technique of learning for [students] which makes education coterminous with life and hence elevates living itself to the level of adventurous experiment. (160; in Knowles 1989, 73–74)

Some of you are taking this class for some reason other than your own choice. For instance, an adviser may have signed you up for it, or maybe the course is a prerequisite. In these cases, an introduction to psychology is a mere hurdle or roadblock preventing you from being where you want to be. Let us acknowledge and accept that this may very well be the case. This is OK. Keep in mind that, while Psychology Land might not be your choice destination, you can use it to get where you want to go.

Psychology (and I trust this goes for any discipline) is an exceedingly broad and intricately nuanced discipline, and this breadth cannot be sufficiently introduced. You will not leave this class with a firm footing in *the* world of psychology. However, if you engage this course, then you might leave this class with a firm footing in *your* world of psychology. This should be the goal. Indeed, forget about emerging from this class as a psychology expert; focus instead on *taking advantage* of this class in order to facilitate your own goals, motivations, and self-understanding. This may seem a bit unnatural, if not unbelievable, but with a little bit of effort on your part, the transition should be manageable.

At this point, I want you to suspend the notion of taking this class. In fact, despite your enrollment status, imagine that you are on the fence about taking this class, and that what you read below along with your experiences in the first few days of class will be the deciding factors on whether you stay. (Incidentally, this is how I have always treated the classes that I have taken.)

Class-time will be split approximately down the middle between professor-led and student-led activities (the side that the majority falls on will be decided by the class). Professor-led time will begin and end each class. Here is where I get to share *my* footing in psychology. Student-led class-time will consist of, but is not limited to, group workshops, experiments, demonstrations, presentations, and exercises. This is where you get to explore the different ways you might be able to take advantage of psychology for yourself and share your interests, successes, and disappointments with one another. In the past, I have had students find ways to take advantage of psychology to develop their acting skills, improve nurse-practitioner bedside manner, investigate cyberbullying on social-networking sites, interview a diagnosed schizophrenic, explore the mind of a serial killer, analyze and interpret their own dreams, mediate delinquent behavior in school and in the home, focus during clutch moments in athletics, wean a roommate off of smoking, and others.

As you can see, student participation will be integral to this class. What you are looking for in the coursework and material, then, are things that relate to *you* and can be used for *your sake* (or the sake of others in your life). For example, if you read something in the above quote (Lindeman) that you found interesting, confusing, or even incorrect, then write it down and bring it to class to share. This is one way that you connect Psychology Land to your everyday life. In time, the rift between what happens in Psychology Land and what happens in life will begin to merge. Indeed, what good is psychology if it does not inform your everyday life?

To make psychology applicable to your life, you're going to need to identify that which is important to you. This seems relatively straightforward, but it is actually quite complicated. Most students who excel at school—particularly in those whose models are typified by the caricature that began this preface—have become increasingly out of touch with their own interests and desires. These have been replaced by desires imposed upon them by parents, teachers, and maybe other friends. For some of you, this may be characterized by a greater interest in *finishing* school than *being in* school—something of which I am often guilty. So, what can you do about it? I trust that after hearing some other students share their interests and concerns related to this class, the uncertainty regarding the application to life will begin to dissolve.

ACKNOWLEDGMENTS

There are many people without whom this book would never have come together. To begin, I would like to recognize the significant role played by Chris Aanstoos, my teacher and the one to whom this book has been dedicated. For many weeks I tried to find ways to integrate his work into this text—trying to determine which examples, insights, and attitudes might best complement my work here. Then I realized that he is already present in all of this, as he is in my classroom. One of the greatest compliments I have ever been paid regarding my teaching was from a fellow doctoral teaching assistant. She said that I reminded her of Dr. Aanstoos. I hope the same may be said of this text.

In addition to the inspiration and motivation that Chris has supplied, I am also indebted to the entire graduate psychology faculty at the University of West Georgia. It was there that I learned the potential of education as a meaningful process, where I learned that it was okay to be directed by my own insights and intuitions, and that my own unique perspective matters. In many ways, this book is a testament to my graduate education (unless the testimony is a poor one, in which case I take full responsibility).

I would also like to thank the support I have received from the faculty and staff here at Darton State College, chiefly to Dean Wendy Kennedy. Wendy has been supportive of my scholarship from the very first campus visit, from funding conference trips to standing behind me as a teacher and scholar. The support for my writing is particularly impressive when it is recognized that she has no official charge of supporting faculty scholarship, as Darton is primarily a two-year-degree-granting teaching institution. Wendy certainly doesn't make it feel that way. Gratitude is also owed to a few close colleagues for their support and encouragement throughout this process as well: Anne Yanez, Reba Goodin, and Jason Goodner. And the many hapless Darton students who have passed through my classroom must not go unnoticed. They have been the ones to serve as unsolicited reviewers of earlier versions of the manuscript—indeed, before I knew it would become a manuscript at all.

I owe a debt to Hans Skott-Myhre, who looked at me askance when I reported that I would post the completed manuscript online, and to Fred Wertz, who recommended that I consider Rowman & Littlefield as a prospective publisher. Finally, I must thank Molly White, my editor at Rowman & Littlefield, for courageously selling this peculiar textbook to the board, and for the expert reviewers who candidly shared their suggestions and commendations for this work.

Chapter One

Introduction to Psychologizing

This book is a work in progress. By this I mean that the content, insights, definitions, and descriptions found inside are still under a process of transformation. This is fitting because the discipline of psychology is itself a work in progress. Psychology shows great diversity with the types of *questions that it asks*, the *methods of research that it employs*, and even the *type of relationship it asks psychologists to form with the world*. Consider this last one: the type of relationship it asks you to form with the world.

Imagine you are a psychologist interested in understanding another person. How will you relate to this person? Will you get to know them the way you might get to know a friend, allowing them to tell you about themselves? Or will you stand at a safe distance—draped in a white lab coat and armed with testing instruments? In this book, we examine both ways of relating to and understanding people as psychologists. As the title suggests, we are looking for the style that is *personal* and *meaningful*.

The American Psychological Association (APA) currently has about fifty loosely related divisions based on their differences regarding psychological subject matter. Indeed, to suggest that this textbook is anything other than a work in progress would be to misrepresent the discipline of psychology. So, if a completed overview of the state of psychology is out of the question, what is the purpose of a course in general psychology? More specifically, what is the purpose of this book?

The purpose of this textbook is to guide you, the student/reader/scholar, in the process of psychologizing. This is to say that rather than learning the capital-P discipline of psychology, where you are given a compilation of all of the actual thinking conducted by every psychologist from 1887 until today, this textbook aims to get you to participate in the process of psychology. Do you see the difference?

In a typical approach, "Psychology" stands as a mountain to be conquered. "Just four months of this and, if I get better than a C minus, I never have to take it again." It is believed that conquering this mountain will bring certain rewards: "Now I will be able to figure out the behavior of my friends and loved ones." "Now I will have the skill to control those around me." "Now I will know everything there is to know about the mind." This book does not dispense this kind of knowledge. Sorry. Instead, *it aims to get you, the student/reader/scholar, to start looking closely at your own experience and the experiences of those around you.* In this way, you begin to see and understand the meaning of experience as it is lived by your friends and loved ones; understand the ways in which your choices and actions influence those around you; and begin to see how much there still is to learn about people. To repeat, this textbook aims to get you to begin thinking like psychologists by understanding actual persons. Of course, this begins with the assumption that psychology is interested in actual persons.

TWO AIMS OF *PSYCHOLOGIZING*

This approach is motivated by two convictions that have come from the psychologists and educators whom I have studied. I call them convictions because "findings" seems too arrogant. "Convictions" acknowledges that my experiences have played a role in their formation. I suspect that you do not have the patience for me to go into each scholar who has played a part in forming this approach, but let me direct you to the bibliographical references if you are interested in understanding or challenging what follows. These convictions defend why I prefer to call this book *Psychologizing* rather than *Introduction to Psychology*. The purpose of this first part is to defend the approach taken in this textbook. This is followed by a more thorough description of the goals I have for readers of this book—namely, what it means to participate in psychology (that is, psychologizing).

Aim One: De-emphasizing the Collection of Psychological Facts

The first conviction I have that supports my approach has many parts, but they each depend on the following recognition: *there is no generic, unisex, uni-gender, uni-class, uni-race, one-size-fits-all introduction to psychology.* There is no such thing as a "basic psychology course." This means that any introduction to psychology will always emphasize some areas and de-emphasize others. What I'm getting at is that there is no defined curriculum for a general introduction to psychology that all instructors must cover at the risk of forever handicapping their psychology students.

Griggs and Mitchell (2002) were psychology instructors who set out to discover the "core curriculum of psychology." They learned that no such core exists today, *nor* was there one fifty years ago. Findings like these need not be met with defeat but instead may be met with a sigh of relief. Since there is no core that must be memorized, we may now embrace the unique perspectives, insights, and interests each of us brings. This means that ours is a unique classroom, and each of our perspectives will be important to consider. Maybe we can even transform the discipline. By the way: twenty-first-century psychology has a big change coming.

This century has already witnessed the passage from the human to the posthuman (Braidotti 2013; Wolfe 2009) or nonhuman (Grusin 2015). Psychology has largely been devoted to what it means to be a person *in the twentieth century*. But many of you already understand that being a person with a smartphone in the twenty-first century is significantly different from being one without *any* mobile devices. What it means to be a person is changing. You can be the one to develop a psychology for that.

Rather than handicapping students by limiting thought to twentieth-century superstitions about what it means to be human, students who are encouraged to psychologize will have the freedom to challenge these. An example of this might be a challenge to the superstition that a face-to-face relationship is always preferable to a technologically mediated one. That is: a date that includes hand holding and dinner at a restaurant is better than one that takes place five hundred miles apart and through video chat.

Finally, presenting psychology as a complete and unerring discipline has the disadvantage of turning students into fact-gathering automatons. You will not be expected to swallow and regurgitate facts. You will see in chapter 3 that doing so is the *opposite* of learning. Instead, you are encouraged to be curious, intuitive, spontaneous, and enthusiastic *psychologizers*.

Consider what it would mean if there were such a thing as a complete and perfect collection of psychological facts. Now imagine that there was some procedure for getting future psychologists to memorize each of these. Would this not result in a perfect psychology program? Hell, no. This sounds dreadful. Such knowledge, Alfred North Whitehead claims, "is the most useless bore on God's earth" (1957, 1). Consider the following degree program that Whitehead has observed, modified to more closely resemble the psychology major:

> The solution which I am urging, is to eradicate the fatal disconnection of subjects which kills the vitality of our modern curriculum. There is only one subject-matter for education, and that is Life in all its manifestations. Instead of this single unity, we offer children—[Introduction to Psychology], from which nothing follows; [Research Methods], from which nothing follows; [Personality Theories], from which nothing follows; History [and Systems], from which nothing follows; a Couple of [Therapeutic Techniques], never mastered. . . . Can such a list be said to represent Life? As it is known in the midst of living it? The best that can be said of it is, that it is a rapid table of

contents which a deity might run over in his mind while he was thinking of
creating a world, and has not yet determined how to put it together. (6–7)

In the absence of personal and meaningful application, even the most
thorough curriculum remains separate from the lives of students. Whitehead
anticipates the failure of content-directed teaching by emphasizing the over-
use of "detail":

> Whatever be the detail with which you cram your student, the chance of his
> meeting in after-life exactly that detail is almost infinitesimal; and if he does
> meet it, he will probably have forgotten what you taught him about it. The
> really useful training yields a comprehension of a few general principles with a
> thorough grounding in the way they apply to a variety of concrete details. In
> subsequent practice, men will have forgotten your particular details; but they
> will remember by an unconscious common sense how to apply principles to
> immediate circumstances. Your learning is useless to you till you have lost
> your text-books, burnt your lecture notes, and forgotten the minutiae which
> you learnt by heart for the examination. What, in the way of detail, you
> continually require will stick in your memory as obvious facts like the sun and
> moon; and what you casually require can be looked up in any work of refer-
> ence. The function of a University is to enable you to shed details in favor of
> principles. (26)

Whitehead's final point is the goal of psychologizing: to learn the principles
of psychology through its practice. Doing so recognizes that the psychological facts change as people change. Familiarizing yourself with the principles
of how to look more closely as a psychologist will ensure that the discipline
of psychology continues to follow its subject matter—namely, people.

The second conviction that supports my approach is that learning which
emphasizes trust is superior to one which emphasizes distrust. This includes
trust in oneself and trust in the process of learning. Integral to this trust is the
relationship between learner and learned. This is where I introduce Whitehead's curious disciplinary gerund: it is where we learn how "psychologizing" comes to replace "psychology." Trust has unfortunately become an
obstacle in the contemporary classroom. Students who do not trust their own
ability or, more likely, students who do not trust that the school recognizes
their abilities as important are forced to cheat or fail. The system has already
failed them. Similarly, instructors find themselves going to great lengths to
separate original thought from plagiarized thought. This culture of distrust
mars the classroom. The only way to replace distrust with trust in this context
is to replace "fact giving" with "knowledge production." The teacher-as-
knowledge-dispenser and student-as-knowledge-receptacle classroom is ex-
changed for a more egalitarian classroom that values and esteems the imagination and creativity of both instructor and students. In addition to respect-
ing, valuing, and challenging students, Whitehead's approach avoids the

problematic consequences that stem from "banking" pedagogies as outlined by radical educator Paolo Freire (2012b).

Aim Two: Trusting Yourself and the Learning Process

I argued in the previous section that teaching and learning do not have to occur at the expense of the unique strengths, talents, and gifts of the students and the instructor. In psychologizing, psychology instructors and students come together and create something new in the world of psychology by closely examining their own experience and the experiences of others. We acknowledge that *a greater investment can always be made in better understanding a person.* Students can take advantage of the expertise and resources that the instructor provides, and the instructor takes advantage of the eager and imaginative minds of students. Indeed, the instructors are old students and the students, young instructors. Whitehead encourages college instructors to treat their students like adults; indeed, he finds it imperative to do so. This is the first important detail in establishing a classroom that features trust. Whitehead writes,

> During the school period the student has been mentally bending over his desk; at the University he should stand up and look around. For this reason it is fatal if the first year at the University be frittered away in going over the old work in the old spirit. (1957, 26)

An introductory classroom is full of expert learners, untrained psychologists, and unique, imaginative, and profoundly curious people. Students are not hopelessly indolent, though much of their formal schooling may suggest that this is the case. These are the classrooms that operate under what Freire has called "banking methodology." See whether this sounds familiar:

> The teacher talks about reality as if it were motionless, static, compartmentalized, and predictable. Or else he expounds on a topic completely alien to the existential experience of the students. His task is to "fill" the students with the contents of his narration—contents which are detached from reality, disconnected from the totality that engendered them and could give them significance. Words are emptied of their concreteness and become a hollow, alienated, and alienating verbosity. (2012b, 71)

Students have spent the past twelve years working their way through formal schooling, and now they have been deposited into the land of psychology, where their instructors stand at the fore. "The students are alive, and the purpose of education is to stimulate and guide their self-development" (Whitehead 1957, v).

On entering primary school, it could easily be argued, the most difficult phases of learning have already been completed. On entering preschool,

children already have a basic grasp of language—and any adult who is struggling to learn a foreign language can explain the difficulty. Toddlers also
exhibit gross and fine motor control—abilities that stroke patients will explain take a great deal of effort to regain when lost. Moreover, these children
even have a developing awareness of personal interests, sociality, music, art,
and so on. Indeed, by venturing into a preschool classroom you are sure to be
met with expert learners. What is more, they will be having fun doing so.

When the emphasis shifts from content to a process that trusts the participation of the student, a transformative classroom takes shape. Clark Moustakas explains:

> [The teacher] must allow the learner's point of view to emerge, be treated with
> respect, and valued. During the initial meetings an atmosphere of mutual ac-
> ceptance, trust, and love must develop which helps free the individual partici-
> pants, including the teacher. The teacher, with his whole being, actively en-
> courages each individual to be and become more fully himself. He recognizes
> the individual perceptions of each person as worthy. (1972, 26)

It is only after the lay psychologists' points of view are allowed to emerge
that knowledge is created and the process of psychologizing begins. Freire
describes a process very similar to what is intended by psychologizing:
"Knowledge emerges only through invention and re-invention, through the
restless, impatient, continuing, hopeful inquiry human beings pursue in the
world, with the world, and with each other" (2012b, 72).

I call this collective production of knowledge or process of learning
psychology "psychologizing." I have borrowed the unusual gerund from the
description that Whitehead gave to his philosophy courses. Knowles (1989),
one of Whitehead's first doctoral students, explains that Whitehead was not
teaching a course on "philosophy" as if it were set in stone. Instead, he
encouraged his students to "philosophize." By this I understand that students
were given the freedom and trust to participate in the dialogue *as* young,
inexperienced philosophers. Inspired by this, I have found it important to
allow students to "psychologize" in order to understand psychology. This
means making mistakes, criticizing the readings, privileging their personal
biases, and, above all, wondering deeply about the topic of people. This also
has the advantage of transforming psychology as a thing into a process.
Reared in classrooms of Freire's "banking" sort, students meet this new
demand with considerable caution. However, as soon as they realize that
they, too, can be insightful, they will blow you away. I maintain that this is
what contemporary psychology demands.

The twentieth-century task of psychology is wearing thin. The dissatisfaction with mainstream psychological methods—methods that emphasize
psychological fact over the understanding of persons—is explored at the
beginning of chapter 2. Psychology is in danger of being dissolved as a

twenty-first-century academic discipline. If it cannot transform to meet the demands of a rapidly transforming world, it will cease to exist as an autonomous discipline and will instead be absorbed into the disciplines of education, cognitive science, philosophy, and biology. During the past decade, the humanities were facing this crisis. The president of the Dutch Consortium of European Sciences concluded that the humanities disciplines had repeatedly failed to evolve beyond a twentieth-century anthropomorphism and anthropocentrism. These perspectives understand that the world can be known only insofar as it matters to humans. Since the humanities include creative writing, rhetoric, literature, cultural studies, foreign languages, and philosophy, it is easy to see how the human perspective is integral to each. However, some have argued that these disciplines have failed at investigating the role the environment plays in shaping culture or even in attempting to understand the role the environment plays in noncultural ways—that is, in understanding the world before or after humans. The humanities have responded in impressive fashion, including an entire book series devoted to the posthuman (Posthumanities series from the University of Minnesota Press). Psychology is next on the list to lose its credential as a still-relevant discipline.

In exploring an introductory course from the vantage point of Alfred North Whitehead, we have begun the process of outlining how this approach will be different from more traditional approaches. I have called this approach psychologizing. Thus far, I have hoped to encourage students and instructors to *trust their intuition* and to *teach and learn from their unique creativity and conviction*. The stale, boring, and tedious "Introduction to Psychology" course might even become as alive as the students and instructors that occupy it. In this textbook, psychologizing is allowed and even encouraged. Life and "Introduction to Psychology" are no longer kept separate but begin to intertwine. This is the goal of this book. I have found phenomenology to be an insightful way of intertwining everyday experience with beginning to think like a psychologist. The following section explains what is meant by psychologizing as well as the significance of phenomenology for this project.

WHAT IS MEANT BY "PSYCHOLOGIZING"; OR, HOW TO PSYCHOLOGIZE

From the previous discussion, you are probably developing some ideas about how this approach to introductory psychology is different from the more traditional and mainstream approaches from high school and maybe even college. A more comprehensive description of these differences follows in the next chapter. For now, our task is to outline the project of psychologizing. This is, after all, what you will be asked to do throughout the duration of this book. Psychologizing is the practice of thinking like a psychologist, and it comprises three key elements. Each of these elements plays a part in understanding the experience of persons. *Experience is the raw data of all empirical, scientific knowledge, and it is our task as psychologists to understand experiences from the vantage point of people who live them.* Since this is precisely the task of phenomenology, I can merge the two descriptions together. Thus, the reader may understand that by "thinking like a psychologist," I intend "thinking like a phenomenological psychologist." You will find in the next chapter that not all psychologists are interested in understanding experience, and this is the reason for the distinction. The three key elements to psychologizing include (1) the adoption of a different attitude in relation to psychological phenomena, (2) an emphasis on first-person and subjective knowledge, and (3) scrupulous attention to the meaning that subjects express in their experience. These three elements overlap a great deal, so each description also includes the significance of the other two. Since understanding experience has been the project of phenomenology, we can use this tradition to help understand how a psychologizing program might be achieved.

Adopting a Different Attitude toward Psychological Phenomena

Before getting into the differences in attitude that are promoted when one practices how to think like a psychologist, we need to define one of these terms: phenomena. "Phenomena" is the plural form of phenomenon, so we will begin with the latter. When I first heard this word, even in the context of psychology, I immediately thought of the John Travolta movie of the same name. In the movie, "phenomenon" had the connotation of something inexplicable, magical, or mystical. While any of these terms could accurately describe what happens when you begin to look more deeply into experience, it is not what is intended here. For psychology, the term "phenomenon" gets its significance from the modern philosophy of science, specifically that of logical positivism. A detour into the history of this term will help set up the project of psychologizing.

Logical positivists believe that the world can be understood entirely, leaving nothing out. The term "positivism" indicates a single positive universe, and it is the task of scientists to slowly uncover all the parts that make it up. Positivism can also be used to describe some of the projects in psychology. For example, the assumption that there could be an introductory psychology class that covers all of psychology's bases is a positivist assumption. This is because it maintains that there are a definite number of bases and that these bases are fundamental to psychology. The term "logical" in logical positivism means what you think it means: it is the assumption that the positive universe can be put together based on the rules of rationalism and logic.

Here's why this is important for psychology: in the nineteenth century, the century in which psychology got its start, logical positivists agreed that there were two ways of understanding the world. The world could be understood in physical terms and in phenomenal terms. An example will help illustrate the differences here.

Consider the example of a rock. A rock can be explored physically or phenomenologically. The rock's hardness, mass, volume, composition, density, and boiling point can all be tested and measured based on the rules of physics and geology. *This is how the physical rock can be understood.* But when we encounter a rock, we do not encounter it in terms of its physical qualities: we are in touch with its *phenomenal qualities*. Place a rock in your hand, and you will recognize a familiar texture, coldness, and heft; you may even have a particular memory of a similar rock from the past that either sweetens or sours the experience. Whatever the case, *quantities* of mass and hardness, while important constituents in the experience of holding a rock, do not define this experience. *There is an incongruity or difference between physical quantities and phenomenal qualities.* This incongruity is where we begin looking as psychologists. To be fair, psychology has had a long history of privileging the physical aspects of logical positivism. This is because of a meeting held in Vienna in 1922 during which a group of philosophers decided that trying to understand phenomenal qualities was a waste of time. They instead decided to focus solely on the physical quantities because these could be measured and verified. The disappointment psychologists have experienced with this approach are explained in the following chapter. Indeed, measuring a person is not a very interesting way of getting to know them.

With this brief overview of the differences between physical quantities and phenomenal qualities, the reader may begin to see what the psychologist's task might be. Psychologists recognize that physical quantities are easy to measure and are important for understanding experience, but this does not mean psychologists should look here and nowhere else. Psychologists also recognize that although phenomenal qualities are difficult to articulate and understand, they are important for understanding experience. In experience, physical quantities and phenomenal qualities are interconnected: you cannot have one without also having the other. How must one begin navigating this complicated relationship between physical and phenomenal? This brings up the first part of adopting a different attitude: avoiding the tendency to settle for any immediate conclusions regarding experience.

Avoiding the Tendency to Jump to Conclusions

When faced with a psychological conundrum, it is quite easy to settle on the first reasonable explanation. This tendency must be avoided. Remember that it is experiences we are interested in understanding, and it is not useful if these are immediately explained away. For example, you might be interested in the psychology of road rage. Without giving it much thought, you could probably come up with an explanation as to why this occurs. However, *psychologists are not content to settle on any reasonable explanation*. If you have had this experience, then you understand that it would be difficult to sum it up with any single causal factor. *Indeed, the experience of road rage occurs within the context of other life events, and any attempt to do justice to the psychology of road rage must consider these additional factors.* By avoiding the tendency to select the first explanation that comes along, psychologists may look more deeply into the experience and learn much more about it.

We already find that thinking like a psychologist is quite a bit different from the usual ways of understanding our world of experience. Psychologizing is not just "common sense." This is because it is typical to feel like we know what is occurring in the world around us. *But as soon as we are asked to think like a psychologist, we find that we are largely out of touch with experience.* A person might recognize that it is difficult to send a text message to her or his romantic interest, but can a deeper meaning be found in this? Do we see the depth of meaning in such an experience? A person might customarily send several hundred text messages per week, but for some reason this single instance is more difficult. As psychologists, we want to begin peeling back the layers from the surface of this experience. In doing so, we find that sending this text message bears all sorts of pressures from the present, past, and future. We learn about the person as well as the phenomenon of sending a text message to a romantic interest, and as a result, we develop a greater appreciation for both.

Consider what is meant by understanding this experience of sending a text message. Such an investigation would likely uncover uncertainties from the present: personal identity, lifestyle choices, priorities, character, and superstitions and beliefs about the connection between happiness and relationship status; unresolved conflicts from the past: failed relationships, successful relationships; and even anxiety about the future: that this casual conversation could change life forever or fail to change life at all. It is easy to imagine a host of more insightful examples of the possible meaning such a text message might have, *but we cannot know for certain until we ask a person about their experience of this*. This is the purpose behind the second element—the emphasis on personal, subjective knowledge. Since it is the person in which the physical and phenomenal worlds collide, it is to the person that we must turn. Before the importance of personal, subjective knowledge is discussed, one more aspect of the psychological attitude must be addressed. Like the familiar tendency to come up with an explanation that covers up a unique experience, psychologists must also avoid assuming that an experience can be understood by a simple fact.

Avoiding the Tendency to Explain Phenomena with the Insistence on "Fact"

By avoiding the tendency to explain away psychological phenomena with the first idea that comes to mind, one is forced to look more carefully. As a result, experience is found to be much deeper and more nuanced than the way it is typically seen. This is an important first step in thinking like a psychologist, but this does not conclude the ways in which your attitude must change. The next tendency to avoid is *the assumption that there is a single best explanation for the phenomenon in question.*

The ability to understand every effect in terms of its cause is a gem of modernity bestowed on us by the likes of Galileo and Newton. This kind of thinking begins by asking the question: Why? Asking "why" is a demand made on the universe to explain itself. It also reduces the events of the world to billiard balls on a pool table. To be sure, asking this question has yielded a powerful system of controlling environments and people, but it is not itself a complete explanation. Newton, after all, relies on the assumption that objects begin in motion. Even the discipline of mechanical physics, caricatured by the pool table, has had to suspend the question of why for more than one hundred years now and has instead been forced to understand the interaction of physical bodies in terms of quantum probability, alinear causality, and entanglement. Thanks, Einstein. This means that over the past hundred years it has been a position of arrogance to assume that a single explanation could be used to understand a physical event. This is rapidly becoming the theme of science into the twenty-first century, and fortunately, psychologists are beginning to catch on.

As practicing psychologists, we recognize that experience has many layers of meaning as well as many contexts in which it can be understood. Consider the road-rage phenomenon once again, only this time as an example of the many contexts within which it might be understood. Is the temporal context important in understanding this experience? Here the instrument of a timeline might be useful. In the very center of the timeline we make a point indicating the experience of road rage. Is what occurred before this dot important? How about those things that are expected to happen afterward? This timeline can also be very narrow: the events of a single day. Or it can be very broad: the life of a person. In the broader case, we might ask: Is it necessary for a driver to have had many experiences driving in order for this phenomenon to occur? Or is it possible for road rage to occur during someone's first time behind the wheel?

By zooming out on the road-rage experience, it is quite easy to see the importance of temporal context. The same can be said of spatial contexts (e.g., on which streets this occurs), social contexts (e.g., who is present, who one is leaving behind, toward whom one is traveling, and even how one views oneself as a skilled or unskilled driver), and physiological contexts (what occurs in one's body as this event unfolds: heart rate, breathing, stom-ach tightness, tension in the neck, clenching of fists, maybe even shouting). Moreover, these contexts are interrelated in certain ways. As psychologists, we know that in order to understand experiences, we must consider the greater contexts in which they occur. This is to say that each context is helpful in understanding the road-rage experience.

Here's a test; see how you do: Sheila is driving her car. She experiences road rage. Why has this happened?

The first tendency is to come up with a familiar explanation as to why this occurs. As practicing psychologists, *we avoid this*. The next tendency to avoid is the assumption that some*thing* explains why it has occurred, even if we don't know what this is yet. This requires that the experimenter decide *which* context is important and, more specifically, *what it is* within that context that explains the road-rage phenomenon. To solve this riddle, the experimenter controls all contexts except one. If you just thought to yourself, "Oops! That is an impossible task," then you're starting to get it. Indeed, the assumption that context can be controlled by brilliant methodological design is an extension of the assumption that an experience can be understood by a single causal factor. If these two tendencies are out, then how do we begin to understand the psychology of road rage? Let's figure this out by returning to Sheila: Sheila is driving her car. She experiences road rage. Why has this happened?

There's a problematic suggestion in this question that forces the reader into the assumption that there is a simple answer. Resist this suggestion. In fact, cross out the question that starts with "Why . . . ?" This question assumes that the experience can be understood without asking Sheila about it. These answers assume that experiences occur independently of the people who live them. This is the nineteenth-century belief that the world can be divided into physical and phenomenal categories. As practicing psycholo-gists, *we begin with the assumption that in human experience, the physical and the phenomenal are always together*. Therefore, to learn about this, we must ask people. For Sheila's case, we will ask her, "What was this experi-ence like?" and see what she has to teach us about road rage.

Emphasizing Personal, Subjective Knowledge

If you have succeeded in following the first element of beginning to think like a psychologist, then your attitude regarding psychological phenomena will be much different than it was before you began reading. By avoiding the tendency to come up with and settle on the first "commonsense" explanation, you acknowledge that you might be able to learn something new. Indeed, through this study, you might develop a deeper sense of understanding about yourself and others. By avoiding the assumption that there is a single cause behind a phenomenon or that the phenomenon could ever in principle be understood in its entirety, you acknowledge that there are many ways of making sense of an experience—none of which should be immediately discarded. So how might one begin such a colossal task?

Many methods have been developed throughout the history of psychology, and with our newly developed attitude, *we recognize that each of these has unique insights to offer*. Indeed, I maintain that any of these methods, if conducted with the attitude described above, is a valuable tool to a practicing psychologist. Many of these will be explored in the pages that follow. However, since we have established early on that we are interested in understanding the experiences had by others and by ourselves, we will depend on methods that *emphasize the meaning of our experiences*. We have already seen that an experience has many layers. How do we determine which one to start with? The answer to this question is actually quite simple, but it goes against many decades of scientific practice: *we begin by trusting the subject*.

Suppose that we were to decide we are interested in the psychology of road rage and that we have also had the good fortune of meeting Sheila, a person who has reported having had this experience. How do we know which of the many layers of experience are most important for understanding her road-rage incident? We allow her to indicate what seems important and what does not seem important by explaining her experience. But as she begins to show you the way, it is important to maintain the attitude discussed in point 1, avoiding the tendency to jump to conclusions.

Trusting the subject begins with the assumption that *subjective knowledge* is important. Subjective knowledge is the knowledge that can be verified only through first-person experience. First-person knowledge is the knowledge that you gain by experiencing something firsthand. A first-person account of a musical concert means that you have attended said concert: it was loud; "my ears were ringing." It is often compared with objective knowledge, whose verification is thought to occur through third-person means. Third-person knowledge is the knowledge that comes to you from an external source. A third-person account of a musical concert is one that discusses the concert in general: it was loud enough for the majority of ears to begin ringing. A more thorough discussion of the differences between subjective and objective forms of knowledge is the task of the following chapter, but for now a simple detail is worth mentioning. As psychologists, whose business it is to understand experience, we know only too well that it is impossible to arrive at a piece of objective knowledge without going through subjective channels. This is to say that even an experimental psychologist (a person) who is vacuum-sealed inside a hazmat suit and shielded from her subjects behind a one-way mirror is still the one collecting data, data which she can understand only through her own senses. No matter how far she tries to distance herself from the experiment, it is still she who has come up with the questions and design and she who must make meaningful sense in interpreting the data (or throw it out). This is to say that there can be no observation that has been collected with perfect objectivity.

With a promissory note to discuss the importance of trusting the subject in the subsequent chapter, we may turn to our final element of thinking like psychologists. Let us first review what we have accomplished so far. To practice thinking like psychologists, we have begun with a shift in attitude: this includes the tendency to come up with the first explanation and thereby ignore the experience as well as the assumption that any single explanation will be sufficient for understanding the experience in question. While this shift in attitude certainly makes the task seem enormous, the second element to thinking like a psychologist provides us with a basic starting place: trusting the subject. After the requirements involved in our shift in attitude, the condition of trusting the subject is accepted with considerable relief. It is understood that subjects who describe their experience will indicate what is important about it. By pairing these first two elements together, it is understood that psychologists must listen to descriptions of experience without giving explanations or assuming that any one explanation will be sufficient. This process leads to the final element of thinking like a psychologist: scrupulous attention to detail.

Paying Scrupulous Attention to the Meaning Subjects Express in Their Descriptions

I began by telling you what *not* to do when thinking like a psychologist. Then I told you *where* to look for data that will inform your understanding of experience. This final section tells you *what* to look for more specifically. The assumption we begin with regarding an experience is that it is always structured, and this structure always indicates the meaning the experience has for the person who lives through it. This assumption actually stems from the psychology laboratory—specifically, the tradition of perception theory known as Gestalt. Gestalt is examined more closely in the chapter about perception, so for now we will only concern ourselves with the facts that experiences are always structured and that these structures demonstrate the meanings a particular experience has for the person living through it. The following description of this comes from Ernest Keen, who has been instrumental in the development of this work:

> One way to clarify experience is to seek what events *mean* to us. In asking this question, we discover that conscious experience has a certain *structure*. Indeed, we might say that the "structuredness" of experience *is* the meaningfulness of experience. Structureless experience would be meaningless experience. (1982, 19)

And he continues, describing more specifically the task we have before us in trying to understand the structure of experience:

> The structure of experience is more or less implicit, but it is absolutely critical for the meanings that events have for us. Or, stated more accurately, because meaning *is* structure, we should say that *meaning* is more or less implicit in experience. Phenomenological psychology seeks to articulate explicitly the implicit structure and meaning of human experience. (19)

We will begin with the statement that experiences are always meaningful, for it is on this assumption that we find the structure of experience. "But what about a meaningless experience? Certainly *this* must be devoid of meaning." There are meaningless gestures, meaningless clichés, meaningless gifts, meaningless platitudes, and meaningless expressions. Still, each of these examples indicates a meaningful experience. The experience that someone's gesture was a meaningless one is not to say that it failed to register any impression. If this were the case, then a more appropriate response might be: "I don't understand what was intended by such and such a gesture." To say that it is a meaningless gesture is to indicate that it failed to express a particular type of meaning, *and this tells you much about the person's experience.* Consider: a card sent to the widowed woman is experienced as a meaningless gesture only when what was hoped for was a visitor. Here the meaningless gesture is perceived as such only against the backdrop of receiving a visitor. Even in the experience of meaninglessness we come to understand psychological phenomena and the people who live them more deeply.

Once it becomes comfortable to suspend any initial judgments regarding the reason for an experience, and you no longer expect that any experience will be easily reducible to a single causal factor, then discerning the structure of experience will become much easier. Consider the above examples of meaninglessness. If you were content with the first simple explanation, then your investigation would be over! It may be concluded that road rage or writing a poem or failing a college class are all meaningless experiences. We resist the tendency of establishing the truth of these experiences by lingering in their descriptions a little while longer. Indeed, you might even think out loud: "That you should describe your experience as *meaningless* is very peculiar." This will encourage a subject to return to the experience she called meaningless and rearticulate what was *meant* by this. Since psychologists are keen on the multilayeredness of experience, you are especially interested in what this subject indicates about the context in which her experience of meaninglessness was had.

Before concluding the introduction, I would like to provide an example of what is meant by the shift in attitude required for psychologizing. This example comes from Eugene Gendlin.

AN EXAMPLE OF PSYCHOLOGIZING:
HOW TO LISTEN LIKE A PSYCHOLOGIST

During a successful career as a psychotherapist and professor at University of Chicago, Eugene Gendlin wrote a book with a bold objective: to teach lay-persons how to understand and solve psychological problems like famous psychotherapists do. Does his objective sound familiar? Gendlin calls his method *focusing*, and he has directed his manual to the nonprofessional. In a section called the "listening manual," Gendlin explains the importance of being a good listener. We can use this example of listening to demonstrate how we might begin to think like psychologists.

Gendlin's "listening manual" is but a part of his larger program of *focusing*, and we are going to look at only a small part of what he describes as listening. So what follows is only a narrow sliver of what Gendlin has provided. To begin, he acknowledges that we generally do a poor job of listening to one another. This is a problem if we have already established that we are interested in the experience of others. Gendlin argues that if one learns how to listen, "People can tell you much more . . . than can ever happen in ordinary interchanges" (1978, 135). Okay, so he thinks that we learn more by listening, but how is this different from what we normally do in a conversation? Gendlin explains:

> In ordinary social interchange we nearly always stop each other from getting very far inside. Our advice, reactions, encouragements, reassurances, and well-intentioned comments actually prevent people from feeling understood. Try following someone carefully without putting anything of your own in. (1978, 135–36)

When you listen to someone describe an experience, do your comments encourage them to go more deeply into their experience or to stop short? Sometimes we say something like "Oh yeah, I know what you're talking about," as if to suggest: "You can stop now because I already understand what you're saying." This would be an example of allowing the first possible explanation to cover over the possibility of learning something new. Since we're interested in thinking like psychologists, we try to avoid this tendency. On this point, Gendlin explains that with listening, you must "never introduce topics that the other person didn't express. Never push your own interpretations. Never mix in your own ideas" (1978, 136). If your goal is to better understand the experience of another, then you would do well to follow these three rules that Gendlin provides. We might also use them as reminders of our task of trying to think like psychologists.

SUMMARY

In this introductory chapter, I first defended the nontraditional orientation of this book's approach by comparing the more typical version of the introduction to psychology course with this version: introduction to psychologizing. In the latter version, the version this book follows, you are asked to practice thinking like psychologists. Doing so recognizes that psychology is a diverse and changing discipline, so it is more important for you to learn how to think like psychologists than to learn the facts of psychology. This approach also has the advantage of preparing you to revolutionize psychology because you are not limited by the litany of superstitions in the history of psychological thought. Another element of a course that emphasizes psychologizing is that it is built on trust: in yourself as a student and in the learning process. This supplies the confidence required for becoming a revolutionary thinker in psychology.

The second objective of the chapter was to give an overview of what is intended by "psychologizing." I have used phenomenology to help us understand how this might be done. I chose phenomenology because it has been developed as a way of investigating and coming to a better understanding of experience. Thinking like a psychologist comprises three elements: (1) adopting a different attitude in relation to psychological phenomena, (2) emphasizing personal and subjective knowledge, and (3) paying scrupulous attention to the meaning that subjects express in their descriptions. I followed with an example of psychologizing supplied by Gendlin's "listening manual."

In the following chapter, we explore the disciplinary objective of psychology. This is where you will have to ask yourself: what am I interested in and motivated by as a psychologist? The answer to this question will shape the types of experiments you design, the questions you find important to ask, and the relationship you take to your work as a practicing psychologist.

PSYCHOLOGIZING IN ACTION

giving their experience, if they are honest in their expres-
derful. —Perls 1974, 77

Accompanying each chapter of this book will be an instance of Psychologizing in Action (PIA). These are included to demonstrate what each chapter is talking about by providing descriptions of experience—that is, actual instances of psychologizing. The first of these describes their purpose.

While reading this introductory chapter, you have likely realized that this text isn't like most introductory textbooks: it doesn't ask you to memorize facts—indeed, it de-emphasizes the importance of such facts. Instead, it asks you to form a different relationship to psychological phenomena by trying to understand a person's experience. Fritz Perls calls this *"isism."* This, he describes, "is called the phenomenological or existential approach. Nobody can at any given moment be different from what he is at that moment, including the wish to be different" (1972, 210). This he discerns from *aboutism. Aboutism* is what most general psychology textbooks accomplish. "Aboutism," Perls explains, "is science, description, gossiping, avoidance of involvement, round and round the mulberry bush" (1972, 210). Aboutists can talk about facts, about people, about concepts, and about psychology without recognizing in it anything personal—without allowing it to be meaningful. "People who have surrounded themselves with thick verbal defenses will accept and argue with such terms and spew back sentences, but they themselves remain untouched. They are *about*ists" (1972, 209).

These sections provide descriptions of experience—the raw data of psychology. Descriptions do not explain why something has happened but how it has happened to an actual person. They recognize the significance and depth that our experiences have and that no concept could ever sufficiently capture. For example, the chapter 11 PIA looks at the experience of loneliness. We find from Moustakas's description that loneliness is much deeper than simply being by oneself or feeling cut off from others. As we read his description, we see that there is an ineffable quality to being lonely.

My hope is that the descriptions in the PIAs will encourage you to look into the depth of not only your own personal experience but the experiences of those around you as well.

Chapter Two

Methods

Let us ask the questions: suppose I wish to know more about the nature of the human person—about you, for instance, or about some other particular person—what is the most promising and most fruitful way to go about it? How useful are the assumptions and methods and conceptualizations of classical science? Which approach is best? Which techniques? Which tests and which measurements? Which a priori assumptions about the nature of knowledge? What do we mean by the word "know"? —Maslow 1966, 6

In this epigraph, Maslow provides an insightful place to start for this chapter. He asks the question you face as someone interested in learning how to think like a psychologist: What is the most promising and most fruitful way to go about learning more about yourself and others—learning about psychology? Maslow has identified an appropriate first step for beginning to think like a psychologist. He reasons that you must first identify your subject matter: for you, this will be actual persons. You must then identify the types of questions you are interested in answering: these are featured as the topic of each chapter from here on out. Only *then* can you decide on the techniques, assumptions, and methods to employ. When I first read this question, I nearly fell over. I had never thought about psychology this way before. *I had learned that psychologists must first master the psychological methods before learning how to ask the questions.* The assumption was that a single method might fit every conceivable problem. Maslow observes this problem in psychology: "I suppose it is tempting, if the only tool you have is a hammer, to treat everything as if it were a nail" (1966, 15–16).

In this chapter, I review the approach to psychology that begins by establishing its method and only *then* asking questions. The problem with this approach is that it forces problems into preestablished methods. This is a Procrustean fallacy. King Procrustes, as the story goes, has a bed in his guest room. The bed is exactly six feet long. Whenever guests come to visit, King Procrustes makes sure that they fit into his guest bed: if they are taller than six feet, then he cuts off any excess height; if they are shorter than six feet, then he pulls on their arms and legs until they are six feet. In this way, King Procrustes is able to accommodate all his guests in his guest bedroom. We recognize that King Procrustes makes the mistake of making his guests fit the bed and not the other way around. The bed is, after all, intended *for* the guest. As psychologists, we must not fit our problems to our methods. Put differently, we must be careful not to let our methods determine our problems but instead allow our problems to determine our methods. Unfortunately, the Procrustean fallacy is a familiar one in the history of psychology, and it has even become mainstream. In the following section, I use Keith Stanovich (2012) to explain the only method that psychologists ought to practice—namely, the theory-driven and data-based experimental method.

TWO APPROACHES TO PSYCHOLOGY: OBJECTIVE AND SUBJECTIVE

The overview of the method-focused approach to psychology is followed by a brief review of the disappointment with which this approach has been met by psychologists, featuring prominent psychologists from each of the past three decades. Then we turn our attention to a problem-focused approach. This discussion features Maslow's *Psychology of Science*, and it serves as an exemplar of how you will learn to practice psychology. I'll use the examples of Wertz (2011) and Giorgi (2009) to demonstrate the contemporary significance of this approach.

Thinking Straight about Psychology

Keith Stanovich is a prominent experimental psychologist at an internationally esteemed department of psychology. His undergraduate methods textbook, *How to Think Straight about Psychology*, is currently in its tenth edition. Its success is understandable given Stanovich's optimistic perspective of psychology's status among the sciences as well as his nuts-and-bolts approach to its practice. This is important for a discipline that has had a history of struggling with its identity and status as a natural science. Stanovich argues quite compellingly that psychology is indeed a science, and he describes how you or I might become psychological scientists too. He begins by defining the discipline of psychology:

> It is easy to argue that there are really *only* two things that justify psychology as an independent discipline. The first is that psychology studies the full range of human and nonhuman behavior with the techniques of science. The second

is that the applications that derive from this knowledge are *scientifically* based. Were this not true, there would be no reason for psychology to exist. (2012, 6)

In one fell swoop, Stanovich asserts that psychology is a science and that it is distinct from the other sciences. This is a relief to anybody who is interested in practicing psychology and who also wishes to be taken seriously: psychologists *are* scientists. Furthermore, his maneuver identifies its subject matter (human and nonhuman behavior) and method (scientific method).

Here's how it works: come up with a topic in which you are interested, for instance, Internet blogging. Now reduce "Internet blogging" to human and nonhuman behavior. Notice what has already happened. This approach, however attractive at the start, has demanded that we begin by reducing a complicated experiential event into a set of observable behaviors—moreover, behaviors that can be controlled, manipulated, and measured in the manner that the scientific method demands.

We find that with Stanovich's approach, the subject matter must immediately be fitted to the method. *This, of course, has certain advantages.* Indeed, the experimental method has been a useful way of asking and answering questions about nature for many centuries. Psychologists may choose to benefit from this heritage, and Stanovich explains how. "Clearly, then, the first and most important step that anyone must take in understanding psychology is to realize that its defining feature is that it is the data-based scientific study of behavior" (2012, 7). *Those of you who are interested in becoming experimental psychologists may wish to write down this definition and practice observing the world in this way.* You can, after all, psychologize in ways that are not necessarily applauded in this book. But for now, let us consider the experimental psychology approach from the starting point that we selected from the outset: we are interested in understanding the experience of others and ourselves.

If Stanovich is suggesting a specific starting point for psychological inquiry, regardless of the question being asked, then what is being left out? That is, if the subject matter is being made to fit the method, then what is it within the subject matter (persons) that is being ignored? From our vantage point, we see that personal experience is immediately disregarded. Experience, it seems, is important only insofar as one can explain it in terms of observable and testable behaviors. While experimental psychology has had, and continues to have, some success, the psychologists who are practicing it have grown increasingly disenchanted. Something important, it seems, has been left out of this formulation. And that something is the subject of psychology—the person.

Disappointment with Experimental Psychology

Former APA president William Bevan shares his reflections on several decades as a psychologist in his "Distinguished Contributions to Psychology in the Public Interest Award Address," delivered at the ninety-eighth annual APA convention. He explains:

> Over the years I have found a disturbingly large proportion of the papers I have read to be trivial, some even contrived. The intellectual processes behind them too often have lacked clarity and crispness; manuscripts have been marked by a mindless and routine recitation of detail, more focused on submerging rather than elevating understanding. Preoccupation has frequently been at the level of data. . . . American psychology at its intellectual foundations remains at best a 19th-century enterprise. (1991, 476)

Bevan is reflecting on the style of psychology I earlier discussed as the scientific ideal. The next three points regard his opinion of psychology when it is practiced this way.

Bevan observes that experimental psychology has become trivial. There has been an emphasis on detail to the neglect of importance; the process seems mindless and not mindful; and the personal element seems to have evaporated. Bevan also notes that the purpose behind such experimental reports seems to be in *submerging* rather than *elevating* understanding. By this I understand him to mean that experimental reports do more to obscure or cover over the importance of understanding something new and personal about experience. *It is as if understanding ourselves and others is less important than being able to evaluate data.* Finally, Bevan accuses mainstream psychology of remaining a nineteenth-century enterprise. This is both a blessing and a curse. It is a blessing because it implies that psychology may finally be counted among the sciences. It is a curse because the definition of science it has finally actualized is stuck in the nineteenth century. Indeed, even the sciences on which psychology was modeled have gone on and changed.

Bevan acknowledges that much about being a scientific psychologist doesn't require an impersonal approach to the subject matter:

> Good science requires good scientists, by which I mean moral, honest, hardworking people who will look at what they are doing from all angles, test their intuitions, check their insights, debate with their colleagues, pay their nickels, and take their chances. There are no formulas that will guarantee success. All of which is not to say that science and the nonscientific disciplines are identical, but it is to say that both are creations of the human mind. (1991, 476)

From this quote we recognize that *psychology begins with psychologists—* people with a deep interest in understanding other people—*and not a partic-*

ular method. Your own observations and relationship to psychological phenomena are the strongest tools in your psychologist tool belt: you strengthen these tools by psychologizing.

Bevan is not alone in the dissatisfaction with a method-centered, fact-oriented practice of psychology. Psychology historians Stephen Toulmin and David Leary (1985) have gone as far as to call this approach to psychology a cult—the "cult of empiricism." They explain what they mean by the selection of such a "prejudicial term":

> Among experimental psychologists in the United States from roughly the 1920s on, a commitment to "empiricism" rapidly became something which (like the doctrine of the Trinity) it was more important to accept than to understand. These experimental psychologists came to regard theoretical questions that were not tied directly to the analysis of "controlled experiments" as self-discrediting. (1985, 607)

Toulmin and Leary have observed a trend in twentieth-century psychology: it begins with the assumption that the only important data is empirical and that it is derived experimentally. Everything else is ignored. Moreover, this position is self-affirming. It can point to all psychological facts and demonstrate that they have been discovered through the scientific method. This is like King Procrustes, who may now point to all his former guests, who are exactly six feet tall, to prove that all guests must be six feet tall.

In a more recent example, Kelly and Kelly (and Crabtree, Gould, Grosso, and Grayson 2007) share their doubts concerning the emphasis marked by psychology as it is practiced into the twenty-first century:

> Our doubts regarding current psychological orthodoxy, I hasten to add, are at least in part shared by others. There seems to be a growing unease in many quarters, a sense that the narrowly physicalist contemporary approach to the analysis of mind has deflected psychology as a whole from what should be its most central concerns, and furthermore that mainstream . . . theories themselves are encountering fundamental limitations and have nearly exhausted their explanatory resources. (2007, xxi–xxii)

In sum, psychologists over the past few decades have grown tired of the narrow, science-at-all-costs approach to psychology. Across each of these lamentations, the sense is that we have missed the part that is most living about psychology—the part that is motivated by profound curiosity and enthusiasm: *the person has been left out of these formulations.*

Psychologizing Science: Maslow's *Psychology of Science*

Abraham Maslow, whose quote introduced this chapter, experienced this dissatisfaction with the psychology in which he had been trained. Like many of you, Maslow began studying psychology so that he could help others. It was when he began asking questions about how to live a satisfying and meaningful life that his dissatisfaction became apparent. He writes:

> My restlessness with classical science became serious only when I started asking new questions about the higher reaches of human nature. Only then did the classical scientific model in which I had been trained fail me. It was then that I had to invent, *ad hoc*, new methods, new concepts, and new words in order to handle my data well. Before this, for me, Science had been One, and there was but One Science. But now it looked as if there were *two* Sciences for me, one for my new problems, and one for everything else. But more recently, perhaps ten or fifteen years ago, it began to appear that these two Sciences could be generalized into One Science again. This *new* Science looks different however; it promises to be more inclusive and more powerful than the old One Science. (1966, xv)

In this passage, we find that Maslow had received training to become a psychologist. Many of you are of the mindset that a couple of psychology degrees will provide the tools you need in order to answer the psychological questions you wish to have answered. Maslow had discovered, like some of the psychologists we heard from above, that the tools he had been given weren't always helpful in answering the questions he had formed.

Notice the assumption about psychology that Maslow had as he was going through training: that "there was but One Science." He capitalizes these the same way that I had capitalized "Psychology" in the introduction. This is a very powerful assumption. With it comes the understanding that you will be able to learn everything there is to know about a particular topic. So what happens when the capital-P psychology fails to answer a question that comes up? This is the scenario that Maslow had found himself in, so he designed a second psychology to answer these questions.

For most questions, Maslow was content to apply the scientific method and publish his results, but occasionally his question demanded a more personal approach. "If [psychologists] were interested in working with animals, or with part-processes in human beings, they could be 'experimental and scientific psychologists.' But if they were interested in whole persons, these laws and methods were not of much help" (1966, 8). In the cases where psychologists are interested in whole persons, Maslow found it best to use a person-centered, phenomenological approach (1966, 45–47).

In this other approach, Maslow also reports that he had to construct his methods *ad hoc*, which means "for this" or "for a particular occasion." This, by the way, is what we do when we psychologize: *we adapt a method that aims at the understanding of a particular experience.* As a psychologist, Maslow realizes that he has two tools: the experimental method and psychologizing. This is what he means by observing that there were "*two* Sciences" for him. But then he realizes that his more personal and spontaneous way of being in relation to psychological experience is but another form of the sophisticated experimental method. By this he means that psychologizing and applying the experimental method go hand in hand. Experimental psychologists still psychologize, and those who psychologize are exploring basic experimental psychology. This is also what Bevan means when he mentions how "good scientists" still "take chances" and can never rely on a single method for success.

Maslow has shown us that we can be invested in the game of psychology by practicing how to think like psychologists. Moreover, by practicing how to think creatively as psychologists from the beginning, we will be better equipped to adapt a method to fit the questions we find important to ask as established psychologists. Since Maslow echoes many of the principles guiding the practice of thinking like psychologists outlined in the introduction, we will consider what he has to say about practicing psychology. This will have the added benefit of reviewing what was outlined as our approach.

The first important detail that Maslow describes is that of subjective reports. Recall that this was introduced as the best way to begin to understand personal experience. Maslow explains, "By far the best way we have to learn what people are like is to get them, one way or another, to tell us, whether directly by question and answer or by free association, to which we simply listen" (1966, 12). This should be a review for you, from the conclusion of the previous chapter, where Eugene Gendlin explained how a psychologist must listen. Maslow tells us that this is an important first step in thinking like a psychologist. Remember also how Gendlin mentioned the importance of listening in a manner that does not interfere with what your subject (the person you are trying to understand) is trying to say. Maslow, too, emphasizes the importance of noninterference:

> Slowly and painfully we psychologists have had to learn to become good clinical or naturalistic observers, to wait and watch and listen patiently, to keep our hands off, to refrain from being . . . too interfering and controlling, and— most important of all in trying to understand another person—to keep our mouths shut and our eyes and ears wide open. (1966, 13)

As bourgeoning psychologists, we are interested in people. To investigate people, we allow them to demonstrate for us what their experiences are while we try to stay out of the way. When we investigate in this way, we learn a great deal about the meaning that experience has for people. Notice how this is different from the relationship taken up by an experimental scientist: experimentalists are interested in manipulation and testing. *While poking, measuring, and taking apart objects might be a beneficial way of understanding physical things, it is not a helpful way of understanding living things—most specifically human persons.* "If you do this to human beings, you *won't* get to know them" (Maslow 1966, 13). This was something Maslow had experienced firsthand as a clinician.

What we learn from this is that people—the subject matter of psychology—demand a more personal method of investigation. In the following section, philosopher and advocate for a human science Edmund Husserl will be used to outline the difference between naturalistic science and humanistic science. His conclusion is that the study of humans requires a method different from those used for physics and geology: humans require a human science. His discussion will conclude this chapter on method.

HUSSERL AND PSYCHOLOGY: SCIENCE OF THE NATURAL WORLD OR OF THE HUMAN WORLD?

In the introduction, I asked you to make two changes to the way you think in order to practice thinking like a psychologist. The first was a shift away from the tendency to use the first explanation that comes up while making an observation. This shift allows you to go deeper into the meaning that an experience might have. The second was a shift away from the expectation that any *one explanation* would be sufficient for understanding an experience. This shift recognizes that experience and life are more complicated than a simple explanation. Hopefully you have seen how Stanovich and Maslow, discussed earlier, have both succeeded in the first shift: psychologists are good at letting the subject matter—be it numerical data or personal experience—speak for itself. The two psychologists differ with regard to the second shift: Stanovich argues for a correct way to think about psychology (that is, a *straight* way), whereas Maslow leaves this up to the subject.

These two shifts—the latter in particular—are suggestions made by philosopher Edmund Husserl. Husserl, who is widely recognized as the man responsible for developing a school of thought called "phenomenology," spends a great deal of time arguing *against* psychologists. This is because psychology was in the best position of all scientific disciplines to understand the complexity of the human world. Yet it had become customary to try to explain psychology as simply one more manifestation of the natural world (like geology, astronomy, and chemistry). A *natural* psychology is an objective one. A *human* psychology is a subjective one. "Objective science means straightforwardly taking the world as one's subject matter; humanistic science means taking the world as one's subject matter *as* the world of the subjectivity which functions for it, the world insofar as it is subject-related" (Husserl 1970, 326). Bevan (1991), Toulmin and Leary (1985), and Kelly and colleagues (2007) have been used to demonstrate how disappointing a naturalistic approach to psychology can be. Now we will use Husserl to try to understand what a human psychology might be like.

Husserl explains the "humanistic world" in terms of the subject matter of psychology—that is, persons. Moreover, he explains that such a world is no different from the world of natural science. *This is the world that we are investigating in this chapter.*

> The world toward which [persons] comport themselves, which motivates them, with which they constantly have to deal, is of course precisely *the* world, the one existing world. . . . In this sense what is in question is not the world as it actually is but the particular world which is valid for the persons, the world appearing to them with the particular properties it has in appearing to them; the question is how they, as persons, comport themselves in action and passion— how they are motivated to their specifically personal acts of perception, of remembering, of thinking, of valuing, of making plans, of being frightened and automatically startled, of defending themselves, of attaching, etc. (1970, 317)

How about the above description as the subject matter of psychology? Investigating the world that motivates persons? Or the way that persons are startled or defend themselves? This is the world of experience. This is the world that we look for when we begin thinking like psychologists. Husserl explains how this approach might be practiced:

> Humanistic science is the science of human subjectivity in its conscious relation to the world as appearing to it and motivating it in action and passion; and, conversely, [it is] the science of the world as the surrounding world of persons, or as the world appearing to them, having validity for them. (1970, 318)

This passage effectively outlines the approach that will be maintained throughout the remainder of this book. Instead of looking at thinking, learning, biology, perception, and memory in terms of causes and effects, we will look to the human relation to the world vis-à-vis thinking, learning, biology, perception, and memory. That is, memory is not a component of being a human like a tool in one's backpack; it is a particular way of relating to the world. We will not look at what memory *is* but at how we relate to others, ourselves, and the world through memory. Notice where we are focusing: not on memory per se, but on persons who are experiencing through the modality of memory. "What the person does and suffers, what happens within him, how he stands in relation to his surrounding world, what angers him, what depresses him, what makes him cheerful or upset—these are questions relating to persons" (Husserl 1970, 322). And these are the questions we will begin to ask by learning how to think like psychologists.

While Husserl's push for a humanistic science provides a general framework for how we will practice psychology throughout the course of this book, psychologist Amedeo Giorgi (2009) has sought to develop a psychological method based on the phenomenology of Husserl. Since a phenomenological method had never been articulated, Giorgi first had to fill in some of the theoretical gaps in the philosophy. The result was a rigorous method that psychologists could use when they were interested in practicing psychology in line with what Husserl has termed "humanistic science" above. The method has subsequently been fruitfully applied in doctoral dissertations, academic books, and a great variety of published papers and conference presentations. There are even a few international conferences that feature this approach to psychology as well as other disciplines: the International Human Science Research Conference and the Interdisciplinary Coalition of North American Phenomenologists.

Humanistic Psychology Today

The application of Husserl's humanistic science to psychology is but one example of a shift that psychology has been undergoing for some time now. While it was nearly impossible to study anything but the objective style of psychology in the 1940s and 1950s, a subjective or qualitative approach has been gaining steam in the later parts of the twentieth century and into the twenty-first. We have seen this already through Maslow's "psychology of science." Since it concerns the subjective qualities of experience instead of the quantitative measurements of behavior, this humanistic approach may be called qualitative. Giorgi (2009, 15–55) traces the history of qualitative approaches in psychology, demonstrating that such pockets have always existed. Psychology was even marked by such qualitative approaches in the nineteenth century. (An example from William James will conclude this chapter.)

Though qualitative approaches have existed, they have been marginalized by the more explicitly scientific formats of psychology. Psychologist Frederick Wertz explains:

> Powerful institutions place high value on, accord privilege to, and reward research methods that have achieved such tangible success in natural science and technology. By employing research methods of natural science, university departments of psychology have built laboratories, funded graduate assistants, and won economic support or research that is the exclusive privileges of the science, technology, engineering, and mathematics (STEM) disciplines. Psychology's aspiration to be a STEM discipline has always been strong and continues to become stronger. (2011, 85–86)

The method outlined by Keith Stanovich (2012) earlier demonstrates how neatly a psychological experiment might fit in with the STEM disciplines. Indeed, the only difference between biology and psychology is *what* is being measured (quantified); the methods remain constant. These kinds of experiments are more likely to receive funding and are more likely to be taken seriously by the academic and scientific communities.

But something happened recently that indicates a change in tide. The division of the American Psychological Association that is responsible for defining and articulating the methods and procedures for psychological research—APA Division 5—added a section that recognized the importance of qualitative methods. Wertz describes the efforts of qualitative psychologist Kenneth Gergen and others in bringing about this change:

> In 2008, Kenneth Gergen, Ruthellen Josselson, and Mark Freeman assembled a petition of 863 members of the American Psychological Association to establish a new division of qualitative inquiry in the APA. The initiative won strong support from divisions in the areas of counseling (17); theory and philosophy (24); humanism (32); women (35); psychoanalysis (39); and lesbian, gay, bisexual and transgendered issues (44). Additional support came from industrial organizational (14), psychotherapy (29), religion (36), health (38), family (43), ethnic minority issues (45), media (46), group psychology and psychotherapy (49), and men and masculinity study (51). Although the majority of APA's Council of Representatives did not vote for the new division, APA Division 5—Evaluation, Measurement and Statistics—welcomed the qualitative psychologists to join it as a section called the Society for Qualitative Inquiry in Psychology (SQIP), and would promote both qualitative and quantitative methods. Psychologists on the SQIP e-mail list, now numbering 1,300, are joining Division 5 and making this prestigious and centrally positioned organization more pluralistic. (2011, 87)

As a result of their addition to Division 5, qualitative approaches to psychology have been granted a legitimacy they did not have in the previous decades. Wertz summarizes the growth of qualitative approaches to psychology:

> There has been an explosion of new journals, scientific associations, conferences, textbooks, prolific publications, workshops, training materials, computer software programs for data management and analysis, university courses, and faculty positions. The common core is a commitment to understand the world contextually and from the point of view of the acting subject through rich everyday language and a broad range of other expressive vehicles. (2011, 81)

It is an exciting time to be exploring the world of psychology—a time during which it has once again become okay to try to understand a person through the complicated network of their experiences. Indeed, there has been a long history of ignoring the personal component of psychology in order to look at the natural component of psychology—as if psychology were only another appendage of the hard sciences. We do not reject this approach, but we also do not accept any approach to the neglect of all others. This is because we understand that human experience is more complicated than any one explanation would allow. But enough talking *about* psychology. Let's practice it.

SAMPLE PSYCHOLOGIZING EXPERIMENT: INTROSPECTIVE ANALYSIS OF BEING GIVEN A "YES"/"NO" ANSWER

This sample experiment is a simple one to do with friends or family, and *you* get to be the psychologist. It also demonstrates *three* neat elements of psychology. The first is that it serves as an example of one of the first methods in the history of psychology; the second is that it gives you an opportunity to conduct a simple experiment on friends or family; and the third is that is also demonstrates something about the consequences of telling someone "yes" or "no"—consequences that reach a little further than the simple answer to a question.

Introspection and William James

The purpose here is not to give a thorough historical overview of the James-ian method of introspection but to set up the experiment. You may, however, wish to look up his chapter on the method in *Principles of Psychology*. You will find that William James was not only a brilliant psychologist but also a talented writer.

James proposed the method of introspection as the chief tool in the psychologist's tool belt (2007). He explained that "introspection is what you have first, foremost, and always." To apply the method, you need only to go into your mind and explain what you find there. The book itself provides a great number of psychological topics that James explored through this meth-od. Introspection begins with the mind-world relation and focuses on the role of the mind.

If the topic were memory, introspection would begin by paying careful attention to the experience of memory, specifically how the processes seem to unfold in the mind.

How You'll Do It

To carry out a successful introspection, your test subjects need to be trained ahead of time. Wilhelm Wundt, who was responsible for the first psychology laboratory ever (1887), trained his test subjects a minimum of ten thousand hours. You won't need to have your test subject undergo such training, but you will soon understand why Wundt felt it necessary. Here is how you will train your subjects: ask them to get into a comfortable position because they will be there for a few minutes. Now ask them to notice where they are. Not which room they are in, but how they are feeling—where they are at experientially. Are they upset? Tense? Relaxed? Just ask them to notice how they are feeling right now. You might suggest that they recognize how shallow or deep their breathing is, how tense their shoulders are, the weight of their feet on the ground, where their thoughts are going, and so on. The purpose is to give them a baseline so that they will notice any changes that occur. Once you're confident that they have tuned into themselves, tell them you will begin the experiment shortly. As neutrally as possible—that is, without raising your voice or changing your inflection—repeat the following word to them: "no." Give some space between repetitions; there's no need to gun them down with the term. You'll feel pretty weird doing this, but repeat it maybe five to six times. Then ask your subjects to write down what changed (if anything). If they are able to tune into any changes that occurred in their experience—perceptions, thoughts, feelings, emotions, and so on—then they introspected. You may repeat the experiment with the word "yes."

What You Will Find

When told "no," even though there was no context for the answer, it is remarkable how frequently students explain that they felt as though they had done something wrong, they felt small and unappreciated, or they felt closed off, shut down, sad, guilty, or other similar feelings. Many explain how memories from childhood came back up. With the word "yes," students report a weight lifting off their chest, an openness to possibility, and a sense of affirmation and happiness.

We learn from this brief and simple introspection experiment that words carry a lot more emotional power than the context of questions in which they are asked. You might even have noticed that you felt differently telling somebody "yes" than you did telling them "no." This scenario was actually borrowed from a lecture given by the pediatric neuropsychiatrist Daniel Siegel (2009). He used it as a demonstration of how we are interpersonally connected—part of his theory of interpersonal neurobiology (2012).

SUMMARY

This chapter looked at how one goes about the practice of psychology. In order to accomplish this, the terms "objectivity" and "subjectivity" were introduced. These two approaches to knowledge were considered alongside Maslow's question that all psychologists must ask: what is the best and most fruitful way to go about understanding another person?

With objectivity as it has been outlined by Stanovich, it is believed that a person can be held at a safe distance from the psychologist so that the psychologist does not interfere with the facts she hopes to discover. Here the aspects of a person have an existence and are available to be tested and measured. The tool of the objective psychologist is the experiment. Although this approach has a long history in the discipline of psychology, it has customarily left psychologists feeling disconnected from the people they wish to understand.

With subjectivity as it has been demonstrated by Maslow, the psychologist aims to get to know the person she wishes to better understand—even doing so personally. Her aim is in understanding the meaning that people's experiences have for themselves, so she directs her attention to this world of meaning (and not the world of objective fact).

Beginning with Wundt, we have learned that a psychologist must recognize the importance of both approaches: objective *and* subjective. Both have merit in their own right, and both, when practiced by themselves, are missing something.

PSYCHOLOGIZING IN ACTION

"Tears of Wonder-Joy": A Transpersonal Approach

- Seeing a watercolor painting by kindergarten children on "one big happy community"—crude yet colorful continents with hands reaching for one another
- Witnessing simple, natural acts of animals—good, innocent, artless
- Witnessing anything truly honest, open, free from guile or craft
- Experiencing Nature's beauty—for example, the coastal mountains shrouded in morning mist

I have had such experiences many times. I have come to call them my "tears of wonder-joy." The tears and chills are, to me, my body's way of indicating that the eye of my heart is open and functioning and encountering something of vast importance and meaning. I have come to recognize these wonder-joy tears as direct responses to the true, the good, the beautiful. Such tears are not tears of pain or sadness or sorrow. Rather, for me, they are accompanied by positive affect—by feelings of wonder, joy, gratitude, yearning, poignancy, awe, intensity, love, and compassion. With them comes a feeling that my heart is going out to what I am witnessing. The tears, chills, and special feelings come upon me, unexpectedly and spontaneously, as experiences of grace—as bodily signals, signs, or indicators of encounters with the numinous; as my body's way of letting me know I am having an unplanned, unavoidable encounter with the Real.

These experiences, for me, are pointers: They serve as affirmations or confirmations of valued qualities that I am truly seeking, and provide immediate indications of how those qualities are recognized. Their aftereffects serve as reminders of my direction, help me stay on course, and allow me to make useful corrections in my path. So, they and their memories serve a guiding function in my life. The experiences themselves even serve a more direct guidance function—my body and feelings are automatically moved in certain directions, and a greater valence is added to the events or qualities that precipitated the wonder-joy tears, so that these former are valued more and approached more readily in the future. [. . .]

Wonder-joy tears also serve as confirmations or affirmations of Something More. They lead me to appreciate the great power, wisdom, and goodness that is behind things and shines through things—the ground that shines through the figure.

Source: Braud 2001.

Chapter Three

Learning

In chapter 1 we examined the project of psychology by asking the question: as psychologists, what is it that we're interested in? While there are many possible answers to this question—indeed, as many as there are psychologists to ask it—we saw that these may be divided into two categories. The first category aims at uncovering all the facts about psychology, and Keith Stanovich's *How to Think Straight about Psychology* was provided as an example of this. To answer this type of question, lay psychologists would do well to first master the procedures for asking and answering such questions before attempting any practice. The second category aims at understanding persons, and it argues that anything that is learned when one focuses on a person is of importance to the project of psychology. Abraham Maslow's *Psychology of Science* was provided as an example. To answer this type of question, lay psychologists must psychologize.

In this chapter, we explore the psychological topic of learning. Like the method of psychology, the topic of the previous chapter, learning can be divided into two categories. In the first category, learning is something that can happen to a person. In the second category, learning is something in which a person must participate. The type of learning we are interested in at present is the second of these two. This is because we recognize that learning cannot occur independently of a learner and that learning is always a personal and meaningful process. While this perspective might sound quite obvious from the outset, it has not always been the case in the history of psychology. Indeed, the field of psychology has a long legacy of an impersonal and meaning*less* definition of learning. This follows the history of psychology as a science of behavior. We will see that behaviorists argue that all learning can be explained in terms of cause-and-effect relationships. Such an approach has a certain appeal worth noting, but it is unsatisfactory because it ignores the role of the learner in the learning process. The legacy of behaviorism is explored, and its shortcomings are summarized. This is followed by an approach to learning that honors the role of the learner as the most important part. The personal form of learning can then serve as our model of learning to become psychologists.

THE LEGACY OF BEHAVIORISM IN BRIEF

A comprehensive review of the science of behaviorism is not necessary here for a few reasons. The first is the appeal of its simplicity. To say that its method is simple and then proceed to meticulously examine its procedures would be counterproductive. Second, the insights that behaviorism have for the classroom—which are of obvious concern to the present chapter—come almost exclusively from the *promises about* the science of behavior and not the experimental laboratories themselves. Finally, the reports from the experimental laboratories have yielded robust evidence to the contrary of the promises of behaviorism. Indeed, were exclusive attention paid to the behaviorist lab reports, one would see little advantage to its continued application in the classroom or elsewhere. Its failure as a comprehensive system of learning has been well documented. Instead, we'll focus on the initial promises proposed by early behaviorism and how these alone have resulted in its history as a theory of learning.

To a historical epoch that had delivered on the promises of flight, wealth, protection from infectious diseases, and telecommunication, credulity for outrageous promises was not in short supply: people were of the mindset that anything was possible. Indeed, imagination was no limit for what modern technology was shown to have in store. We can imagine that it came as no surprise when an American psychologist supplied outlandishly optimistic hypotheses regarding the rearing of children. Watson writes:

> Give me a dozen healthy infants, well-formed, and my own specified world to bring them up in and I'll guarantee to take any one at random and train him to become any type of specialist I might select—doctor, lawyer, artist, merchant-chief and, yes, even beggar-man and thief, regardless of his talents, penchants, tendencies, abilities, vocations, and race of his ancestors. I am going beyond my facts and I admit it, but so have the advocates of the contrary and they have been doing it for many thousands of years. (1930, 82)

Notice what Watson has done from the vantage point of practicing psychologists. First, he guarantees his method despite a lack of supporting evidence. The statement is his *hypothesis* about the benefits of behavioral conditioning. Second is the breadth and depth of the promise: he can take anybody— provided the person does not occupy the margins of human ability—and turn him into anything. The appeal to a newly developed institution, responsible for turning out occupational specialists as though they were automobiles, must have been impressive.

Watson's insights began in a Russian laboratory, where a medical student by the name of Ivan Pavlov had mistakenly conditioned a dog to do something unusual. Pavlov was researching digestion in dogs. The salivation response was the key to his research because it was the easiest to observe: if the dog was salivating, then the digestion response had begun. Since digestion is something that occurs naturally while someone is eating, part of his work required that he feed the dogs. It is not until dogs are presented with food that the digestion response begins. Try to begin salivating at will. You will find that this is impossible. You might be able to initiate this process if you are hungry and you begin to imagine food, but even here you must concede the precondition of food (real or imagined). Pavlov would feed the dogs and then measure salivation production. One day he realized that the dogs began to salivate before any food had been presented. He later discovered that the bell sound that always preceded the presentation of food had become *paired* with the food itself. Thus, the commencement of the digestion process *in response to the bell* had been learned.

Watson reasoned that any and all behaviors could be learned in this way. This was how he arrived at the outlandish promise quoted earlier. He even succeeded in demonstrating how a child might "learn" a phobia (Watson and Rayner 1920). This is classical conditioning in a nutshell: by pairing a neutral stimulus with an unconditioned stimulus, a response that normally follows the latter will be conditioned to follow the former. We'll define some terms and then go over this once more. A stimulus is *anything* in the environment that produces a behavioral response. A behavioral response is *anything* an organism (or person) does that can be observed. An unconditioned stimulus needs no learning; it will always produce a particular (unconditioned) response. Blow into someone's eyes from six inches away. This is an unconditioned stimulus that produces an unconditioned blinking response. Blinking is the behavior, and blowing is the stimulus. Now add a neutral stimulus before you blow into the person's eyes: say something like "Hello?" and then blow. Saying "Hello?" does not get people to blink their eyes, but you can condition this to happen. After a few times of saying "Hello?" and *then* blowing in a person's eyes, the person will be conditioned to blink after you say "Hello?" This is a learned response. Watson believed that you could turn a child into a premier criminal defense attorney through such pairing procedures.

If you look more closely at classical conditioning, you realize that it has a huge limitation: the classical behavioral psychologist is limited to reflex behaviors such as salivating and blinking. Such unconditioned reflex behaviors fall well short of turning a child into a doctor, lawyer, or artist. Watson did not spend very much time as a psychologist after his method had proved so limited. He did, however, do very well for himself in advertising. Can you think of how classical conditioning might be useful in designing advertisements? Pick up any magazine and see the continued application of the principles of classical conditioning.

Even though classical conditioning was limited in scope, behaviorism still found its way into the classroom. Edward Thorndike provided the first comprehensive science of learning theory, basing his methods on the findings of Pavlov.

In the early twentieth century, it seemed as though only education had yet to reap the benefits of modernity. With the growing fields of the social sciences, education would not be left in medieval darkness much longer. Enter Edward Thorndike. *A propos* of the themes of modern science, educational historian Joel Spring explains that "Thorndike's dream was to turn all of teaching into a scientific profession in which all educators would be guided by the scientific method and spirit" (2011, 257). Just as mechanical engineering had delivered all varieties of transportation by adhering to the rigorous processes and methods of modern science, so too might education deliver capable instructors and pupils.

The behaviorist method is straightforward and rather simple. Indeed, it is really as simple as "stimulus" and "response." It also follows the dictates of modern science. Thorndike explains in *The Principles of Teaching Based on Psychology* the method as it pertains to teaching: "Using psychological terms, the art of teaching may be defined as the art of giving and withholding stimuli with the result of producing and preventing certain responses" (quoted in Spring 2011, 257). Instructors may be trained in the art of the "what," the "when," and the "how" of manipulating stimuli, and the students will respond naturally. Thorndike argues that all intellectual development may be understood in terms of these laws.

With the addition of such simple, albeit rigorous, guidelines for classroom instruction, one may now employ the tools of measurement. Students (and their teachers) may be tested on how well the transfer of learning has come along—that is, how well the conditioning has come about. If students are not demonstrating the necessary learned behaviors, then teachers must pay greater attention to factors such as stimulus strength and latency between the unconditioned and conditioned stimuli and make the necessary adjustments. Cognitive psychologist George Miller had grown up in classrooms dominated by this approach to learning. He explains the typical scenario in an interview with Bernard Baars: "There was a tradition of human research from Ebbinghaus through Thorndike . . . [that] tried to interpret all the verbal learning data in terms of Pavlovian conditioning or operant conditioning" (Baars 1986, 205). Even with its profound limitations, behaviorism was and still is a popular theory of learning. The approach that B. F. Skinner had proposed has probably made the greatest waves in the history of psychology and learning theory.

Skinner's operant method of behavioral conditioning began to deliver on Watson's promise. Entire laboratories full of dogs, rats, monkeys, pigeons, and children, to name a few, were being conditioned to demonstrate a host of learned behaviors. Skinner notes that "[i]n spite of great phylogenetic differences, all these organisms show amazingly similar properties of the learning process" (1955, 50). Indeed, these organisms were "learning" much more than the reflex responses to which Watson's stimulus-response protocol was limited. Moreover, Skinner infiltrates the classroom in an earnest attempt to enhance pedagogical practices, though his suggestions might surprise you (even though they shouldn't).

To operantly condition an animal, one needed to manipulate the consequences that followed the behavior. Before providing an example, here is the quippy explanation from Skinner himself:

> Behavior which operates upon the environment to produce consequences ("operant" behavior) can be studied by arranging environments in which specific consequences are contingent upon it. The contingencies under investigation have become steadily more complex, and one by one they are taking over the explanatory functions previously assigned to [learning]. (1971, 16)

What exactly does this definition entail? Say an experimenter puts a pigeon in a box with the hopes of making the pigeon twirl around counterclockwise for a full revolution before pecking the ground twice. The experimenter need only "reinforce" any action that most closely resembles this target behavior. All of the strutting, pecking, nodding, and wing flapping that might happen is ignored until the pigeon begins to turn left. Then the reinforcement is given. Provided the reinforcement is strong enough, the pigeon will continue turning left. Once the full revolution is "learned," the experimenter must withhold reinforcement until a pecking motion follows a single revolution, and so on.

Control of details, however, is exceedingly important. Failure to present a stimulus that is *reinforcing enough* will not result in learning in the manner of Skinner. Also, failure to present reinforcement in *close enough* temporal proximity will also fail to result in learning. Skinner explains:

> It should be emphasized that this has been achieved by analyzing the effects of reinforcement and by designing techniques which manipulate reinforcement with considerable precision. Only in this way can the behavior of the individual organism be brought under such precise control. (1955, 50)

Also note that Skinner pays considerable attention to the manipulation of punishing stimuli—that is, consequences that follow particular behaviors that reduce the latter's occurrence. After sufficient experimentation, Skinner himself admits to the ineffectiveness of a purely punitive method of conditioning (or learning). "Punished behavior," he writes, "is likely to reappear after the punitive contingencies are withdrawn" (1971, 58). Despite the failure of punitive contingencies within the behaviorist paradigm, they still enjoy membership as a respected method in contemporary education.

Like many respected psychologists who dabbled in applied learning theory, Skinner (1955) also made visits to the classroom. As was his wont, he applied his customary experimental rigor and detail to the process that must necessarily be "learning." He describes the procedure of learning arithmetic in such detail:

> Let us consider, for example, the teaching of arithmetic in the lower grades. The school is concerned with imparting to the child a large number of responses of a special sort. The responses are all verbal. They consist of speaking and writing certain words, figures and signs which, to put it roughly, refer to numbers and to arithmetic operations. The first task is to shape up these responses—to get the child to pronounce and to write responses correctly, but the principal task is to bring this behavior under many sorts of stimulus control. This is what happened when the child learns to count, to recite tables, to count while ticking off the items in an assemblage of objects, to respond to spoken or written numbers by saying "odd," "even," "prime," and so on. Over and above this elaborate repertoire of numerical behavior, most of which is often dismissed as the product of rote learning, the teaching of arithmetic looks forward to these complex serial arrangements of responses involved in transposing, learning fractions, and so on, which modify the order of the original material so that the response called a solution is eventually made possible. (1955, 50–51)

Like the pigeon in the Skinner box, these students might wander about aimlessly for a period before happening upon the "response called a solution." At this point the "teacher" has only a few seconds to provide necessary reinforcement (lest the target behavior be lost among the repertoire of random classroom behavior). Skinner's laboratory sensibility provides a keen insight into the difficult context of a classroom, namely, that "the lapse of only a few seconds between response and reinforcement destroys most of the effect"; and he continues that given the "long periods of time [that] customarily elapse . . . it is surprising that this system has any effect whatsoever" (1955, 51–52).

It may come as a surprise that Skinner immediately denies the plausibility of behaviorism's efficacy in the classroom. However, he protects the status of his method by throwing teachers under the school bus. Skinner explains this concern and offers a solution:

In the experimental study of learning it has been found that the contingencies of reinforcement which are most efficient in controlling the organism cannot be arranged through the personal mediation of the experimenter. An organism is affected by subtle details of contingencies which are beyond the capacity of the human organism to arrange. Mechanical and electrical devices must be used. . . . The simple fact is that, as a mere reinforcing mechanism, the teacher is out of date. (1955, 55)

Once again, were educational administration to take seriously the notion of a scientifically informed praxis, then the employment of behaviorism in the classroom would include the outsourcing of teaching jobs to machines— or, put more contemporarily, to computers. This raises an interesting point: when drawn to its logical conclusion, a rigorous, objectively scientific teaching method demands that the instructors be removed from the classroom. The person, it seems, gets in the way of the learning process.

What happens when the learner is allowed to participate in the learning process? To understand what this means, a contrast with Skinner's approach can be made. In the example of teaching a student to solve math problems, it is important to identify *what is counted as important* from the perspective of behaviorism. Skinner differentiates between two types of behavior: emitted responses and elicited responses. An emitted response is anything that a person does: a student might look at the problem and try to think about what it is asking, maybe even experiment with a few equations. An elicited response is anything that occurs with greater frequency because it has been given priority. Students learn by reducing unnecessary emitted responses and increasing the elicited responses. In fact, a surplus of emitted responses might even be identified as "problem behavior." This may be found in recent educational scholarship such as *Getting the Buggers to Behave* (Cowley 2010) or *Bad Students, Not Bad Schools* (Weissberg 2010). The behaviorist approach to learning finds individual differences to be a problem; it succeeds when these are reduced, replaced by the learned target behaviors. Since we are interested in understanding people, we recognize that these individual differences are important, and losing them should be frowned upon. Indeed, we might even be so bold as to suggest that learning begins with these. This is the position taken by psychologist and educator Carl Rogers. His perspective will be followed through the conclusion of this chapter.

Rogers begins by explaining that he is interested in learning,

[b]ut *not* the lifeless, sterile, futile, quickly forgotten stuff which is crammed into the mind of the poor helpless individual tied into his seat by ironclad bonds of conformity! I am talking about LEARNING—the insatiable curiosity which drives the [high school student to spend hours familiarizing him or herself with a complicated piece of technology known as a smartphone, and without any formalized instruction at all]. (1969, 3)

I have taken a bit of artistic license in providing a more contemporary exam- ple. But consider the tireless enthusiasm, curiosity, and insight that goes into mastering your smartphone (or tablet, or computer, etc.). These often come packaged with a user's manual: a guidebook for operation. A user's manual might be likened to a textbook. To be sure, the manual has engineer-tested answers for a lot of the possible questions that might come up as you begin navigating your new phone. But do you always consult with the manual before exploring? I imagine that the user's manual was a helpful guide when- ever you found yourself stumped by a problem but that it did not dictate your every action.

Consider also how much time you spent familiarizing yourself with your phone. Did you have to set time aside from your normal day called "smart- phone study time"? And when the time approached, did you try to come up with some excuse as to why it could be put off until later? I imagine that your answers to each of these questions has been "no," and hopefully you're realizing that learning doesn't have to be a drab and tiresome experience. You might even realize that it can be an exciting and self-initiated experi- ence. To continue the example, how did you discover whether or not you had solved a problem correctly? Did you have to call up the technician and see whether you had arrived at the correct answer? Probably not: the correctness and incorrectness is something you experience firsthand. You know that the answer is right because it works. You're also uninterested in a "close enough" answer because this doesn't quite work. You might want to send a mass text message to selected contacts but know only how to send them one at a time. Close enough, right? Probably not: you will spend another few minutes (or hours, depending on the sophistication of the problem you face) until you have mastered the task.

We are all familiar with this type of learning, but we do not always identify it as learning. This is because we have grown accustomed to equat- ing the impersonal and boring classroom procedures with learning. When learning occurs rapidly and spontaneously, we are tempted to call it some- thing else—something fun but certainly not learning. Carl Rogers, a human- istic psychotherapist and educator, argues that the kind of learning that is personal and meaningful—the kind that gets us to spend hours figuring out our technology or getting to know our close friends—is the only type of learning that matters. Let us more closely evaluate how he defines learning. Rogers (1969, 5) lists five elements that make up significant learning. These will be considered alongside the example of learning how to operate the complicated device with which people have become more and more familiar: the smartphone.

1. The first element of significant learning is that *it has a quality of personal involvement*. Remember that not all definitions of learning take this element for granted. The behaviorist theory maintains that learning is some-

thing that happens *to* a learner. This turns the learner into a passive recipient of learning. Rogers argues that for significant learning to occur, the learner has to be involved. In learning how to operate your smartphone, the chances are good that each of the little tricks you have employed is specific to the ways in which you use your phone. This is to suggest that you use your phone in a way that is different from the way your parents use their phones. You have even tried to explain to somebody something you have learned— such as how to edit a digital picture—only to find out that such a task is impossible since that person doesn't use his phone in the same way. We also see that there is more than one, or five, or fifty ways to use a smartphone, none of which is necessarily better than the others. This means that learning is not general to all but is specific to each learner. This is another way of saying that learning is personal.

2. Through this example you might also see how significant learning is *self-initiated*. As soon as you remove the smartphone from the box, learning is under way. I don't know of anybody who required the discipline from their mom, dad, or smartphone representative in order to begin learning its features. Learning occurs spontaneously and without the supervision of an expert. In many cases, future smartphone owners begin learning how to use the phone before it arrives or even becomes available. Now what would happen if somebody had given you a list of smartphone applications to master, and each had its own description of how to best go about doing so? It would require that you follow the rules that somebody else had determined were most important. You would probably ignore the instructions and master each procedure by playing around with it. This is what is meant by self-initiated learning. But does this mean that it is impossible to learn something when you are asked to learn it? By no means. Learning can (and does) occur in the most unlikely of circumstances. When students are being drilled with multiplication tables in math class, some of them might realize the significance of calculating a product: they might look up from their worksheet and see the desks arranged in five rows of six desks and understand that there are thirty desks without having to count each of them. In this case, the student who has recognized the meaning behind multiplication has learned something significant; this is different from being able to repeat that $6 \times 5 = 30$.

3. When significant learning has occurred, we find that *it is pervasive*: it actually changes the way somebody interacts with their world. I remember that learning how to use the GPS map system on a smartphone was frustrating. I wished that I simply had a map. But as soon as I mastered this (and "mastered" might be too generous a term), I found that this smartphone application began to change the way I gave and received directions, looked for restaurants, and estimated how long it would take me to travel somewhere. This instance of learning was significant because it was reflected in

small but noticeable changes in my life. This is what Rogers means when he says that significant learning is pervasive.

4. Since significant learning is pervasive, which means it can be seen through various changes that it brings about in a person's life, we also see that it is *meaningful*. You may have asked, "What significance does this have for me?" when asked to learn something. This is a brilliant question that we would do well to ask more frequently. Learning how to drive a car is a good example of this. In the United States, receiving one's driver's license is usually preceded by some formal driving classes. In my state, this was called "driver's training." It was here that future drivers learned a great deal about operating an automobile, navigating in traffic, and following the rules of the road. I memorized a great number of facts in this class and did quite well on the written exam. But memorizing facts is not the same as driving a car in traffic. Over the six months that followed the conclusion of driver's training, many of these facts were forgotten. Those that stayed were the ones I encountered on a regular basis. These were no longer known on the basis of their factuality but had been learned in the context of driving: the road and its other drivers became my teachers.

5. Finally, Rogers explains of significant learning that it can be *evaluated by only the learner*. Whether or not you have learned how to master the camera functions, GPS functions, or calling functions of your smartphone can be evaluated by only you. You might take a picture in a dark setting and the flash doesn't turn on. Nobody else can decide for you whether the picture this captures is satisfactory. If you decide that it *is* satisfactory, then you are confident that you have a good understanding of your smartphone's camera function. If you decide that it could be clearer, then you have a bit more to learn. After you learn something, you might ask the question: could I do better? The answer to this question is almost always "yes," and this shows us that learning is almost never complete. So instead, we must decide where we invest ourselves for learning.

After looking more closely at the experience of learning, we find that this is something we know quite well and are rather good at. Young children still remember this. If you ask three- or four-year-olds, they will demonstrate the wonder, curiosity, and enthusiasm that marks learning. Children spend most of their day learning about this and that because they know that learning is fun. Carl Rogers has identified five elements of this kind of learning. He explains that significant learning is personal, self-initiated, pervasive, meaningful, and self-evaluated. Children are masters of this kind of learning, but somewhere along the line this significant type of learning is replaced by the procedure of learning. It is difficult to determine where this happens exactly, but we recognize it when we stop seeing the importance that learning has for us; we no longer look for the significance in learning. Learning in this fashion is something of which we are passive recipients. We sometimes wish we could learn in our sleep or just skip to the part where we have already learned a discipline: we say, "I wish I knew French," as if learning a language didn't require a supremely personal investment of time and attention.

The topic of this chapter is learning, but we also see how it relates to the greater topic of psychologizing. Learning to be a psychologist is a process that requires lots of practice—practice in thinking like a psychologist. You cannot learn to be a psychologist in your sleep. You also cannot start collecting college degrees in the hopes that this will turn you into a psychologist. Psychology is a way of looking at the experiences of yourself and others, and, like learning, the process of psychologizing is personal, self-initiated, pervasive, meaningful, and self-evaluated.

In the following chapter we consider a topic that is very much related to learning: intelligence. For this, we will ask the question: is intelligence something that you *have* or something that you *acquire* or both? Looking more closely into the phenomenon of intelligence will also require us to look at the topics of knowledge and thinking.

SUMMARY

This chapter looked at the experience of learning. As the first topic covered in the textbook, it also serves as a demonstration of how subsequent topics will be handled. Instead of looking at learning as a thing that is engineered by teachers in the classroom, we saw that learning is a way of relating to the environment. Learning happens all the time, sometimes when we don't even try to do so.

Behaviorism was the approach that educators adopted in the early part of the twentieth century. Behaviorists assume that learning must be done to students through conditioning. Aside from ignoring the meaningful aspects of learning, it can sometimes interfere with the process of learning—such as when you promise a student goodies for doing good work.

The behaviorist approach to learning was delineated from the kind of learning that Carl Rogers describes. This kind of learning is self-initiated, personal, pervasive, meaningful, and self-evaluated. With this approach, we realize that learning need not be a chore but can actually be as fun as we remember it being in our first years of grade school.

PSYCHOLOGIZING IN ACTION

Discovering an Occupational Calling

By the time I realized that I should have been an English major, it was too late to make the switch. But what was I going to do with my life? . . . So there I was, a couple of years after college, bitter from the fact that I had thrown away the chance to get an education, working a job that meant nothing to me, my career essentially dead in the water, my self-belief in ruins, with no idea what I wanted to do or where I should go next.

And then I happened to be visiting a friend in architecture school. She wasn't happy, either; her program was way too pretentious and theoretical. We were walking along—I can practically point to the spot where it happened—and she said, "I have to get out of graduate school." And I immediately thought . . . "I have to go to graduate school." Meaning, I'll never be happy until I give myself the chance to study English after all. Meaning, goddam it, it's not too late—I'm not going to let it be too late. That was it: that was the lightning bolt. Everything was suddenly clear and calm. I understood what I needed to do, because I'd let myself become aware of what I'd always known.

It wasn't easy getting in at that point. I was rejected by something like nine of the eleven programs I applied to, and the ones that did admit me were going to make me fight to keep my place by cutting half the class at the end of the initial year. But for the first time in a very long while, I performed at the top of my ability, and for the first time ever, I loved being in school. I'd study for seventy, eighty hours a week, reading until 4 a.m. in my crummy little room in graduate student housing, and I had never been happier. I had finally learned to listen to my gut, or in more sophisticated terms, had come to recognize the moral significance of desire. I had found out that I could do what I wanted, and that I could do it just because I wanted to.

Source: Deresiewicz 2014, 107–8.

Chapter Four

Thinking, Knowledge, and Intelligence

Psychology is responsible for the concept of intelligence. In fact, we would hardly want any part in a version of psychology that didn't provide a theory of intelligence. That is what this chapter is designed to explain. We also explore the relationship that intelligence has to knowledge and to thinking—elements that are no doubt significant for understanding intelligence, though this significance might be unclear at the moment. Like many of the topics that can be investigated through the lens of experience, the topics covered in this chapter can be taken in one of two ways. In the first and most traditional way, it is assumed that these topics can be understood *without going through the channels of experience*: this would be to suppose that intelligence could exist without a person. In the second way—the way that we are practicing in this book—it is assumed that these topics can be understood only through our experience of them.

The chapter begins with the topic of intelligence, and this is followed with discussions about thinking and its relationship to knowledge. You might notice that this seems to be ordered in reverse. This is because psychology has concerned itself with intelligence before it began to worry about the roles of knowledge and thinking. We will see how the early positivist definitions of intelligence took the meanings of knowledge and thinking for granted. What we often think of as intelligence is a measuring scale with which we can reliably compare one person with another. The higher somebody is on the scale, the more intelligent that person is. Here we might even introduce the concepts of "knowledge" and "thinking." People who score high on intelligence scales have lots of knowledge while those at the bottom have very little. And those who score high tend to be good at thinking while those at the bottom demonstrate poor thinking skills. I argue that this conception of intelligence (extending to knowledge and thinking) is a damaging one, and I

47

propose a new one that emphasizes our unique talents and gifts. This new conception requires a reconsideration of the concepts "thinking" and "knowledge."

INTELLIGENCE

The first theory of intelligence emerged around one of the first educational psychology problems: how do we know which types of schools to place students in? The educational system in which many of us grew up had already solved this problem by starting students at the same time and thus progressing at the same rate (assuming, of course, that this is possible or even beneficial). Students who could not keep up or who were having trouble keeping up were put in special programs where they received more attention. Alfred Binet was the first person tasked with figuring out which students required the additional attention. He designed a series of questions aimed at identifying the ability levels of students. The questions included some basic motor tasks, drawing tasks, and problem-solving tasks. Binet proposed the concept of mental age, which means exactly what it sounds like it means. We understand our chronological age as the number of years we have been living: a ten-year-old has been living ten years. Binet defines the mental age (of ten, for example) as the mental skills that an average ten-year-old would possess. If a ten-year-old had the mental age of an eleven-year-old, then she could be expected to succeed at the higher-level courses. The intelligence quotient (IQ) is the calculation of someone's mental age divided by their chronological age and then multiplied by one hundred. This girl's IQ would be 110, which is considered just above average.

Binet's test was an important development in educational psychology, and there is much that can be learned from it. But since general psychology textbooks are limited and provide little space for in-depth study into a single topic, we will instead jump right to some of the problems with such a test, including the relationship between knowledge and intelligence as well as thinking and intelligence. In outlining what Binet implies about knowledge and thinking, maybe we can anticipate some of the problems with his theory of intelligence.

Binet's test is an example of a standardized test. Most of us who have survived any formal schooling system have been subjected to a battery of such tests. These tests are used to gauge how well schools are doing, how well prepared students are for higher education, and whether or not a student qualifies for special conditions for learning. Perhaps we are already seeing one of the problems of Binet's intelligence test by such a comparison. While the questions and topics of a standardized test are varied, the assumption is that a single *standard* test will accurately measure a student's mental age.

The chief question is this: for *whom* is it standard? I could come up with a test that anybody living in downtown Albany would do quite well on. A simple question might be this: "How many stops does the bus make between the Flint River Aquarium and YMCA?" Students who have used the bus to make this commute would find it quite easy to answer this question. But students who had never been on the bus would be at a considerable disadvantage. We see that such a question, even though there is a simple answer to it, puts some students at an advantage and others at a disadvantage. This question actually benefits students who do not have the luxury of owning their own car, but this is seldom the case for the people who are designing question items. We might instead expect to see a transportation question that concerns gas prices or navigating the system of highways in southwestern Georgia. In this example, students who have never left Albany or who can count on two hands the number of times they have left Albany in their lives are going to do poorly. It was quickly discovered that the Stanford-Binet—the IQ test that had been established and tested by Binet—was biased along lines of race, ethnicity, culture, socioeconomic status, and religion. Take a moment to imagine how a question written by a white middle-class suburban man might be biased along any of these lines.

Efforts can be made to mitigate bias on standardized tests. For example, tests might be specific to nationality. Here we could find that questions aimed at students in the United States concerning geographical familiarity might ask about the United States: name two states that border California. Again, this would be a simple question for anybody who has traveled to California or to a neighboring state, but it may as well be asking about wine regions in Australia for a student reared in urban Chicago. We quickly find that the problems of standardized intelligence tests—and the problems about the intelligences they propose to measure—are complicated. Indeed, to solve them we must either make a judgment call about what is most important in determining intelligence regardless of who is being asked to demonstrate it (for example, that US geography is more important than individual city geography) or we must change the definition of intelligence. This is a problem that we can consider as psychologists: what does our experience tell us about the important elements in determining intelligence? In trying to understand the psychology of intelligence, we will look at the experiences of thinking and of knowing. This is because intelligence tests are designed to measure student knowledge and skills in thinking; thus, by understanding these two elements through experience, we may better understand what intelligence is (even though "intelligence-ing" isn't likely to be an experience we have had).

THINKING

> Many are of the opinion that men do not like to think; that they will do much to
> avoid it; that they prefer to repeat instead. But in spite of many factors that are
> inimical to real thinking, that suffocate it, here and there it emerges and flour-
> ishes. And often one gets the strong impression that men, even children, long
> for it. —Max Wertheimer, *Productive Thinking*

What does it mean to think? Thinking is something with which we are each
so familiar that we seldom stop to consider it. Are you thinking as you read
these words? Or are you just repeating them in your head as your eyes pass
over them? Can we really do something without thinking? Or think about
something without doing it? In this section, we look at the two most popular
examples of thinking: logic and factual recall. Much of schooling can be
divided into these two categories. Intelligence, as it is measured by standardized instruments, is no more than logic and recall. My argument is the same
as that of Max Wertheimer: that school has done nothing to teach students
how to think. Put more bluntly: I would guess that you, the reader, do not
know how to think.

What We Normally Call Thinking: Logic and Recall

Two strategies most often define thinking: the strategies of applying rules in
the fashion of deductive logic and the association method of rote recall. Let
us consider them both in turn.

Logic

Logical thinking, Wertheimer tells us, "is concerned with truth. Being true or
false is a quality of assertions, propositions, and only of these" (1959, 5).
Much of what we understand about the world can be discussed in terms of
logical relationships between various things. Indeed, the goal of classical
physics is to be able to predict all of the possible relationships between
earthly bodies. Wertheimer continues:

> Some psychologists would hold that a person is able to think, is intelligent,
> when he can carry out the operations of traditional logic correctly and easily.
> The inability to form general concepts, to abstract, to draw conclusions in
> syllogisms of certain formal types is viewed as a mental deficiency, which is
> determined and measured in experiments. (1959, 7)

Imagine that you are asking another person for directions. You want to get
from your classroom to the campus library. You are *here* but you want to get
there. We see that *here* and *there* stand in definite relationship to each other.
There are many ways to get from *here* to *there*, but we understand that the

value of the logical formula is that it gets you to the library. You might be given three or four directives to follow: walk toward the front of campus until you reach the fountain, then turn toward the nursing building, and so on. Wertheimer finds the following benefits with the application of logic: "its emphasis on proof; in the seriousness of the rules . . . ; in the . . . rigor in each individual step" (1959, 7). If, after following each of the directions, you should find yourself at the library, then you know that the directions were good ones! Look now to the second procedure that we are likely to call thinking.

Associationism

Wertheimer explains the associationist type of thinking:

> Basically, the items are connected in the way in which my friend's telephone number is connected with his name, in which nonsense syllables become reproducible when learned in a series of such syllables, or in which a dog is conditioned to respond with salivation to a certain musical sound. (1959, 8)

College students are quite familiar with the associationist style of thinking. What do we do in preparation for an exam—the night before, for example? Cram sessions. Cram sessions are events where students stare at concepts alongside definitions and hope that the two will eventually become linked. If this task is a success, then when the student sees a concept on an exam, she knows the definition with which it is associated. Anybody who has suffered through flash cards knows this operation quite intimately.

To be sure, we are familiar with each of these operations, and we have little difficulty referring to them as "thinking." Wertheimer argues that this is why we have grown so tired of it: "what was vital, forceful, creative in it seems somehow to have evaporated in the formulations." We understand that logical drills and associationist repetition are *re*productive forms of thinking because they can be performed without any personal investment in the thinking process. Reproductive thinking is entirely impersonal; indeed, we see that one need not think at all since this is left to somebody else. Reproductive thinking replaces creative and insightful forms of thinking.

Reproductive thinking, Wertheimer explains, can be represented by the ability to replicate certain activities when prompted to do so. For instance, if a student has learned how to calculate the area of a rectangle in a reproductive manner, then she knows to gather the number designating the figure's base and multiply it by the number designating the figure's height, therefore arriving successfully at the figure's area. Notice that she does not understand what this procedure indicates about the relationship between width and length or base and height. She simply knows that multiplying these numbers arrives at a new number, and that this number is the same as the figure's area.

In such a simple geometry problem, we might have difficulty imagining how this answer can be given without understanding what this means. If this describes you, then wait for a moment until we come up with a more complicated problem. Back to this student who *knows* how to solve for the area of a rectangle: she will likely be able to generalize these instructions to any size of rectangle, as long as the dimensions are provided, because the task and problem are the same. Notice what happens when the type of problem changes; for example, the same student is then given a *triangle* of the same dimensions. Will she understand the new relationship between base and height, or will she simply recall that these must be multiplied? Students who can solve the rectangle problem but fail to do so in the triangle problem exhibit reproductive thinking. We see that reproductive thinking is limited to instances of rote recall.

Compare this example of reproductive thinking with an example of productive thinking. In this instance, the student will understand why she is multiplying length by width or base by height. This student would be able to take account for the new figure. She will recognize that the triangle is different from the rectangle in terms that are important to area measurement. In a rectangle, each of the angle measures is ninety degrees. A triangle can have at most one ninety-degree angle. This difference is not immediately important in understanding the difference between rectangles and triangles. If, however, the formula for calculating area is understood, then this student will recognize that one of the dimensions must be halved. Actually, she will understand that an average between sides must be taken, as with a trapezoid, but this amounts to halving one of the values because one of the sides has no length (where two lines come to a point).

Still having trouble imagining how someone can give a correct answer but not understand how that answer was obtained? The following example is another simple problem that comes from trigonometry. I have had several hundred students give me the correct answer immediately upon looking at the figure. Not a single one has been able to prove the answer. This is to say that they *knew* the answer but did not *understand* the answer. In the language of this chapter, they thought about it reproductively and not productively. The question concerns the angles created by two intersecting line segments (figure 4.1). Their intersection results in two acute and two obtuse angles. This is the question: What is the relationship between angles *a* and *b*? The angles opposite each other, as one recalls from grade-school geometry, have the same angular measure. If asked to prove this relationship, however, it is not enough to simply state the identity of *a* and *b* by way of their known geometrical relationship. Despite the expression of an accurate fact regarding the relationship between angles *a* and *b*, this fails to demonstrate an understanding of the problem, a structural understanding; it is instead an example of reproductive thinking. See whether you can prove this relationship.

Here's the fact that we can establish: $a = b$. How, then, might we go about solving the proof? Students typically begin by gathering all that is known about the figure, for example, that the sum of all of the angles of the intersecting lines is 360, which may be further broken down into 180 degrees from endpoint to endpoint on each line segment. Therefore, the top and bottom unlabeled angle measures (call them c and d, respectively) could be written as $(180 - a)$ or $(180 - b)$. Thus conceived, however, we will never be able to solve the proof because a and b never occur in the same equation. We are no closer to solving the proof than we were when we stated the identity of a and b. It is not until it is understood that c could be written as $c = 180 - a$ or $c = 180 - b$ that the proof may be solved. The dual identity of c in terms of its contribution to the 180-degree angle measure with angles a and b must first be discovered before one can, using the identitive property (i.e., $c = c$), find that $180 - a = 180 - b$ and prove that $a = b$.

We see that in order to solve the angle-identity proof, we must first understand the status of a and b as they relate to a third angle—for example, angle c. The problem can be solved only *in terms of this third angle*. To simply say that $a = b$ is to ignore the role played by angle c in this identity. It assumes that the relationship $a = b$ could occur independent of, or segregated from, angle c (or d).

Productive Thinking

Throughout the pages of his book, *Productive Thinking*, Wertheimer makes clear what he means by thinking in a productive way. We see that with the opposite angles problem, the relationship between angles a and b can be understood only within the context of a third angle—c. It is only *with c* that one may use the knowledge about the number of degrees on a line about a

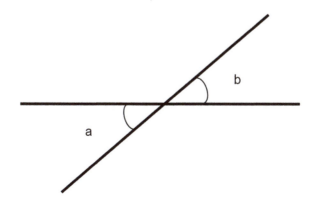

Figure 4.1. Opposite Angles Proof

single point (180). We have seen this proof worked out. To consider the relationship between a and b without the context of c demands reproductive thinking, but expanding one's perspective to include angle c and thus to better understand the $a = b$ identity is an instance of productive thinking.

It is difficult to define what productive thinking is because this suggests that there is some procedure that counts as "thinking productively." Were we to arrive at such a definition, then we could imagine somebody piously and obediently following the directions for "thinking productively," thereby making it reproductive. With this in mind, Wertheimer has designed his book with a series of examples where problems can be solved or experiences can be understood reproductively or productively. Since we are chiefly interested in understanding experience, consider his example of a girl describing her office (specifically the relations between staff). When asked the size of the office at which she worked, this girl responded:

> "Well," she said, "there are a number of people in the office. I have to do directly with a Mr. A, a Mr. B, and a Mr. C, who often come to my desk, ask questions, bring me letters, etc. There are others in the office with whom I do not have to do directly. Mr. A has dealings with a Mr. D, Mr. B with a Mr. E, and Mr. C with a Mr. F. D and E also have dealings with each other; so do E and F. Let me see, that makes six people in the office besides myself." (1959, 136–37)

Were you able to follow her logic? To be sure, she has stated everything with tedious specificity, but are you given an overall impression of the relations in her office? Wertheimer uses this example to demonstrate how a logical description, though accurate, might not be informative or even helpful. With a little bit of work, we find that this girl works directly under her boss, Mr. B, and has two people below her and for whom she is the boss. This description, though objectively less informative, actually expresses more about the social-professional situation at her office. This is because it provides the structure of the relationships between the office mates (e.g., who is the boss of whom). Though we can think productively in a great variety of ways, we understand that it always includes attention toward the context in which an experience or problem occurs. Since the essence of productive thinking can be given only through examples, we will consider one more. It comes from the radical teaching approach of Paolo Freire. His example is helpful because it demonstrates the serious consequences of reproductive thinking.

Critical Thinking: A Case Study with Paolo Freire

Freire was a revolutionary educator. He did not simply revolutionize education but used education to lead a revolution. He taught hundreds of Brazilian peasants how to read and write. This was particularly important at the time because Brazil had passed a piece of legislation that limited voting privileges to the literate. When the authorities realized that Freire was giving the farmers a democratic voice by encouraging them to learn literacy, he was exiled from Brazil. Why was literacy so revolutionary?

Freire not only gave these peasants literacy, he gave them critical consciousness as well. In the context of this chapter, critical consciousness may be understood as productive thinking. It has been demonstrated that with reproductive thinking, one does not actually have to understand the importance of context within which a problem makes sense. All that is important to a reproductive thinker is the facts, and these facts are understood to occur without any context or reason. Facts are facts, the reproductive thinker says. For the farmers in 1960s Recife, Brazil, the facts were that they were illiterate and that democracy was not theirs to practice. This was embedded deeply in their consciousness, in the same way we know that opposite angles are always equal.

The reader might be thinking, "Well, why didn't they simply learn how to read and write and thus take democracy into their own hands?" Such a question misses out on the embeddedness of reproductive thinking. "This is just the way it is." Newspapers were not written for the peasant farmer but for the urban businessmen who began to populate the larger cities. Freire recognized that illiteracy was an identity these peasants had resigned themselves to—one that was "inexorably given" (2012a, 10). Teaching somebody who *knows* he or she cannot learn is an impossible task. So how did Freire accomplish this task? He began by giving up on the reproductive idea that literacy must be learned. "Acquiring literacy does not involve memorizing sentences, words, or syllables—lifeless objects unconnected to an existential universe—but rather an attitude of creation and re-creation, a self-transformation producing a stance of intervention in one's context" (2012a, 43).

A literacy course that follows linguistics might begin with phonemes: the irreducible parts of spoken language: ta, te, ti, to, tu, and so on. Freire's lesson plan did not. Instead of drilling the parts of speech into the peasant farmers, Freire conducted what he called "cultural circles." In a cultural group, men and women look at pictures that depict events with which they are all familiar. For example, one such picture shows a woman drawing water from a well. Their task is to discuss what about each picture demonstrates *nature*, and what demonstrates *culture*. In the woman-drawing-water example, the need for water is recognized as natural while the well itself is a cultural artifact. If we have never considered the possibility of getting water by some means other than a well, then we might argue that using a well is natural. But then a fellow culture-group attendee might explain how some people collect water from a stream, some collect it from a spring, and still others collect rainwater. Participants are asked to examine these events critically. In doing so, they ask the question: could this be another way? It is understood that some elements are natural while others are cultural. We can imagine many ways to gather water but would struggle to imagine a woman who could manage without water. The culture groups continue for several days until the group reaches the final picture: a picture of a cultural circle. The participants are asked to turn their critical lens on illiteracy: could this be another way? Literacy suddenly becomes a possible way of interacting with the world, no longer limited to a select class of affluence or privilege. Once they realized that they too might be literate, the peasant farmers began to learn how to read and write quite rapidly. Freire explains one such example:

> Not infrequently, participants would write words with complex phonemes (*tra*, *nha*, etc.), which had not yet been presented to them. In one of the Culture Circles in Angicos, Rio Grande do Norte, on the fifth day of discussion, in which simple phonemes were being shown, one of the participants went to the blackboard to write (as he said) "a thinking word." He wrote: "*o povo vai resouver os poblemas do Brasil votando conciente*" ("the people will solve the problems of Brazil by informed voting"). (2012a, 47–48)

In summary, Freire reminds us that in teaching people how to think, we must "avoid a rote, mechanical process" and instead "make it possible for them to achieve critical consciousness so that they can teach themselves to read and write" (2012a, 48).

INTELLIGENCE BASED ON PERSONAL KNOWLEDGE

We initially looked at intelligence as a collection of skills and types of information upon which a judgment call has been made: namely, these skills and this information count as being intelligent whereas others do not. Insofar as they have been standardized, intelligence tests are biased since they privilege certain types of knowledge and skill over others. While we see the problem with the standardization of intelligence, it is difficult to imagine an experience of this. We then looked more specifically at thinking, since this is an experience with which we are all familiar and would agree has much to do with intelligence. Thinking, as argued by Wertheimer, is largely obscured by the procedures of logic (e.g., obediently following rules) and association (e.g., repetition or rote recall). These procedures are referred to as reproductive thinking since they don't require that one do any actual thinking, but merely reproduce the thinking that someone else has done. Reproductive thinking separates fact from meaning, giving the impression that meaning is insignificant while fact is of chief importance. Productive thinking, while impossible to define, involves recognizing the meaning of a particular fact. Here problems and experiences are seen within their context, and it is only within this context that the fact has any meaning at all. Wertheimer has explained the deficiency of reproductive thinking, but the example from Freire's literacy education program demonstrates the serious problems that accompany reproductive modes of thinking. If content to think reproductively, you are party to your own subjugation. In this respect, it becomes understandable that Wertheimer might look on an arithmetic class in horror when students are swallowing reproductive procedures "piously" and "without any reaction" (1959, 26).

While the standardization of intelligence is itself a problem, we have also seen that the kind of thinking that this fosters is also problematic. We have yet to see a conception of intelligence that aptly recognizes and balances the personal and meaningful tasks of thinking and knowledge. Howard Gardner (1983) supplies this.

Gardner developed a laboratory at Harvard where he studied intelligence along a variety of axes. Instead of beginning with the assumption that "intelligence" was something of which an individual has a little or a lot, Gardner began with the assumption that "human beings are capable of developing capacities of an exquisitely high order in at least seven semi-autonomous intellectual realms" (1983, 48). He realized that it is misleading when we refer to intelligence as a single thing. This mistake eventually leads to an unquestioned confidence in the standardized intelligence exam. As we have seen, such a conception of intelligence leads to the preference for *reproductive* thinking to the neglect of *productive* or *critical* thinking.

Instead of speaking of intelligence as a single individual construct, Gardner prefers to speak of it in terms of multiple intelligences. More specifically, Gardner argues that "as a species, we have the potential to develop our intellectual potentialities in the following realms: 1) language; 2) music; 3) logic and mathematics; 4) visual-spatial conceptualization; 5) bodily-kinesthetic skills; 6) knowledge of other persons; 7) knowledge of ourselves" (1983, 48). The exact number of intelligences is unimportant. What is important is that this conception of intelligence recognizes, validates, and celebrates a variety of important capacities in humans. Gardner does not arrive at this list by sitting in his office and speculating about what might constitute intelligence. He arrives at these realms by observing a great many people in a great many contexts and carefully considering the variety of cultural, social, and historical skills and talents that people have been able to develop. For each of these realms, there are people who demonstrate supreme capability. This is to say that each of these realms indicates a different type of intelligence that someone might possess. Rather than saying that individuals vary in how much intelligence they have, it may instead be maintained that individuals differ in their intellectual profile. Notice how this approach changes the way we understand the impetus behind schooling.

With his theory of multiple intelligences, Gardner is arguing that "individuals differ in their potentials in various domains" and not a single domain.

This means that it would be misleading to compare two people on the basis of a single intelligence because this ignores the other possible types of intelligence. Intelligence testing, instead of finding out how much intelligence someone has, can be a way of discovering an individual's strengths. Gardner explains:

> Such an assessment of an individual's "intellectual profile" should be thought of as informative rather than limiting. Armed with this kind of knowledge, parents and educators have the option of developing a child's strengths, and of supplementing weaker areas. (1983, 49)

Think about how schooling might change if this were the approach to intelligence. There wouldn't be any intellectual ideal toward which all students must inexorably march. Instead, students would be seen to represent different capabilities—different intellectual profiles. Students are then recognized for the skills and talents they possess, and schooling would be geared toward developing these capacities. There couldn't possibly be one single standard of intelligence because such a standard could emphasize only one of the seven (or however many) intelligences.

This, however, is not how we normally think of intelligence. Of the seven that Gardner lists above, can you decide which ones are held in the highest esteem? Try asking yourself these questions: Who is smarter—the mathematician or the athlete? Who is more successful—the girl who keeps to herself or the girl who is popular? Who makes the most money—the man who can read and write well, or the talented ceramics sculptor? Gardner realized, as many of us have gathered from our own experience, that we judge certain intelligences as more important than others. He explains:

> According to my analysis, we have tended in our own society to accord excessive weight to linguistic and logical-mathematic intelligences, while giving relatively short shrift to other intellectual domains. Our aptitude and achievement tests are also far more sensitive to accomplishments in these domains. In order to test an individual's ability in the bodily or musical domains, for example, it is clearly inadequate simply to use paper-and-pencil measures which can be administered in an hour. Rather, one should ask individuals to participate in activities which actually call in significant measures on these "intelligences"—to dance, play a sport, to sing, to learn an instrument. (1983, 49)

Have you ever taken a standardized test—aptitude, intelligence, or achievement test—that has asked you to recite a melody from memory or practice a dance move? Why aren't these included on standardized tests? The way that you answer this question will probably indicate what you have been taught about intelligence. It might sound something like this: while dancing or singing is important, these are not as important in determining intelligence as reading, writing, and arithmetic. Have we forgotten that during the Renaissance, scientists were indistinguishable from artists? Or that all of the epic Greek literature that has survived has been passed along as songs (and not written down)? That we privilege reading, writing, and arithmetic over the other intelligences merely reflects a judgment we currently have about what is important. This should not be confused with intelligence.

SUMMARY

We began by looking at the common conception of intelligence and how psychology brought this about. We then looked more closely at some of the problems with this approach. These problems forced us to carefully consider the role played by thinking and knowledge—both important to the topic of intelligence. It seems as though there is no room for actual thinking in the common conception of intelligence. This is because thinking is replaced by various modes of reproducing the thought that is held in the highest esteem. This is the idea that "there's a right answer to everything." When we learn to think for ourselves, we find that there are many answers to things, and by exploring alternative answers, we express and develop our own unique insights and gifts. This type of thinking requires us to investigate our own lives and our relationships to other things. Paolo Freire was used as an example of the liberating benefits of this approach to thinking and the subjugating detriments of reproductive thinking. It was against this backdrop that we returned to intelligence—this time from the vantage point of Howard Gardner.

For Gardner, intelligence is an individualized collection of a variety of abilities and inabilities. Instead of comparing people in terms of their abilities in one or two of the realms of intelligence, we might do better to recognize that each of us varies in the type of intelligence we have. Once these differences are recognized and appreciated—that is, without the addition of a judgment call—then thinking, learning, and schooling can be directed toward the further development of specialized talents. Intelligence testing becomes an opportunity to celebrate what you're good at. This is different from the current sense that intelligence tests tell us the ways in which we are deficient. The theory of multiple intelligences shows us that more than one realm counts for intelligence and that there is room for growth in each of them. Moreover, having a deficiency in one realm doesn't mean that you are unintelligent—even if that realm is reading. To be sure, we find that these can be further developed, but this does not need to be developed at the expense of recognizing the supreme musical or artistic intelligence that someone might have.

PSYCHOLOGIZING IN ACTION

I Consider a Tree

I can look on it as a picture: stiff column in a shock of light, or splash of green shot with the delicate blue and silver of the background.

I can perceive it as movement: flowing veins on clinging, pressing pith, suck of the roots, breathing of the leaves, ceaseless commerce with earth and air—and the obscure growth itself.

I can classify it in a species and study it as a type in its structure and mode of life.

I can subdue its actual presence and form so sternly that I recognize it only as an expression of law—of the laws in accordance with which a constant opposition of forces is continually adjusted, or of those in accordance with which the component substances mingle and separate.

I can dissipate it and perpetuate it in number, in pure numerical relation.

In all this the tree remains my object, occupies space and time, and has its nature and constitution.

It can, however, also come about, if I have both will and grace, that in considering the tree I become bound up in relation to it. The tree is now no longer *It*. I have been seized by the power of exclusiveness.

To effect this is not necessary for me to give up any of the ways in which I consider the tree. There is nothing from which I would have to turn my eyes away in order to see, and no knowledge that I would have to forget. Rather is everything, picture and movement, species and type, law and number, indivisibly united in this event.

Everything belonging to the tree is in this: its form and structure, its colours and chemical composition, its intercourse with the elements and with the stars, are all present in a single whole.

The tree is no impression, no play of my imagination, no value depending on my mood; but it is bodied over against me and has to do with me, as I with it—only in a different way.

Let no attempt be made to sap the strength from the meaning of relation: relation is mutual.

Source: Buber 1958, 7–8.

Chapter Five

Biological Psychology

To move from physics to physiology is an interesting step. The phenomenon of movement no longer plagues us, the soul is dispatched to limbo or some other place, and the mind is explicable in terms of the reflex arc or conditioned reflexes. —Eugene Kaelin 1964, 169

By reviewing the table of contents of any general psychology textbook, we quickly find that psychologists hold the biological bases of behavior in high esteem. It is understood that the introduction and methods chapters provide the minimum overview necessary for preparing students to start learning psychology, and the first content chapter provides the next most fundamental element of a psychology course. It is here that we find biological psychology. What sense are we to make of the significance of biology in our project of understanding experience?

Our bodies and the biology that goes along with them are necessary in each of our experiences. This is to say that there can be no experience *without* a body and its associated biology. Try to imagine standing in relation to something without a body. To directly investigate experience, we must consider the body as an important part of the context that gives the experience meaning and a necessary component through which an experience can happen. In this respect, it is fitting that a psychology textbook begin with a chapter on the body. While the body is an important detail that cannot be ignored, this does not mean that it must be considered at the expense of everything else. We unfortunately find an overemphasis on the role played by the body in experience, a strong tendency to reduce all experience to biological mechanisms. This is the conclusion Sally Satel and Scott Lilienfeld drew in their 2013 book, *Brainwashed: The Seductive Appeal of Mindless Neuroscience*. They write that "problems arise . . . when we ascribe too much importance to the brain-based explanations and not enough to psychological or social ones" (xvii). Similar concerns have followed biological explanations of psychology throughout history: William James noticed this as early as 1890, Karl Lashley in 1930, and Kurt Goldstein in 1934.

When biological bases of psychology are overemphasized, experiences such as depression, loneliness, anticipation, and anxiety are reduced to neurotransmitters and nervous-system activation. To say that "depression gets reduced to nervous-system activation" is to say that "depression is *nothing but* such-and-such a nervous-system activation." The meaning that surrounds these experiences as they are lived gets disregarded as unnecessary or unimportant. This is clearly a problem for psychologists who are interested in understanding persons and their experiences. Since we have decided to concern ourselves with understanding experience, we avoid the assumption that psychology can be understood exclusively by any system of explanation. We called this "avoiding the natural attitude" in the first chapter. We will instead consider biological mechanisms as a possible explanation *among many*. This means trying to see the ways in which biology helps us better understand our experience.

To begin, we will use Karl Lashley (1930) to demonstrate how biology is often used as a substitute for understanding experience—what we are trying to avoid. Lashley explains why biology falls short of its aim because biological mechanisms fail to explain all phenomena—even the biological ones. Lashley's concerns will lead into a more in-depth consideration of the role biology plays in experience. This will be supplied by Kurt Goldstein. After critiquing the model of biological reductionism for understanding humans, Goldstein suggests an alternative: a holistic model. We find that a holistic conception is fitting for psychologists who are interested in understanding experience. This is because holism considers the importance of things such as context and meaning; holism recognizes that experience occurs in wholes—each whole includes biology, environment, history, spirituality, and so on. This is appropriate for our project because we begin with the recognition that experience is complicated and that it can be understood from a variety of standpoints. Furthermore, none of these standpoints is itself sufficient for understanding experience.

LASHLEY'S CRITIQUE OF NEURAL ASSOCIATIONISM

Karl Lashley (1890–1958) was a bold researcher in the areas of biology, zoology, and neuropsychology—publishing some of the first papers on the psychological effects of brain damage. Lashley had had enough first-person experience with brain-injured persons to understand that the relationship between the brain and experience was not as simple as the modern scientific theories had anticipated. At the time of his (1930) paper, psychology was the newest target for a reduction to neuroscience. Here is Lashley's tongue-in-cheek analysis of the state of psychology into the middle of this past century:

> Among the systems and points of view which comprise our efforts to formulate a science of psychology, the proposition upon which there seems to be most nearly a general agreement is that the final explanation of behavior or of mental processes is to be sought in the physiological activity of the body and, in particular, in the properties of the nervous system. The tendency to seek all causal relations of behavior in brain processes is characteristic of the recent development of psychology in America. Most of our text-books begin with an exposition of the structure of the brain and imply that this lays a foundation for the later understanding of behavior. It is rare that a discussion of any psychology problem avoids some reference to the neural substratum, and the development of elaborate neurological theories to "explain" the phenomena in every field of psychology is becoming increasingly fashionable. (1930, 1)

If one has struggled to find Lashley's opinion of the popularity of neuroscience, he candidly admits: "I have been impressed chiefly by its futility. The chapter on the nervous system seems to provide an excuse for pictures in an otherwise dry and monotonous text. That it has any other function is not clear" (1930, 1). To be sure, the popularity of sexy, full-colored shots of cross-sections of the brain indicating blood-flow patterns has increased even into the twenty-first century.

His concern has some precedent. Lashley was one of the early scholars of associationism. This term was introduced in chapter 3 and in the context of thinking. Associationistic thinking is the ability to associate a problem with an answer: for example, we all know that $5 \times 5 = 25$ even though we may not immediately recognize the relationship between five groups of five units. In biology, associationism is the theory that a brain state always equals a behavior or a mental state. That is, "happiness" is associated with a particular brain state; "depression" is associated with a particular brain state; and so on. Associationism is most impressive with its demonstrations of the primary motor cortex. The primary motor cortex is the thin strip of cerebral cortex that is responsible for all physical movement in your body. Neuroscientists can trace every motor behavior—from head to toe—onto the primary motor cortex. If the "right-big-toe" region of your brain is activated, then you are moving your "right big toe." In his studies, Lashley shares his review of many cases of damage to the motor cortex and explains how associationism works through the analogy of the reflex. If associationism is correct, then irreparable damage to a given area of the motor cortex will result in the loss of the motor ability with which the area was *associated*. This, as demonstrated with stroke patients, is not always the case. Lashley first explains that the nervous system is far more complicated than this theory provides:

> The model for the [associationist] theory is a telephone system. Just as two instruments can be connected only by certain wires, so the sense organs and muscles concerned in any act are connected by nerve fibers specialized for that act.
>
> Perhaps few neurologists would agree to such a bare statement. They point to the incalculable number of nerve cells, the interplay of inhibition and facilitation, and suggest that in so complex a system there are limitless possibilities. But the fact remains that the essential feature of the reflex theory is the assumption that individual neurons are specialized for particular functions. The explanatory value of the theory rests upon this point alone. (1930, 3)

Next, Lashley explains that the nervous system does not always behave in ways that are conducive to the reflex theory. Even the firing of a neuron seems to follow rules other than this. "The adequate stimulus in such cases may be described in terms of a pattern having definite proportions but always, within wide limits, it is a matter of indifference to what receptor cells this pattern is applied" (1930, 4). Taken together, the complexity of the cerebral cortex and the limited predictability of the nerves themselves are used as proof that the business of neuropsychology as the only useful approach to psychology, save sexy full-page images in textbooks, is futile.

Even as early as 1930 (a date that could be extended back to 1890 with William James), psychologists expressed their concern about an overemphasis on neurological reductionism. Once again, "neural reductionism" means that any part of psychology can in principle be reduced to what happens in the nervous system. With this approach, it is understood that all psychology can be reduced to the rules of nervous-system functioning. Lashley has shared a major limitation of this approach: the associationist account of psychology fails to explain how rehabilitation is possible with functions that have been impaired due to cortical damage. If the wire that connects the brain to the right hand has been damaged—which is the case with stroke patients who lose considerable amounts of brain tissue—then how is it that right-hand operations can be relearned and rehabilitated in left-brain-damaged stroke patients? Lashley argues for a more inclusive theory of neuropsychology.

Goldstein (1995) makes a similar argument against associationism and suggests a holistic conception instead.

BIOLOGY FROM MECHANISM TO HOLISM

As a medical doctor, Kurt Goldstein had received comprehensive training in the dominant medical and biological theories of his time. At the beginning of the twentieth century, these theories had been characterized by an emphasis on the machine metaphor. This means that it was assumed that organisms work the same way as machines work, that is, in the way we understand a machine as a system of discrete parts with specific functions, so too can we understand an organism. Consider what this means: just as one can replace or fix any part to improve the operation of the machine, so too can one isolate and manipulate any part of the organism for its overall benefit. The chief method of doing so in the organism was supplied by the "reflex theory." Goldstein explains:

> According to the view underlying the reflex theory, the organism represents a bundle of isolable mechanisms that are constant in structure and that respond, in a constant way, to events in the environment (stimuli). . . . This is the view held not only of the nervous system but also of all phenomena. For example, even chemical processes are considered as related to the activity of very definite mechanisms. (1995, 69)

It was the business of the medical biologist to understand the sum total of "isolable mechanisms" that make up the organism and thus complete the biology of the human. Goldstein explains how the purposes of the laboratory and research were to disclose the relationships between causal events (stimuli) and their subsequent organismic responses. He continues:

> To work out these laws exactly, one exposes the organism to single stimuli, using various means to control conditions so that the reaction, which corresponds to that particular stimulus, may occur in almost complete isolation. . . . Therefore, for those who adopt this view, "analytical" experimentation has become the ideal foundation of knowledge. (1995, 69)

To repeat, Goldstein had entered the field of medical biology at a time when it was customary to view the person as a machine so that instead of beholding a person, one sees only a "bundle of isolable mechanisms." It is important to understand how much of modern medicine is owed to this system of explanation. It is through this approach that the specialized function of any particular organ system has been identified and understood. Moreover, without this system of explanation, medical specialization would be impossible. Indeed, this part-by-part system of explanation can work for everything that occurs within a person! A vertical jump may be understood by the series of muscular contractions from your feet all the way up through your trunk. Or even more specifically: every neural synapse that occurs therein. There is an explanation for everything, because everything can be understood in increasingly smaller parts that operate based on the laws of the reflex theory.

While it is an eminently helpful system of explanation for the biological organism, this does not mean that one need look no further than the reflex theory. That is, *a record of all of the reflexes inside an organism can never complete the picture of the organism*. Take, for instance, what might be the most common of all reflexes: the patellar reflex. Assuming this is still done, anybody who recalls having undergone a medical examination will remember the miniature rubber-mallet blow to the tendon just below the relaxed knee. Whoop! Up the foot goes. No matter how many times this demonstration has been done to the right leg, the left foot has never mysteriously lifted. This is because it is understood that the sudden impact to the relaxed patellar tendon *causes* the latter's contraction. Thus, provided the knee is bent and relaxed, the reflex contraction causes a slight "kick" forward of the lower part of the same leg. This is profoundly impressive to one who has been caught unsuspecting. I remember my experience with this as a child. I was completely dumbfounded by the mysterious occurrence: "My leg just kicked but *I* didn't cause that." The reflex theory maintains that one may be enraptured in a dialogue or a good book and yet, "Whoop! Up the foot goes." One could even focus one's attention on remaining still and yet, "Whoop! Up the foot goes." Despite the simplicity of this particular reflex, it eventually breaks down as a *complete system of explanation*. That is, it is useful if understood as a general tendency, but even this must not be endorsed as an absolute, "cause and effect" law. Goldstein explains:

> The "patellar reflex," for example, has proved to be by no means invariably constant in the same individual. It varies, depending, among other things, on the position of the limb, on the behavior of the rest of the organism, and on whether or not attention is paid to it. . . . A certain kind of attention diminishes the response, another kind exaggerates it. . . . To explain all these variations, it was necessary to go beyond the process in the so-called reflex arc and to assume that the course of a reflex is influenced by other factors. (1995, 70–71)

Once again, the purpose here is not to discount the benefit of the reflex theory—it has certainly contributed to a vast sum of knowledge pertaining to the biological organism. What is intended here is a limitation on the theory's breadth of explanatory power: *the reflex theory, while eminently helpful, does not provide an absolute system of explanation of the biological organism.* Namely, while the reflex theory as an abstraction is helpful in understanding the experience of a human, we cannot understand the human entirely in terms of reflex theory. The human being does not allow this reduction, as demonstrated in the breakdown of the patellar reflex.

Notice how this recognition comes about. It may be understood that Goldstein cuts his medical-student teeth on the mechanical explanation of the organism. One might even imagine that several years of medical coursework had been completed without ever coming into contact with a living biological organism. Nevertheless, it would still be assumed that living organisms could be understood in exacting detail, provided the laws of the reflex theory were learned. This extensive knowledge of the organism, abstracted into the biology of mechanism, might even have been exacted on the cadaver. At every step of medical training, one could imagine that there is no contact with an organism, only contact with the organism-as-a-machine. Once again, this is useful if it is understood that the model is never sufficient to replace the living person. The problem begins when the medical student treats her human patient as a cadaver or, what amounts to the same thing, a "bundle of isolable mechanisms." Goldstein describes the gravity of this reduction:

> The real crisis arises when, even in the face of new findings, the investigator cannot free himself from the former theory; rather, the scientist attempts to preserve it and, by constant emendations, to reconcile it with these new facts instead of replacing it by a new theory fitted to deal with both the old and new facts. (1995, 35)

This is to say that scientists who begin with the assumption that the human being is "nothing but a bundle of reflexes" will be incapable of understanding anything to the contrary. Thomas Kuhn (2012) has likened scientists of this kind to a horse wearing blinders: they easily miss what lies just beyond the narrow scope of their assumptions. This problem in medicine is evident in the experience of chronic pain. Chronic pain is an example of the crisis that Goldstein warns against. Had medical specialists been more open in interpreting their patient's reports, "chronic pain" would not exist.

The bold proclamation "chronic pain could have been avoided" is protected in two respects. In the first respect, the very designation of "chronic pain" wouldn't make sense: it is only within the biology of mechanism that such a category is necessary. But it is the second respect, in which the mechanization of the human has resulted in chronic pain, that is the most troublesome. This may be understood by the stigma attached to illnesses that fall outside the pale of medical explanation.

To understand this enigmatic medical phenomenon currently referred to as "chronic pain," Gillian Bendelow has emphasized the importance of the mind/body problem in the history of biomedicine's success. She explains:

> The critique of biomedicine, with its emphasis on high-technology, cure and the mind/body divide has developed alongside the decline of high mortality rates from infectious diseases. In the "developed" countries mortality tends to be largely replaced by degenerative illnesses such as cancer and cardio-vascular disease, and morbidity patterns increasingly dominated by conditions closely associated with "lifestyle" such as diabetes, anxiety and eating disorders, and increasingly, with illnesses associated with increased life expectancy such as Parkinsons, Alzheimers and rheumatoid arthritis. Thus, both biomedicine and medical social sciences have been challenged by a host of illnesses with multifactorial etiologies and complex mind-body relationships. (2010, 22)

Bendelow notes the impressive success biological medicine has had in completely wiping out what had, for many centuries, been the leading cause of mortality. Indeed, it was not until infectious diseases were done away with that medicine could face the next generation of killers, which she identifies as "conditions closely associated with 'lifestyle'" and "illnesses associated with increased life expectancy." To these I would add stress (Allan and Fisher 2011). It is important to keep in mind that with "chronic pain," new problems are faced with which the biomedical model is not immediately effective.

Given the impressive success that the biomedical model had already demonstrated (e.g., by almost eliminating the mortal consequences of infectious diseases), it would be understandable, nay condoned, that the biomedical model be the first choice in trying to understand a new illness. However, as Goldstein has warned, this does not mean that all illnesses are always best explained through this model. Consider the following fictional vignette:

During his checkup, John reports to his doctor that he has been experiencing continued discomfort in his lower back. His doctor has John try a series of flexibility procedures before examining the thoracic vertebrae with his hands. He takes a few X-rays and brings them back for inspection. "I'm afraid I don't see anything wrong, John." John holds his breath. Then, with the entire hospital snickering outside the door, his doctor adds, "Do you think that the problem might be in your head?"

John did what millions of people do every day: he had gone to the doctor with the experience of discomfort and hoped to go home with a diagnosis. Go in with an experience and come out with a biological explanation. "Please explain the biological mechanism that is causing my behavior." Mechanisms can be fixed, whereas experiences are complicated. Things can be understood in terms of their cause, but with experiences, one is forced to consider context and meaning. While this differentiation is a start, it fails to get to the heart of the injustice that John has experienced. John did not go home with the onus of a more complicated problem than he had hoped. He went home with *nothing*. If his pain wasn't a thing, then it was nothing. When the tendency is to turn an experience into a biological mechanism, then the absence of a mechanism is *nothing*. The doctor's report of "nothing" informed John's experience of pain so that to John, even his experience was not real.

John had hoped that his discomfort was real and not imagined. He had hoped that his back pain was a thing and not no-thing. Fritz Perls explains the difference between nothingness and no-thingness: "Nothingness in the Western sense can also be contrasted with the Eastern idea of *no-thing-ness*. Things don't exist; every event is a process; the thing is merely a transitory form of an eternal process" (1972, 70). Left with no-thing, one must instead countenance the meaning of one's experience as pain the process. To be sure, this latter antinomy is daunting and exceedingly consequential as it pertains to the entire fabric of one's existence. But it is one's being. Since Sartre, author of *Being and Nothingness*, is not there to consult John in the waiting room, his pain story does not end here.

To understand the relationship between biomedicine and the experience of pain, Bendelow provides a commentary:

> Medical theories of pain have traditionally concentrated upon its neurophysiological aspects, both in diagnosis and treatment and scientific medicine reduces the experience of pain to an elaborate broadcasting system of signals, rather than seeing it as moulded and shaped both by the individual and their particular sociocultural context. A major impediment to a more adequate conceptualization of pain is due to the manner in which it has been *medicalised*, resulting in the inevitable Cartesian split between body and mind. Consequently, the dominant conceptualization of pain has focused upon sensation, with the subsequent influence that it is able to be rationally and objectively measured. Medical practice has concentrated on the nociceptive or sensory aspects of pain. . . . One of the most complex and difficult types of pain to treat is *idiopathic* pain—that is, pain for which there is no established physical pathology—often termed *chronic pain syndrome*. (2010, 24)

To further complicate an already difficult matter, Bendelow explains how "'mental' or emotionally triggered illness is, and always has been, consistently stigmatized and marginalized" (2010, 22). Now, in addition to the pain with which his story began, John has to deal with the shame and ridicule of a possibly "mental" problem. When the pain presents, John can do nothing because the pain does not exist as a physical thing—it is a mental thing, which amounts to no-thing at all. This added understanding does little to abate his pain but much to increase his stress. In fact, John has fallen into what has been termed the chronic pain cycle.

After several hundred thousand instances of patients who, like John, left the doctor's office with their pain *and* nothing, doctors conspired against the biomedical model and created a faux-diagnostic category called "idiopathic pain," which, as Bendelow notes, is "often termed *chronic pain syndrome*." The prefix "idio" refers to a single case or a subjective report. Recall the discussion in chapter 2 on methods where "ideographic knowledge" is personal whereas "nomothetic knowledge" is general. Idiopathic pain is a pain that is experienced by an individual yet fails to satisfy any diagnostic criteria. Nothing changes in the way of understanding the experience of chronic pain, but now it has a legitimate (or illegitimate) biomedical name.

Now John is able to return home with his pain; he has also been disabused of the stigma of a mental problem. If asked about his pain, he need not hang his head in shame but may choose, depending on his mood, whether to explain that the problem is chronic or idiopathic. His friends and family will be impressed by the official-sounding biomedical diagnosis, which is in reality no diagnosis. While this obviously does nothing in the amelioration of his pain, John has been freed from the stigma—and the stress associated with it—of having a mental problem. That is, the faux-diagnostic category has only undone the problem that the insistence upon diagnostic categories has caused in the first place.

Chronic pain is not the only instance of faux-diagnostic categories. "Psychosomatic" is a term that identifies the interrelationship between mind and body, and it has been around for quite some time. In looking forward toward a solution to these instances that create a "diagnostic limbo" with which the traditional biomedical models have been unsuccessful, Bendelow suggests an integrative, holistic approach (2010, 23). By doing so, the experience of pain might be further understood as a process in which a person is participating rather than as a thing that a person has. Bendelow concludes with a suggestion that fits the present project:

> Using a focus on the person, rather than measuring so-called objective symptoms, allows us to encompass more easily the notion of *total* pain, which includes psychological, spiritual, interpersonal and even financial aspects of chronic pain, as well as its physical aspects. (26)

THINKING LIKE A BIOLOGICAL PSYCHOLOGIST

The beginning of this chapter outlined the importance of biology in understanding experience: there is no experience that has not been mediated by a body. This was followed by a warning—Goldstein's "crisis"—that the body mustn't be assumed to be the most important. Such a position fails to consider the additional contexts in which experience also always occurs. In the latter part of this chapter, we discuss how a biological perspective might be useful in understanding our experience, guided by Kurt Goldstein in his book *The Organism.*

Like many young medical doctors during wartime, Goldstein was asked to enlist as a field doctor. During one of his assignments, Goldstein was given a very specific task, to separate possibly brain-injured soldiers into groups: who can be rehabilitated and who cannot. Despite the comprehensive systems of classification in which he had been trained, this task proved impossible. I caricature an example here for the purposes of illustration:

> Supervising Doctor: Every patient that I have sent you has been recommended for rehabilitation.

> Goldstein: Yes, it's wonderful.

> SD: You were supposed to weed out those who could not be rehabilitated.

G: That is correct.

SD: What about patient number 21012? His behavior looks severely pathological to me.

G: Indeed.

SD: Does he always just stand in the corner?

G: Yes, isn't that brilliant?

SD: Excuse me?

G: His solution to the problem—it's brilliant.

SD: Solution? Oh, I see why each of your patients has been recommended for rehabilitation. You seem to be confusing "solution" with "problem."

G: With all due respect, doctor, it is you who have confused the patient's "problem" with his solution.

This fictional account is intended to demonstrate two things. The first is the crisis about which Goldstein had earlier warned us, illustrated by the observations of the supervising doctor. The second is the importance of context in understanding this soldier's pathology.

This doctor observed the peculiar behavior—standing in and facing the corner of the examining room—as the pathology. This would be the chief pathological symptom that would need to be removed. In this instance, the patient would be rehabilitated once he left the corner and sat in the chair that faced the examining physician. Goldstein has termed this tendency the "problem of determination of symptoms" (1995, 35). He explains how, in the medical profession, "we have become so accustomed to regard symptoms as direct expressions of the damage in a part of the nervous system" that "we forget that normal as well as abnormal reactions ('symptoms') are only expressions of the organism's attempt to deal with certain demands of the environment" (35). In this example, the supervising doctor saw the symptom—namely, standing in the corner—as a problem; Goldstein viewed this as a solution.

The difference between these two perspectives of the situation could be understood by the context of the symptom. Goldstein emphasizes context by proposing a methodological postulate to avoid future misunderstandings: "No phenomenon should be considered without reference to the organism concerned and to the situation in which it appears" (1995, 40). That is, the pathology is not to be understood as a problematic thing or "symptom," but as an experience of a person. This fits quite naturally with the project of this book: to try to understand the significance of a particular aspect of experience. In this chapter, that aspect is biology. To meet our goal, we must avoid the first explanation that comes to us: to immediately identify a behavior as a problematic symptom would take no longer than a few seconds. This is what Goldstein's supervising doctor has done. But Goldstein looks more closely: he understands that behaviors are always meaningful. However, to see the behavior as a meaningful experience had by the patient takes extra careful attention over a length of time. Goldstein has done well to understand even the meaning behind the peculiar behavior that follows severe brain damage. He goes on to explain what he has learned:

> First of all, we find that the patients avoid, as far as possible, all situations that would occasion catastrophic reactions. Of course, this avoidance by no means implies that the patient has consciously recognized the situation and its danger. . . . When an objectively endangering stimulus is on its way, a catastrophic reaction sets in immediately, precluding any adequate response to the situation. The patient then appears completely aloof from the world. It is not so much that the endangering situation has been actively avoided, as that the patient has been passively protected from it. (1995, 51)

Seeing the "symptomatic" behavior as a flight from a potentially catastrophic situation certainly helps make standing in the corner seem somewhat understandable, even advisable. Through careful observation, Goldstein was able to see that the unusual behavior demonstrated by the brain-injured soldiers was not arbitrarily pathological but pathological in ways that betrayed the singular meanings of the existence as lived by the various soldiers. He did so by psychologizing. It is not as though Goldstein one day decided to give up the whole project of giving the first mechanical explanation that came to mind; his subject matter demanded that he look more closely. And this he does. What followed from his experience in the examining room was a list of thirteen general rules or tendencies that characterize organismic life—that is, a holistic biology (1995, 48–59).

SUMMARY

The body, along with the biological processes this includes, is an important aspect of psychology. You cannot have an experience without a body that mediates this experience. However, this does not mean that experiences can be understood only by looking at the body. To examine only the body is compelling, and it has been increasingly common in the human sciences and even the humanities, as Satel and Lilienfeld (2013) showed us.

Although it might seem like an organ/thing, the brain is actually a process—just like you. Moreover, it changes through your experiences just as you change with it. Kurt Goldstein was used to demonstrate how even the simplest activities in the body (like the knee jerk) is not as simple as action and reaction. Indeed, this is a meaningful process, just like learning how to ride a bike. By changing the way we understand the body (that it is a process and not a thing), we can better understand the psychology underlying some of the poorly understood medical problems such as chronic pain.

PSYCHOLOGIZING IN ACTION

Patient with a Frontal Lobe Lesion

> The destruction of one or another substratum of the organism [lesion of the frontal cortex] gives rise to various changes in behavior, showing how these substrata and forms of behavior are interrelated and giving an insight into the organization of the total organism. —Goldstein 1966, 38

The patient whom I have first in mind is a man thirty years of age, with a lesion of the frontal lobe. His customary way of living does not seem to be very much disturbed. [. . .]

Let us take as an example the behavior of this patient in a simple test. We place before him a small wooden stick in a definite position, pointing, for example, diagonally from left to right. He is asked to note the position of the stick carefully. After a half minute's exposure the stick is removed; then it is handed to the patient, and he is asked to put it back in the position in which it was before. He grasps the stick and tries to replace it, but he fumbles; he is all confusion; he looks at the examiner, shakes his head, tries this way and that, plainly uncertain. The upshot is that he cannot place the stick in the required position. He is likewise unable to imitate other simple figures built up of sticks. Next we show the patient a little house made of many sticks, a house with a roof, a door, a window, and a chimney. When he is asked to reproduce the model, he succeeds very well. [. . .]

At first sight the difference may seem inexplicable, but the following experiment clarifies the situation. We put before the patient two sticks placed together so as to form an angle with the opening pointing upward. The patient is unable to reproduce this model. Then we confront him with the same angle, the opening pointing down this time, and now he reproduces the figure very well at the first trial. When we ask the patient how it is that he can reproduce the second figure but not the first one, he says: "This one has nothing to do with the other one." Pointing to the second one, he says, "That is a roof"; to the first, "That is nothing."

Source: Goldstein 1966, 39–41.

Chapter Six

Sensation and Perception

By this point, you have probably developed a sense of what to expect in the forthcoming chapters. We began this journey by considering the subject matter of our discipline: persons. In order to understand a person, we have found it best to investigate his experience. Finally, we investigate his experience by standing back far enough to allow him to describe it or to demonstrate it to us. We explored this approach to psychology through the topic of learning, where the argument was that significant learning is always personal and meaningful; we also explored it through the topic of intelligence, where the argument was that productive and critical thinking demand a personalized definition of intelligence (and not a generic, one-size-fits-all definition); we also explored our approach through biological psychology, where we saw a demonstration that the body is an important context for experience and through which we can better understand experience.

The topic of sensation and perception finds an interesting place in the history of psychology. This is because it could almost be argued that psychology emerges as a way of dealing with the problems *of* sensation and perception. The problem is as follows: how do we sense one thing but perceive another? For example, I received my Internet bill, and it was addressed to "Patrick Whickhead." This was a first for me. How was it that the person collecting my information on the other end of the line had heard "Whickhead" when I had said "Whitehead"? From the classical approach to perception, this is an example where a listener had heard one thing ("Whitehead") but had perceived another ("Whickhead"). The same phenomenon occurs in vision: imagine that your desk is situated in front of a window and that dusk is approaching such that a few rays of sunshine are stretching through the window and across the back corner of your desk. Imagine also that there is a blank sheet of computer paper positioned on your desk such that part of it reflects the sunlight and the rest of it remains in the dark. What color is the sheet of paper? Where it reflects the sunlight it will appear white, but where it sits in the shadows it will appear grey. If you set up this scenario and bring in a friend or family member to answer the question: "What color is this piece of paper?" they will reliably say "white," even when you point to the grey part. From the classical perspective, psychologists determine that such a perception is a *mistake*—we mistakenly generalize the color of paper to the entire sheet—even when it appears in a shadow. Psychology emerged as the discipline equipped to tackle this issue: Why do we see or hear things that aren't really there? How can we explain these mistakes?

In this chapter we consider examples of perception that challenge this classical approach. Instead of beginning with the assumption that paper has a true color or words have a true meaning, we will begin from the perspective of perception: namely, that perception is always understood from a particular vantage point and within a meaningful context. Viewed from this perspective, there are no "mistaken" perceptions; instead, perception becomes a window into the meaning by which persons understand their world and experience. I will try to explain this problem through the example of the Kanisza Square (Kanisza 1979), shown in figure 6.1.

The Kanizsa Square is an interesting figure because it is no square at all; the square is something that we add in perception. Before we consider the nuts and bolts of this illusion, if this is what we want to call it, notice the two ways that this perception might be considered. In the classical approach, the square is understood as a *problem*: why do we see a square when there isn't actually one on the page? This perspective begins with the assumption that there is a difference between stimulus and percept. The stimulus is the sense data from the objective figure: in the Kanizsa Square, this would be the four three-quarter black circles. The percept is how the stimulus appears to an observer: in the Kanizsa Square, this would be a white square atop four black circles. Classical perception psychologists attempt to explain the disparity between stimulus and percept. To resolve the disparity between stimulus and percept would be having the ability to see the stimulus for what it actually is. So now that you know the square is not actually there, can you see the stimulus for what it is? Probably not: the square remains front and center.

Now notice what happens when we start with experience. We have no need to try to undo perception, nor do we assume that some perceptions are more accurate than others. We may then try to understand how a certain perception has come about and not another. That we should all see a square in the Kanizsa image is remarkable: now what can we learn about this? To begin, we learn that sometimes the absence of something is more important than the presence of something else. In this image, the *negative space* is what emerges as the foreground figure. Moreover, the negative space itself has a division. When subjects are asked to count the number of brightnesses in this

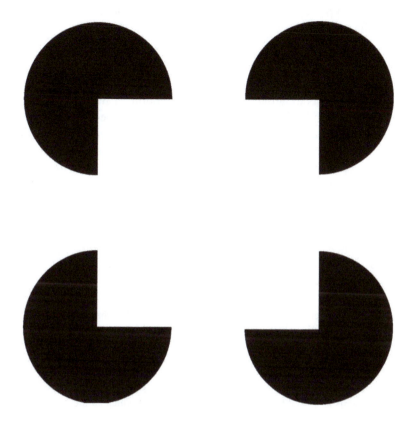

Figure 6.1. Kanizsa Square

figure, they reliably count three. There are the black circles, the white background, and the whitest square. Subjects report *two* brightnesses of white.
When a square is perceived, then a faint line is found where there isn't one.
On the inside of the square, this line is bright; just outside of this line is a
shade darker. Do you see two whites as well? If so, try covering up the black
circles with your hands and seeing whether this line disappears. What you
find is that manipulating the context of the square alters the perception of the
square. This means that the square's context is just as much a part of the
square as the shape itself. This is to say that the boundaries of the square
extend beyond the square itself!

Beginning with perception allows us to understand the experience that is
the backdrop for how we see, hear, smell, taste, and feel the world the way
that we do. Even in the previous examples we are starting to see this. But in
order to begin looking this way, we have to disabuse ourselves of the classi-

cal approach to perception, which assumes that a true or most correct way to perceive the world exists.

THE CLASSICAL APPROACH TO PERCEPTION

When I ask students to define "sensation/perception," I find that the definition gets divided in half in the same way as I demonstrated at the beginning of this chapter. Namely, that an object causes perception, along with the mental or imaginative side of perception. This is the division between stimulus and percept. *On the stimulus side, students place the real world of brightnesses, loudnesses, textures, hardnesses, scents, and so on; on the percept side, students place feelings, emotions, imaginations, and meaning.* Such a division demonstrates how deep the classical approach to perception goes. In this chapter, I explain an approach that collapses these two perspectives on each other. That is to say that there is no difference between the stimulus and the percept. This position goes against the classical psychology textbook. Maurice Merleau-Ponty explains:

> If we consult a classical psychology textbook, it will tell us that an object is a system of properties which present themselves to our various senses and which are united by an act of intellectual synthesis. For example, this lemon is a bulging oval shape with two ends *plus* this yellow color *plus* this fresh feel *plus* this acidic taste. . . . This analysis, however, is far from satisfactory: it is not clear how each of these qualities or properties is bound to the others and yet it seems to us that the lemon is a unified entity of which all these various qualities are merely different manifestations. (2008, 45)

And he continues,

> The unity of the object will remain a mystery for as long as we think of its various qualities (its color and taste, for example) as just so many data belonging to the entirely distinct worlds of sight, smell, touch, and so on. (2008, 45–46)

Merleau-Ponty explains that with a lemon, what we first perceive is the lemon. The sense qualities do not congregate and present to us their case for being a lemon. Texture, taste, and color are each manifestations of "lemoning." What if I were to then add that its skin has an oily texture? Have you ever felt the skin of a lemon? There is a moisture to it—an oiliness to its texture. This is particularly noticeable after the lemon has dried out, when its skin becomes rough. A lemon has an oiliness quality. But this is not the same quality as the oiliness I use to describe gasoline. In the context of discussing lemons, the idea of oily gasoline might actually initiate a gag reflex. What I am trying to explain is that the sense qualities of a lemon do not exist independently of one another. They do not have any specific meaning by themselves; this meaning only happens in the context of the object in question. Oily gasoline is not the same as oily lemons.

We may also understand the Kanizsa Square on the basis of this perspective: as a system of properties, the Kanizsa Square comprises four three-quarter black circles. As a system of properties, this image has two brightnesses: black and white—the circles are black while the background is white. Visual perception, then, is the recognition of the Kanizsa Square's visual properties. How are we to understand the apparent line that is connecting the gaps in the circles—that is, the square shape? The properties of the image do not allow a square to emerge. Moreover, it is only in the context of the square that the circles become circles. It is understood that the square somehow obscures part of the completed circles.

Christof Koch Explains Why We Do Not See with Our Eyes

Christof Koch is a neuroscientist at the California Institute of Technology. He began studying consciousness back when scientists were looked down on for doing so. Other neuroscientists were busy explaining that consciousness was a waste of time—a relic of nineteenth-century mysticism in the academy—but Koch remained interested. His 2012 book, *Consciousness*, summarizes much of the work he has done with a neuroscientific approach to consciousness. It is a fascinating book. Let's focus on one of the many interesting points he makes: that we do not see with our eyes. This is a neuroscientist at one of the most advanced scientific institutes in the world who has spent the past few decades studying consciousness, and he argues that we do *not* see with our eyes.

Koch explains three reasons he argues that we do not see with our eyes. This is not to say that the eyes are unimportant for understanding visual perception—indeed, Koch would be the first to explain the significance of neural explanations for conscious perception. What he means is that vision is more complicated than the processing of information that has been captured by your eyes. The three reasons he gives demonstrate that vision is *more* than this; otherwise, these phenomena would not occur. Koch begins, "Let me give you three examples of why you don't see with your eyes—something that painters have known for centuries" (2012, 50). His first example refers to the tiny movements that your eyes make. These are known as saccades. We might feel like our eyes pan across a scene, but actually they dart from point to point. Ask a partner to try to follow your finger with her eyes as you slowly move it side to side. Notice how her eyes do not move smoothly but make tiny, rapid movements. Koch explains how we don't perceive our visual field this way:

As you saccade to the right, the world should shift leftward—but it doesn't! Consider what would happen if you were to move a video camera with the same cadence across the book: watching the resultant movie would make you nauseated. To avoid this, television cameras pan slowly across the scene; their motion is completely different from the way your eyes dart about as you take in salient aspects of an image. If retinal neurons were the ones communicating the percept of a stationary world, they would have to exclusively signal motion in the outside world, but not respond to motion of the eye in which the cells are themselves located. However, retinal nerve cells, like those in the primary visual cortex, are incapable of distinguishing between object motion and eye motion. They react to both. (2012, 50)

Have you found yourself sitting in a parked car or at a stoplight and suddenly had the experience that you were moving? Maybe the car in front of you rolled backwards toward you or a car parked beside you began to exit the parking spot in reverse. For a moment, you were unsure whether you were moving and the other car was remaining still or the opposite. Why doesn't this always happen whenever we move our head? Is the world rotating about my eyes, or is my head moving about the world? We see in these examples that vision encompasses more than the sensory information that comes in through the eyes. The next example Koch gives is that of the blind spot. If you have never tested your own blind spot, here is a way of doing so: close your right eye and look at the *X* with your left eye. Now slowly move your focus to the right of the *X* mark. It will depend how closely you are holding the book to your eye, and you may even have to continue moving to the right until you have left the page. But eventually the *X* will disappear. If you continue going even farther to the right, the *X* will reappear. It works best if you hold the book about six inches from your eye.

X +

Now that you have discovered your blind spot, consider what this means about the relationship between vision and the structure of your eye. Can you predict what Koch will say? He writes,

Second, consider the "hole" in your retina at the blind spot: This is the place where the optic nerve leaves the retina; the axons making up the nerve fiber displace the photoreceptors, so none of the incoming photons are captured at the blind spot. . . . You would be annoyed if the camera on your cell phone contained a few bad pixels that were always off: The black spot in the photos would drive you nuts. But you don't perceive the hole in your eye because cortical cells actively fill in information from the margins, compensating for the absence of information. (2012, 50)

As his third piece of evidence for why you do not see with your eyes, Koch reminds us that we dream in color and that this most often occurs in the dark and with our eyes closed. He explains how "the world of your dreams is colored, animated, and fully rendered." While you are dreaming, even though you are perceiving color, "the nerve cells in your eyes don't signal anything about the outside world. It is the cortico-thalamic complex that provides the phenomenal content of dreams" (2012, 50, 51).

GESTALT APPROACH TO PERCEPTION

We have looked at the "problem" that classical psychology has assigned to perception, and the list of examples of how we do not see with our eyes lead us to conclude that science is unlikely to come up with a conclusive definition of perception anytime soon. Merleau-Ponty asks us whether, in principle, it ever could: "Rather, the question is whether science does, or ever could, present us with a picture of the world which is complete, self-sufficient and somehow closed in upon itself, such that there could no longer be any meaningful questions outside this picture" (2008, 34)

The experience of perception makes it impossible to come up with a one-and-only scientific definition of perception. For those of you who wish to reduce the experience of perception to the brain, Alva Noë (2009) has written a comprehensive volume explaining why you are *not* your brain and has used perception experiments to demonstrate this. After perception has proven so unyielding to scientific operationalization, it is easy to throw our hands up in defeat: if it cannot be operationalized, then we haven't anything to say about it. However, an alternative exists. But this alternative requires that we take a different approach to understanding perception. For the remainder of the chapter, we will look at an approach to perception that does not attempt to explain away the experience of perception. It is Gestalt perception theory. From here on out, the goal is not to explain why we perceive one thing and not another. Instead, we will try to understand how we come to see anything at all. That is, we will look at the ways in which stimuli organize themselves into meaningful percepts. The story begins in a railway passenger car.

Before writing his seminal paper on the "Laws of Organization in Perceptual Forms" in 1938, Max Wertheimer was sitting beside the window in a passenger train that had stopped at the station. Like us right now, he was wrestling with the problem of perception. He knew that "when we are presented with a number of stimuli we do not as a rule experience 'a number' of individual things, this one and that" (np). If perception cannot be divided up this way, then how are we to understand what we see? He began staring at the railroad crossing sign—the *X* with the flashing red lights. Suddenly it dawned on him. Do you know what he saw?

When two lights on a railroad crossing sign flash, do you understand what is happening? The one on the right flashes, and then the one on the left flashes, then right, then left, then right. Any rudimentary understanding of a closed electrical circuit will help us understand that two lights are flashing in succession. But this is not how it *seems*. Stare at a railroad crossing sign: what do *you* see? Wertheimer realized that what he was perceiving was a single light bouncing back and forth. "[L]arger wholes"—namely, movement—"separated from and related to one another are given in experience: their arrangement and division are concrete and definite" (np). Something about the pattern of two flashing lights had been organized into a single light movement. This phenomenon would later be called stroboscopic motion, which is how we perceive movement on the big screen at the movie theater (when what we're actually looking at is a series of still photos).

Gestalt means "whole." Perception is not a combination of little things. When I see that somebody is happy, I gather his happiness at once! I do not add up the smile, dimples, pleasant tone, and twinkling eyes and arrive at a conclusion that he is happy. Merleau-Ponty liked to speak of the physiognomy of things. The physiognomy is the "face," or how things appear to us. When we are looking at apartments or houses, we get an overall sense of it being an appropriate home for us; when we are invited into someone else's home, we get an overall sense of it being welcoming or unwelcoming. These are not logical deductions but perceptions. The purpose of Gestalt perception theory is to understand how stimuli gather themselves into meaningful wholes. This is why Wertheimer outlined the "laws of *organization* in perceptual forms."

The details of his study may be found by looking it up through its reference information at the conclusion of the book. It is provided free of charge by a neat "History of Psychology" initiative at York University. You will find that Wertheimer explains the laws of perceptual organization with great clarity and through the aid of simple examples. Instead of going through each of these, I leave this for those of you who are interested in looking at it in a bit more depth. I will instead discuss some of the consequences of the change in perception for which I am arguing: a change that emphasizes the significance of personal meaning. That is to say: perception *is* a meaningful experience that occurs as a single Gestalt, an all-or-none threshold. This explains why experience is always meaningful and not meaningless and why we always perceive something and never nothing.

Notice the change for which I am arguing: perception is not *caused* by stimuli but *emerges* from stimuli *in the meaningful context of the observer*. Upon walking through a potential residence, you or I would both come away with a sense of its appropriateness for living. The stimuli (kitchen, bedroom, study, etc.) organize themselves into the way that they might best meet our needs. It isn't accurate to say that we project our desires onto them: that we only see what we want to see. If this were the case, then every house would seem ideal. It also isn't accurate to say that the bedrooms themselves cause our perceptions of them. It is something in between these two explanations. If I am interested in raising a family, then the bedrooms will organize based on this type of Gestalt; if I am interested in saving money, then I am going to be paying attention to energy-efficient appliances, square footage, and expected maintenance. The potential residence will be perceived in a manner that is personal. Merleau-Ponty explains these perceptions:

> It is to describe a particular relationship between us and the object or to indicate that we are moved or compelled to treat it in a certain way, or that it has a particular way of seducing, attracting or fascinating the free subject who stands before us. [Home] is a particular way the world has of acting on me and my body. (2008, 47)

Bruner and Postman Observe the Playing-Card Gestalt

In 1949, two cognitive scientists performed an experiment that demonstrated how we understand our basic perceptions in terms of Gestalts. Their experiment involved a normal deck of playing cards with a few additions. Jerome Bruner and Leo Postman included a black four of hearts and a red six of spades. Within the playing-card Gestalt, a four of hearts is red and a six of spades is black. But Bruner and Postman had reversed these expectations. The experiment proceeded by asking subjects to report color, number, and suit of the cards that were presented. They were interested in *how much longer* it would take subjects to report the unusual or "trick" playing cards than the normal playing cards. Sure enough, the "trick" playing cards took about four times as long to identify. Fortunately for us, their experiment did not conclude here. Bruner and Postman explored the experience of the "trick" card in more detail: what was happening during the extra time that it took to identify the playing card?

Remember, Bruner and Postman were showing their subjects a playing card that they had never seen before and one that does not follow the rules of color and suit. A spade is black and never red; a heart is red and never black. How might a subject reconcile a *red* spade or *black* heart? The experimenters identified four types of reactions used to identify the "trick" playing cards: dominance, compromise, disruption, and recognition of the trick.

With *dominance* reactions, subjects relied on a piece of pertinent information (color or form) for determining color and suit. For example, if you notice color first, then the rounded edges of a red suit would necessarily be a heart. But if you recognize form, then the heart shape would necessarily be red. "Red heart" is the Gestalt—whether you see red first or heart first, you will arrive at the answer if you are looking at a traditional playing card. However, with the "trick" playing cards, this perception doesn't work very well: if you see form first, then you'll see a red heart; if you see color first, then you'll see a black spade. Get it? Dominance reactions demonstrate one way in which perception emerges as a Gestalt and not a sum of individual sensations.

In *compromise* reactions, subject expectation (red heart or black spade) interfered with stimulus presentation (black heart or red spade), and this resulted in a compromise. Bruner and Postman (1949, 216) share a list of some of the colors subjects reported when presented with a red spade:

Brown	Black on reddish card
Black and red mixed	Olive drab
Black with red edges	Grayish red
Black in red light	Looks reddish, then blackens
Purple	Blackish brown
Black but redness somewhere	Blurred reddish
Rusty color	Near black but not quite
Rusty black	Black in yellow light
Lighter than black, blacker than red	

Fifty percent of subjects gave such a compromise response to trick playing cards.

In *disruption* reactions, subjects take much longer to identify the playing card in question. This reaches such a duration that the subject gives up, loses confidence, and reports confusion. One subject reported: "I can't make the suit out, whatever it is. It didn't even look like a card that time. I don't know what color it is not or whether it's a spade or heart. I'm not even sure what a spade looks like! My God!" (1949, 218).

And finally, some subjects *recognized* the incongruity in the "trick" cards. This usually began with the recognition of an erroneous detail: a pip on the heart (a "pip" is the triangular handle on the spade-suit) or an upside-down spade.

Bruner and Postman's study provides an impressive demonstration of what goes into our simple perceptions. Perception can be explained in part by the stimuli that lay before us but also in part by our expectations for a particular perception. This entire chapter defends a rather dramatic shift in how we might come to understand perception. Perception is not the sum of stimuli that have been collected by our senses. We don't see or hear this way. We do, however, participate in our world in a way that is always meaningful. Perception is how we interact with it and make sense of it. Merleau-Ponty argues that perception might be understood as a way of living. I will let him conclude:

Our relationship with things is not a distant one: each speaks to our body and to the way we live. They are clothed in human characteristics (whether docile, soft, hostile, or resistant) and conversely they dwell within us as emblems of forms of life we either love or hate. (2008, 48)

SUMMARY

This chapter examined perception as the experience of deciphering meaning in our world. Perception is not, as it has long been believed, that act of capturing the reality that lies outside. This is the assumption that stimuli cause our awareness of them. How can this be the case when we see things that are not present and fail to see things that are?

The rather ridiculous example of Koch was explored. Vision, Koch maintains, has nothing to do with the eyes. Indeed, through his example, we *see* how vision is a process that involves many sense modalities along with things like memory and expectation.

To be sure, stimuli have their own unique way of being sensed by our bodies—through our eyes, ears, skin, nose, and so on—but they do not communicate independent bits of information. These senses give rise to an experience of perception—of meaning about our surrounding. It is a way of being aware of your surrounding and interacting with it.

PSYCHOLOGIZING IN ACTION

Description of a Heather Branch

Never have I been so touched and almost moved by the sight of heather as the other day, when I found these three branches in your dear letter. Since then they have been lying in my Book of Images, penetrating it with their strong and serious smell, which is really just the fragrance of autumn earth. But how glorious it is, this fragrance. At no other time, it seems to me, does the earth let itself be inhaled in one smell, the ripe earth; in a smell that is in no way inferior to the smell of the sea, bitter where it borders on taste, and more honeysweet where you feel it is close to touching the first sounds. Containing depth within itself, darkness, something of the grave almost, and yet again wind; tar and turpentine and Ceylon tea. Serious and lowly like the smell of a begging monk and yet again hearty and resinous like previous incense. And the way they look: like embroidery, splendid; like three cypresses woven into a Persian rug with violet silk (a violet of such vehement moistness, as if it were the complementary color of the sun). You should see this. I don't believe these little twigs could have been as beautiful when you sent them: otherwise you would have expressed some astonishment about them. Right now one of them happens to be lying on dark-blue velvet in an old pen-and-pencil box. It's like a firework: well, no, it's really like a Persian rug. Are all these millions of little branches really so wonderfully wrought? Just look at the radiance of this green which contains a little gold, and the sandalwood warmth of the brown in the little stems, and that fissure with its new, fresh, inner barely green.— Ah, I've been admiring the splendor of these little fragments for days and am truly ashamed that I was not happy when I was permitted to walk about in a superabundance of these. One lives so badly, because one always comes into the present unfinished, unable, distracted. . . . I found reality as indescribable, down to its smallest details, as it surely always is.

Source: Rilke 2002, 9–10.

Chapter Seven

Memory

Retrospection and Prospection

[M]emories do not exist in a vacuum. Rather, they continually disrupt each other through a mechanism we call "interference." Virtually thousands of studies have documented how our memories can be disrupted by things that we experienced earlier (proactive interference) or things that we experienced later (retroactive interference). —Loftus and Pickrell 1995, 720

In this chapter our focus will be on memory. We find out quite quickly that the concept of "memory" carries with it a fair amount of metaphysical baggage. By this I mean that the concept of memory is kept alive by certain assumptions about experience—assumptions that we have made it our business to unravel by learning to look closely as psychologists. To have a memory, it is first assumed that a particular event or experience occurs *in fact*. In the previous chapter on sensation and perception, we learned that when we are dealing with experience, it is difficult to determine whether what we are sensing is actually there. Indeed, to say that you are definitely sensing the thing in question is itself an assumption. With memory, the second assumption is that we may then carry our events and experiences with us in the same way that a thumb drive carries our files. But do your thumb-drive files "interfere" with one another? Do new pictures saved to your thumb drive change those already saved on it? Of course not, but this is how our memory seems to work.

Instead of looking at memory as the filing away of events in one's mind, we will try to understand the experience of remembering. In this chapter, we will replace memory with the term "retrospection," which means looking into the past from the perspective of the present. Doing so will recognize that a memory is not the act of returning to something that has already occurred in the unchanging past. We may instead look to the past as a context for understanding our experience of the present (or of the future). This change in terminology also enables us to consider the experience of "prospection"—or looking into the future from the perspective of the present. We thus exchange "memory" for the experiences of "retrospection" and "prospection." We also turn memory as a thing into the experience of remembering. At the conclusion of this chapter, you will understand how temporality—the relationship of past-present-future—influences your daily experience. Instead of understanding a unidirectional line of time pointing from past to present and from present to future, I will use the psychology of memory to demonstrate how this line is more a network wherein past, present, and future all interconnect.

LOFTUS EXPLAINS HOW WE REMEMBER WHAT ISN'T

In 1995, psychologist Elizabeth Loftus tested a hypothesis that she had regarding memory: she wondered whether it would be possible to implant a completely false memory into a person's mind.

While this might sound like the aspirations of a mad scientist bent on ruling the world, Loftus's hypothesis already had some precedent. She had already gathered some evidence to suggest that the memories that we keep are susceptible to manipulation by ourselves and by others. This means that a memory that we have about an experience can be predictably changed after the experience has taken place: the memories that we have already made are susceptible to change. A simple example of this comes from an experiment that Loftus performed to demonstrate the plasticity of eyewitness testimony (Loftus and Palmer 1974): the recollections that subjects had of an event was shaped after the fact by changing one word in a follow-up question. The implications that this study has for memory are profound, so it is worth taking a few minutes to look into it a bit further.

The design is quite simple: 150 subjects were shown a one-minute driver's training video that included a four-second car accident. After being shown the video, fifty subjects were asked to approximate how fast the cars were going when they "hit" each other; fifty subjects were asked to approximate how fast the cars were going when they "smashed into" each other; and fifty subjects were not asked any follow-up questions. Each of the subjects watched the same video clip; the only difference was the wording used in the follow-up question. A week later, these subjects were shown the video once more and asked a series of questions about what they had just seen. The key question in which the experimenters were interested was whether or not the subjects had remembered seeing broken glass on the ground. If, *in the previous week*, subjects had been told that the cars had "smashed into" each other, then they were more than twice as likely to report seeing broken glass in the scene than the other two groups were. Substituting the word "smashed" for "hit" was enough to double the number of subjects who remembered seeing broken glass on the ground. Incidentally, the scene had no broken glass.

The memory of watching a car accident was manipulated after the scene had ended—all based on the suggestiveness of a single term. Imagine if there had been a more elaborate effort made at shaping these subjects' memories: for example, if confederates (faux subjects who are actually working for the experimenter) agreed that *they* had seen glass at the scene. With this example, you might be reminded that your memory is sometimes faulty. You remember putting your car keys in one place only to find out that you had evidently placed them somewhere else. That memories are susceptible to change should come as little surprise to you if you have ever heard a friend or relative embellish a personal story—like the fish your father caught that keeps getting bigger and bigger as the story is told. When telling the story of your first ticket, you were going nine miles per hour over the speed limit when telling your parents but fourteen miles per hour over the speed limit when telling your friends. Loftus demonstrates how each time you tell this tale—adding a detail here and forgetting a detail there—your recollection of the event as it once occurred has fundamentally changed.

To be sure, memories are malleable; but can I remember something that I have never experienced? Could I tell a story from my past with confidence that I had lived through it, even though I never actually experienced it? Loftus thought this was possible and set out to do just that. The consequences this experiment would have on traditional theories of memory are profound. It would certainly challenge the notion that our mind is a warehouse in which memories are stored: a giant network of filing cabinets and shelves of memories, facts, experiences, and thoughts. Is it possible that some of these files are imposters? Loftus finds that she *can* implant false memories into people, but this is not a matter of hacking into someone's mind and changing the file contents. Instead, it demands a more expanded conception of memory—one that takes into consideration the role of experience. Experience, as the introductory quote explains, is capable of interfering with memories. We will first review the example of memory implantation from Loftus and Pickrell (1995), and then we will more closely examine the relationship between experience and memory to see whether we can understand what it means to remember.

In the spirit of William James (2007), I will excerpt at great length the study to which I am referring. Moreover, Loftus and Pickrell write in a manner that is clear and easy to follow. Their report is an exception to those that Bevan (1991) has accused of "submerging understanding" in chapter 1. Loftus and Pickrell discuss a case of memory implantation:

In one of the first cases of successful memory implantation, a 14-year-old boy named Chris was supplied with descriptions of three true events that supposedly happened in Chris' childhood involving Chris' mother and older brother Jim. Jim also helped construct one false event. Chris was instructed to write about all four events every day for 5 days, offering any facts or descriptions he could remember about each event. If he could not recall any additional details, he was instructed to write "I don't remember."

The false memory was introduced in a short paragraph. It reminded Chris that he was 5 at the time, that he was lost at the University City shopping mall in Spokane, Washington, where the family often went shopping, and that he was crying heavily when he was rescued by an elderly man and reunited with his family.

Over the first 5 days, Chris remembered more and more about getting lost. He remembered that the man who rescued him was "really cool." He remembered being scared that he would never see his family again. He remembered his mother scolding him.

A few weeks later, Chris was reinterviewed. He rated his memories on a scale from 1 (not clear at all) to 11 (very, very clear). For the three true memories, Chris gave ratings of 1, 10, and 5. For the false shopping mall memory, he assigned his second-highest rating: 8. When asked to describe his memory of getting lost, Chris provided rich details about the toy store where he got lost and his thoughts at the time ("Uh-oh, I'm in trouble now.") He remembered the man who rescued him as wearing a blue flannel shirt, kind of old, kind of bald on top . . . "and, he had glasses."

Chris was soon told that one of the memories was false. Could he guess? He selected one of the real memories. When told that the memory of being lost was the false one, he had trouble believing it. (1995, 721)

In summary, we find that the subject, Chris, had been given a short description of four events. Three were taken from his childhood, and the fourth was a fabrication. Chris was asked to keep a journal for a week and to write about any details that surfaced about these four events. After a few weeks, Chris was able to recall specific information about the event that had never occurred—so much so, in fact, that he was *more certain* that he had gotten lost in a toy store than he was about two of the other events that were actually a part of his past. Loftus and Pickrell tell us that he had trouble believing this. How are we to understand this result?

The first response might be a dismissive one: memories are faulty and thus untrustworthy. Thus, unless we have documentation that something occurred in a particular way, we are better off remaining in disbelief. Such a position would not last long because we will find that recollection of past events—real or imagined—are always informing our experience in the present. I make decisions about what and when to eat, how to act around others, and how to plan for the future based on the memories that I keep. This is true whether I trust my memories or not. Indeed, being dismissive about memory will not work.

The next response we might have is an idea about how we can take advantage of memory plasticity in ourselves and in others. This response more closely resembles the way we will consider memory at present, even though this could be taken as a mad scientist's mind-control technique. Memories *are* subject to change, and they *do* influence our behavior: why not focus on the ways that the past influences our present and our present, the past? We may view the past as an event that occurred in fact. From this perspective, memory is untrustworthy. We may also understand the past as a context for understanding the present. This is how we will view it for the remainder of this chapter. In chapter 5 I explained how the body is always a context for experience; so too are past, present, and future always contexts for experience. When understood as a context, we may begin to recognize the role that memories play in shaping our present and in orienting our future as well as those of the people around us. We may then use this to our advantage. Indeed, after we discuss memory from the vantage point of experience—the approach we are taking with psychologizing—it will be easy to identify the role that memory has in psychopathology, health, personality theory, and so on. Take quality of life, for example: by recognizing the plasticity of memory in tandem with the role that memories have in shaping our sense of life satisfaction, we can either increase or decrease our sense of satisfaction in ourselves or in others. Martin Seligman (2006) explains a few ways that we can shape our memories to our benefit: for example, by taking five minutes to reflect on anything pleasant or satisfying that happened in your day, those pleasant memories are brought to the foreground whenever you begin reflecting on your life. Subjects who practice this tend to score higher on quality-of-life inventories. Now we will turn our attention to the relationship between experience and memory, or how we can understand memory as an experience.

NETWORK OF TEMPORALITY: THE RELATIONSHIPS OF PAST-PRESENT-FUTURE

Loftus finds that she *can* implant memories into people, but you do not have to worry that someone might break into your memory warehouse and plant false facts. Loftus simply reinforces what we already suspect: that memory (of the past) is a context for experiencing the present. If I look at a restaurant menu, I see entrees in terms of my familiarity with them based on past experiences. Even if everything on the menu is new, I still have an idea of what I will like based on my memories tied to the ingredients used—even memories that have been implanted in me. When viewed as a context and not a history saved on some hard drive, it is perfectly understandable that a memory is susceptible to change. The entire previous chapter was spent exploring the way in which visual perception is not always as it seems; perceptions are also subject to change. For the remainder of this chapter, we will look at *memory as an experience that we can have only in the present.*

Instead of memory, which suggests that actual experiences are kept in a vault as a collection of facts, we will refer to memory as retrospection. When we retrospect, we look into the past. We do not actually go to the past, but we look back onto what we understand are the past events and experiences of our life. Furthermore, we can do this only from the context of the present. When I think back on my 101-Dalmatian-themed birthday party, I do so as a young man and not as the terribly shy six-year-old who was uneasy about the merging of school life and home life. See? A six-year-old is not keen on the social and developmental turmoil in the same way that a psychology professor is. Calling this a memory suggests that I can play the video of my birthday party and examine it as a fixed event that I can recall accurately or inaccurately. Even if I were to find some video footage, I could not help but interpret this past experience in the context of the present. My understanding of this event is from the vantage point of an author trying to give an insightful example from his own life; as such, I am noticing details that the six-year-old is missing. This is why we will use the term "retrospection"—to look into the past from the present. Sometimes retrospection is tied to a feeling: I remember being given a Dalmatian stuffed animal, and tied to this is a sense of warmth, security, and love. I experience this sense in my body right now as I retrospect about the gift. The emotional sense I am experiencing cannot have its locus in the birthday party event, because at that moment it was still a new gift: I had no idea I would carry it with me until the spots had begun to fade. When I look back onto the gifting of this stuffed animal, I do so through a layer of events that have occurred subsequently—such as selecting this stuffed animal as my sleep-mate for several months. These subsequent events transform the gifting of "any old stuffed animal" to the gifting of an "extra-special stuffed animal." There is no such thing as the original birthday-party event left unperturbed by subsequent life experience.

What we have done so far is substitute the word "retrospection" for "memory." This is because memories are often taken as the occurrence of some actual event. Such a conception means little to us after we find that memories are subject to change (or even to implantation). The term "retrospection," however, recognizes the dynamic relationship between present and past. This helps us understand how the present can shape the past as well as the reverse. After we make this word substitution, we find that we can look in yet another direction from the present, a direction that the category "memory" prohibits us from considering: looking toward the future, or prospection. Just as we might look into the past from the vantage point of the present, so too might we look forward toward the future. Moreover, since we have already shed the notion of looking into the past *as it really occurred*, we don't have to worry ourselves about looking into the future *as it will occur*. We recognize that past and future provide contexts for experiencing the present. It is easy to say that the past has influenced the present, but how can the *future* influence the present—how can the cause follow after the effect? This is easy. Many of you who are in college or who are considering attending college will be able to relate to this: when I ask my students why they have decided to attend college, almost all of them explain that they have their future in mind—a response which is typically as generic as "to get a job." Usually, if I pry a bit more, students will have a particular job in mind. If asked, they may even have a particular idea about how a course in psychology might be used to facilitate this goal. The future provides a backdrop for understanding our decisions in the present. Delayed gratification is an example of this: I can resist the single marshmallow (or a twenty-thousand-dollar salary) now for the promise of two marshmallows tomorrow (or a forty-thousand-dollar salary four years from now). Whether or not a marshmallow (or job) is actually on its way cannot be known in advance. Indeed, many things can happen between now and later that will turn something promising into something undesirable. We would much rather take twenty thousand dollars today than nothing, yet many of us choose to take on a twenty-thousand-dollar debt instead (or whatever going to college will cost). Such a decision makes sense only in the context of one's future.

What I propose is an alternative conception of time: instead of thinking about time as a line that connects past to present and present to future, it may be more aptly understood as a network. Figure 7.1 depicts the normal conception of time, which is linear.

Events that happen in the past determine the present, and these along with the present determine the future. Since we have already seen that experiences in the present can change the past and that these changes will subsequently change our future, then this model breaks down for us. Figure 7.2 shows the new model that I propose. It is based on the phenomenology of Merleau-Ponty (1962).

In the temporality network, it is understood that the past may be understood within the context of the present; the past may also be understood within the context of the future; the present may be understood in the context of the past or future; and the future may be understood within the contexts of present or past. Do not worry if your head is left spinning after seeing and reading about the diagram. I can assure you that after we go through each of

Past ⟶ **Present** ⟶ **Future**

Figure 7.1. Linear Temporality

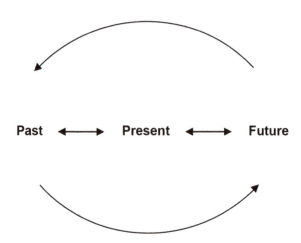

Figure 7.2. Temporality Network

these examples, this diagram will be perfectly clear. Indeed, you will realize that you have understood temporality this way all along. After going through each of these ways of experiencing the relationships between past, present, and future, we will more carefully consider the shift from time as a line to time as a network.

I have decided to use two frames that are familiar to young adults in order to demonstrate the interrelationship between past, present, and future: the first concerns the selection of a career; the second concerns the selection of a partner.

Experiencing the Past within the Context of the Present

At the beginning of the semester, I ask my students to explain a little bit about themselves. This is usually articulated through the description of where students are coming from and where they see themselves going. For this example, what we are interested in with these questions is seeing how the *past* is understood within the context of the *present*. As college students (in the present), many look back at what they were doing in high school and interpret this as "nothing much." When viewed within the context of being a college student, the throes of high school sociality are reduced to "nothing much." Follow high schoolers around for a week and see whether they are doing "nothing much." They will most certainly feel that what they are doing—even if this includes playing video games or hanging out at the mall—is extremely important. It receives the judgment of "nothing much" only from a new frame of reference—namely, being a career-minded individual. Now consider this temporal relationship in the situation of selecting a mate.

Look back to a serious relationship that you have had in the past. This works even if there is no such relationship to speak of because even here, you had a particular idea about why you were single. Let's assume that you remembered a particular person about whom you had become quite serious: looking back, do you have the thought, "I don't know what I saw in him/her?" or, alternatively, "That was obviously going nowhere," or even "I can't believe I didn't see it sooner." That last one works for possible relationships that never happened as well. In each of these cases, the events as they were once experienced are viewed within a new framework of understanding—one that you have in the present.

Experiencing the Past within the Context of the Future

It may have been unusual to think about the ways in which the present changes the past; it is certainly unthinkable that the future that hasn't happened is capable of changing the past that is already finished. However, this is precisely what I argue. When we are in the career selection process, we seldom make our selection based on what we would like to be doing right now. We look forward and anticipate the kind of life that we want to live, the hobbies that we want to have, and the friends we would like to keep. Imagine that you decide to become a medical doctor—even a successful surgeon. This decision is not based on what has happened, but it is an idea about what might happen were you to be successful in developing into a good surgeon. Now that you have selected a possible career path, look back into your past. I have no wish to become a surgeon, but now, when I look into my past, I remember a neuropsychology exam I did well on in college as well as the dissection of a pig's eye that I performed in middle school. I view these as evidence that I was always interested in becoming a successful surgeon. You can try this on your friends or family members: "How did you know that you wanted to be a . . . ?" "Well, I always knew I liked . . . ," and watch their past transform before your eyes.

Our ideas about future occupations are not the only things that change; our ideas about the partner we would like to have (and whether we would like to have one) are also subject to change. Anecdotally, when I decide that I would like to have children, I cannot help but fondly remember my interactions with children in the past; similarly, when I am uninterested in having children, I find that these memories are rather unspectacular. My plans for the future shape my relationship to the past.

Experiencing the Present within the Context of the Past

This is a simple one. Indeed, it is how we often think of memory. Instead of having me provide an example, maybe this is one that you can come up with on your own. Can you think of a specific example of how an experience you have had has influenced a decision you later made? We do this all the time: what we choose to eat and drink, and how much. You may have even selected your major based on your experiences with certain subjects in the past. This may also be seen with the kinds of romantic company you keep. You may even find yourself comparing a possible partner to "the one who got away."

Experiencing the Present within the Context of the Future

Experiencing the present within the context of the past is simple because this is often how we understand the relationship between past and present: the past is why I have become the person that I am today. Now, how can the *future* determine the present? I imagine that you have not picked up this book arbitrarily but have a particular idea about what it might facilitate for you. This is to say that your decision to read this book is based on some idea you have about the future and how reading this book might facilitate that. It might be because you think it will influence your grade in a class, or it will inform a conversation you wish to have, or it might even help you better understand your experience. In each of these, your decision to read *in the present* has been shaped by your anticipations about the future.

This may also be seen in your interactions with potential life partners. Have you ever found yourself in the early stages of getting to know someone and start comparing the person to your future partner? She either *is* or *is not* what you've always wanted. This is how we experience the present in the context of the future.

Experiencing the Future within the Context of the Past

This is another example where the conventional conception of time still holds: we recognize here that past experiences shape the plans we have for the future. Receiving a C minus in a human anatomy course probably bodes poorly for a future as a successful surgeon.

We may also see this with certain expectations about our partners. We might have learned that some expectations are too demanding or that other expectations cannot be ignored. Each of these examples demonstrates that our ideas about the future may be understood through the ways that they have been shaped by our past.

Experiencing the Future within the Context of the Present

This is probably the most difficult temporal relationship to understand—harder still is coming up with an example. However, I have been pleasantly surprised by what my students have been able to come up with. After only a short lecture introducing them to a novel conception of time, students are able to explain this in their own lives. This is why I stated earlier that much of this is intuitive: each of you already understands your own experience of past, present, and future this way. Now we are simply articulating it as such. With this final temporal relationship, we understand that our anticipations about the future are sometimes shaped by our experiences in the present. As you're reading this book, you might see an alternative future flash before your eyes: you once fancied yourself a psychologist, but now you have found yourself so tremendously bored that a career in engineering seems more appealing. This shift in your future occurs *in the present moment*.

You might also be in the middle of a conversation with a close or romantic friend when you suddenly realize that this is or isn't the person with whom you want to spend the rest of your life. Again, the important detail here is that *your future is found transforming based on the experiences that occur in the present.*

NETWORK OF INTENTIONALITIES

We have seen that past and future can be the background upon which we experience the present. Put differently, past and future are found informing our experiences in the present. We use the term "retrospection" when we are looking toward the past from the present and "prospection" when we look toward the future from the present. As such, past and future are understood to exist only in our experience of the present. "Time," as Merleau-Ponty explains, "is not a line, but a network of intentionalities" (1962, 417). We will consider this quote in depth.

The belief that the past shapes our present and then our present shapes our future stems from the assumption that time is a line. As a line, the past is found causing the present, and the present is found causing the future. From this view, the past points to the present and the present together with the past point to the future. But we have already seen that the future is found determining the present and the present, the past. Indeed, we find that time, instead of unfolding in a straight line, is more meaningfully understood as a network of intentionalities: that past, present, and future are always mutually determining and always make sense within a single structure of meaning. Keen explains this network:

> Living into the future is a reckoning of the meaning of present events in terms
> of our anticipations. Living into the past is a reckoning of the meaning of
> events in terms of our memories. In such experiences, the past and future
> literally permeate the present; they invade in a total way and preempt the
> meanings of, the very perceptions of, current events. Such experiential phe-
> nomena are not random; they have a definite structure, and that structure
> would be revealed as orderly, if only we could carry our descriptive work far
> enough to see it clearly. (1982, 6)

Retrospection and prospection are understood as ways of experiencing
the past and future in the context of the present. With this we find that past
and future are topics that we can investigate by asking people about them.
Finally, when we recognize the interrelationship between past, present, and
future, we understand how memories can be manipulated. We may even be
able to predict how a shift in someone's anticipation about the future would
alter his ideas concerning his past.

Something for you to try at home: keep an eye out for the scenario where
you remember a specific event differently from the way someone else does.
You might have remembered that he said the party started at 8:30, but he
swears that he told you 7:30. Perhaps it's more serious than this even. Rather
than speculate about who has the best memory, try to understand how the
differences in retrospection are important. What would it mean for this person to have misinformed you about the starting time of an event? What
would it mean for you to have been an hour late to the event? Each person
has much at stake when the contexts in which the memories occur are examined.

SUMMARY

This chapter challenged the assumption that human memory works the same
way as a computer's memory works. Our memory, it turns out, is not like a
thumb drive. Following the research of Elizabeth Loftus, we learn two troubling details about how our memory works (or, rather, doesn't work): (1) that
the memories we keep are subject to change and (2) that some of the memories we keep are of events or experiences that have never happened to us at
all.

Freed from the assumption that memory is a way of capturing the truth of
events that have occurred in the past, we may consider memory as an experience that takes place in the present. That is, memory is a way of recognizing
how the past influences us in the present (or the reverse). This shift addition-
ally allows us to look at the role that the future plays, too. This sets up a
three-by-two matrix of possible interactions between past, present, and future.

PSYCHOLOGIZING IN ACTION

Memory of a Madeleine Cookie

The sight of the little madeleine had recalled nothing to my mind before I tasted it; . . . the forms of things, including that of the little scallop-shell of pastry, so richly sensual under its severe, religious folds, were either obliterated or had been so long dormant as to have lost the power of expansion which would have allowed them to resume their place in my consciousness. But when from a long-distant past nothing subsists, . . . the smell and taste of things remain poised a long time, like souls, ready to remind us, waiting and hoping for their moment, amid the ruins of all the rest; and bear unfaltering, in the tiny and almost impalpable drop of their essence, the vast structure of recollection.

And once I had recognized the taste of the crumb of madeleine soaked in her decoction of lime-flowers which my aunt used to give me (although I did not yet know and must long postpone the discovery of why this memory made me so happy) immediately the old grey house upon the street, where her room was, rose up like the scenery of a theatre to attach itself to the little pavilion, opening on to the garden, which had been built out behind it for my parents (the isolated panel which until that moment had been all that I could see); and with the house the town, from morning to night and in all weathers, the Square where I was sent before luncheon, the streets along which I used to run errands, the country roads we took when it was fine. And just as the Japanese amuse themselves by filling a porcelain bowl with water and steeping in it little crumbs of paper which until then are without character or form, but, the moment they become wet, stretch themselves and bend, take on colour and distinctive shape, become flowers or houses or people, permanent and recognisable, so in that moment all the flowers in our garden and in M. Swann's park, and the water-lilies on the Vivonne and the good folk of the village and their little dwellings and the parish church and the whole of Combray and of its surroundings, taking their proper shapes and growing solid, sprang into being, town and gardens alike, all from my cup of tea.

Source: Proust 1982, 50–51.

Chapter Eight

Development

Development is a dangerous and exciting area of psychology. It is exciting because everybody and everything can be understood from within a developmental perspective. This is to say that everybody—including yourself, the starting ten for Manchester United Football Club, and the blokes across town at Manchester City—and everything—including the edifice you call home, the Amazon rainforest, and Amazon.com—can each be more deeply understood when considered developmentally. It is dangerous because the developmental lenses through which one looks are necessarily limiting. This is often because "development" typically privileges a particular lifestyle: the assumption is that in order to correctly develop, an adult must have a specific type of job with a specific type of workweek, live in a specific type of house in a specific type of neighborhood, and keep specific types of hobbies with specific types of people. Should one fall short of any of these specific aims, one runs the risk of being dubbed "undeveloped" or immature. Developmental psychology, then, presents an opportunity to consider an event of someone or something within the context of a greater life. Economists study the development of small businesses ventures, ecologists study watershed and forestry development, and developmental psychologists study the development of persons.

Few would expect that an ecosystem develops the same way as a small business: a business is subject to different forces entirely, and the anticipated goal—profit margin or excess growth—is quite different from that of a flourishing ecosystem. Even within the world of business, many end goals are possible. For example, a not-for-profit company succeeds when it adequately fulfills its mission, whereas a privately owned business has a different definition of success. You might even imagine how a substantial sum of money, given to either the private business or the not-for-profit, might mean entirely different things to each company. In each case, however, the event of a substantial donation (for the not-for-profit) or investment (for the private business) could either be understood as a simple addition of revenue or understood within the context of a developing company. *This is to say that the event of a substantial donation or investment gets its meaning within the context of the life of the company—where it has come from and where it aspires to go.* Even within a type of business model, companies will change quite a bit: a three-million-dollar donation to a five-person, two-year-old not-for-profit would be received quite differently from the way the same donation would be received by a thirty-five-year-old, hundred-person not-for-profit. While variety abounds across and within businesses, some general tendencies of businesses are useful for understanding the development and growth of businesses.

The same goes for understanding the development and growth of a person. Different communities of class, ethnicity, religion, nationality, and epoch are each subject to different forces as well as measures of maturity or success. Even within each of these categories of people, we see great variety. Moreover, a person will often straddle many of these categories, making it difficult to discern what development should look like for any individual person. The difference between economic development of businesses and the development of persons is that with persons, the meaning of an event is lived immediately—the significance of an event is indicated in the gestures and on the face of the person for whom it matters. For a business, one could imagine that a meeting must first be conducted to "crunch the numbers" before deciding the meaning of a particular event (such as a three-million-dollar investment). With a person, the significance of an event is impossible to hide from a keen observer. This chapter will be a first step into turning you into a keen observer of developmental significance. We will closely follow the developmental theory of Erik Erikson (1990), which will be supported by that of Daniel Levinson (1986) as well as a few others.

Before looking at the developmental import of life experiences, a word of caution regarding the danger mentioned earlier: the purpose of this chapter, and of the work of Erikson and other developmental psychologists, is *not* to outline what development *must* look like. Instead, it is designed to be an example of how development might be understood. Erikson, for example, was a follower of Freudian psychoanalysis. As such, much of his language and many of his examples employ the language of Freud: he gives much emphasis to benign sexual behavior in children. Without discounting the import of his insights, we can understand Freud within the context of a supremely sexually inhibited Victorian era. Such a perspective provides a meaningful background for understanding the celebrated sexual freedom of many neo-Freudians, such as Fritz Perls (1969), who explored the therapeutic benefits of sexual disinhibition at Esalen Institute. Sexuality has changed significantly over the past hundred years, and it is reflected differently in the significance it is given at various stages of the life cycle. We will avoid the possibility of arriving at an all too narrow or, worse still, an outdated model of development by emphasizing flexibility in a person's life structure. For example, it has become perfectly acceptable for young women to emphasize their professional life structure over their family life structure—a tendency that would have been scarcely believable only fifty years ago. With an inflexible model of development, one might be compelled to assume that a childless woman had evidently failed at starting a family before focusing her energies on her occupation. Similarly, an inflexible model of development might lead one to assume that a young father had first failed (or succeeded) at developing a professional life structure before working on his family structure.

HOW WE WILL LOOK AT DEVELOPMENT

We have already seen that development provides a context for understanding the significance an event has for somebody's life. This is what we mean when we say that we can understand experience developmentally. A developmental perspective can be helpful in understanding a person more deeply. But we also find a danger when this perspective becomes a platform from which we may more easily jump to premature conclusions as psychologists: stay-at-home dads are professional failures. Such a position fails to allow for the evolution of the family, society, occupation, and so on. It is in this manner that development can be dangerous since it prevents us from understanding how the meaning of particular events might change from generation to generation. The remaining dangers of development will be sorted out as I explain the key factors that will help us avoid an inflexible approach to development: these are that development is not hierarchical; that it is not a line but a web; that it is continuous *and* discontinuous; and that it is holistic.

Development Is Not Hierarchical

This goes along with another key factor, that development is not linear. But we consider these separately because this first key factor is famously difficult to remember. Even though I will spend a great deal of time explaining why development is not hierarchical, and even though you will doubtlessly agree, we will all make the mistake of assuming that certain developmental hangups are more important than others and that, ultimately, development will be used as a measuring scale on which people can be compared (e.g., as more or less developed than another). DEVELOPMENT IS NOT HIERARCHICAL. The problems that a child faces are fundamentally different from the kinds of problems that an adult faces. I say fundamentally different because the child understands the world in a much different way. For example, the child might well be a fraction of the size of a given adult. As such, the world will either be easier or more difficult to navigate, depending on the situation. I am careful to give an example of how children and adults differ *physically*. This is a helpful perspective because it is difficult to predetermine whether it is better to be big or small. If we assume that bigger is always better, then we might hierarchize height (which is actually somewhat true in a patriarchal society). But we can see how with some problems, it is actually beneficial to be smaller. Without privileging size, we can say that children and adults occupy different worlds, even though they may face similar problems. Moreover, this can be done without saying that one is always preferable to the other. The same may be said about cognitive and social worlds. The problem arises when it is assumed that the problems that children face are *in principle* less important than the problems that adults face. This is what happens when development is understood hierarchically. This perspective makes it impossible to understand how serious developmental issues are for the person going through them. We must avoid this.

The most famous example of a hierarchical theory of development doubles as the first psychological theory of development. It is Clark Stanley Hall's theory of recapitulation. Not only does recapitulation demonstrate the problem of a hierarchical conception of development, but it also provides an example of the dangers of an inflexible developmental model. Hall likened the development of a person to the evolution of civilization. He explained that the infant could be understood as having the same level of cognitive, social, and physical sophistication as our earliest Neanderthal ancestors. Human development could be understood alongside the increasing complexity and sophistication that marks the evolution of mankind until the present, modern industrial era. Recapitulation begins with the assumption that modern industrialization marks the pinnacle of human development. This is anthropocentric and ethnocentric, which are serious problems. What I want to focus on, however, is the problem of hierarchy that recapitulation presents. Recapitulation assumes that an infant is simply an undeveloped child and a child, an undeveloped adult. It is as if a newborn infant could be understood as a little adult—a fraction of a person. Viewed as such, the baby will be treated accordingly. This perspective also assumes that children and adults see similar problems in the same way: if I want something but cannot have it, I am going to be upset. It is expected that the child handles this frustration in the same way as the adult because "eventually she is going to have to learn this" (because she is really just a little adult). This perspective does not show children respect; it assumes that children have not yet earned respect and do not deserve to be understood. The problems of a hierarchical conception of development will surface again later in this chapter.

It will seem contradictory that I have made such a show of the nonhier-archical nature of development and will proceed to follow Erikson's seven stages of psychosocial development. Some of this contradiction will dissipate in the following section, which outlines how development is more aptly understood as a web and not as a line. In the meantime, I must address why numbered stages are important at all. It is common to see theories of human development split into numbered stages. When the numbers start low and increase from stage to stage, it is easy to confuse this as a hierarchical growth. Stage two is higher than stage one and stage six is near the end, and so on. It is more complicated than this. The following section explains this complication in more detail, but for now an important detail must be briefly stated: the stepwise progression merely indicates that a successive stage is marked by a quality that the former stage did not have. For example, while an infant is incapable of leaving the setting in which she has been placed, a toddler is capable of doing so (because she is physically capable of locomo-tion). By practicing locomotion for no other reason than mastery, this child will inadvertently stumble upon the phenomenon of choice, such as being in this room or going elsewhere; this is the case even if she is unaware of this as a conscious choice. Here we find that the toddler's physical development makes it possible for her to explore the problems of autonomy or indepen-dence—a problem unknown to the infant. With locomotion, the world begins to get really big, and it does so really quickly. The problems faced by the toddler are new, but this does not mean that they are any more or less serious than the problems faced earlier. Also, we may understand that this expansion of world does not mean that the problems faced in infancy are over and done with. This last point is the focus of the following section.

Development Is Not a Line but a Web

To say that development is marked by a stepwise progression through prob-lems of increasing sophistication is not to say that it is linear. To suppose that development is linear is to assume that once I find myself with the ability to navigate from room to room and the ability to reach countertops and rifle through drawers does not mean that I am entirely autonomous—that I no longer need to trust that my needs will be taken care of by my social, emo-tional, and physical environment. Indeed, it only means that I am now faced with an entirely new dilemma: one of choice. I can stay here or go there; I can keep this or throw it away; I can open this or . . . nope, can't open that yet; and so on. That is, in addition to the problem of trusting the environment for my security and safety, I am now faced with a second, albeit related, problem—one that emphasizes my own abilities as a physically, cognitively, and socially autonomous person. Erikson explains that with development, "each item of the healthy personality . . . is systematically related to all others" (1990, 54). A linear conception of development suggests that I pass from one stage to the next. A web recognizes the continued relationship between present stages of development and those that follow you from the past—it even recognizes the stages that await you in the future. Even though I might be navigating the throes of an early adult life structure, I am still very much faced with the problems of identity (Who am I?) and industry (Does my work matter?), and I may even begin facing the issues of generativity (investing in the next generation), albeit in a rudimentary way.

This section should further illustrate the nonhierarchical structure of development. It should instead emphasize that problems in childhood not only are important but will be faced again and again, even into adulthood. As we explore Erikson's stages of psychosocial development, I will provide examples that are unique to the ages in which the issues first arise—like autonomy that is experienced for the first time by toddlers, as well as an example as it plays out later in life. These illustrations will further demonstrate that development resembles a web more than a line.

Development Is Continuous and Discontinuous

Consider both of these terms: "continuity" and "discontinuity." What do these mean in the context of life? To say that something is discontinuous means that there is a point of separation between two of its elements: junior high and high school. Students finish junior high and on the first day of the next school year they enter as high schoolers. Even on the first day of the school year, a distinctive difference is evident between junior high school boys and girls and those in high school. In this way, the graduated arrangement of secondary schools is discontinuous. Discontinuity is marked by definite changes: the character of high school is qualitatively different from that of junior high. Moreover, there is a definite shift (in school building, for example) that marks this discontinuity.

Now consider high school: even within this secondary schooling institution, we can see a marked difference between the upperclassmen and lowerclassmen—a difference that isn't as easy to mark as which grade one finds oneself in. When does this change happen, exactly? It is difficult to pinpoint because the change is a gradual one. Social, physical, and cognitive changes are all occurring to varying degrees; at the end of these changes, one resembles an upperclassman. This is because the change is ongoing or continuous. To say that development is both continuous *and* discontinuous is to say that it is an ongoing process that is difficult to divide up with neat lines of demarcation; however, it is also marked by definite changes and divisible into stages (Erikson 1990) or seasons (Levinson 1986). It is from Levinson's conception of life seasons that I have borrowed the notion that development is both continuous *and* discontinuous. His reasoning for this term also provides an example of the nonhierarchical relationship between "seasons" of development. Development, Levinson explains, is

> a series of periods or stages within the life cycle. The process is not a simple, continuous, unchanging flow. There are qualitatively different seasons, each having its own distinctive character. Every season is different from those that precede and follow it, though it also has much in common with them. (1986, 6)

And he continues:

> To say that a season is relatively stable, however, does not mean that it is relatively stationary or static. Change goes on within each, and a transition is required for the shift from one season to the next. Every season has its own time; it is important in its own right and needs to be understood in its own terms. No season is better or more important than any other. Each has its necessary place and contributes its special character to the whole. It is an organic part of the total cycle, linking past and future and containing both within itself. (1986, 6–7)

Development Is Holistic

This key factor will likely come as little surprise to those who have been reading this book chapter by chapter. In the psychological literature, development is customarily divided into separate units: social development, physical development, cognitive development, emotional development, moral development, and so on. Adolescence, it is maintained, can be understood socially *or* cognitively *or* physically *or* emotionally *or* morally, and so on. Sometimes textbooks are even organized this way. When I say that development is holistic, I mean that adolescence can be understood only as a social-cognitive-physical-emotional-moral phenomenon. Is puberty physical, social, or emotional? Such a question makes a great debate if one assumes that these areas must be explored independently of each other. However, if one understands that they are interrelated, then one sees how physical development directly impacts social and emotional spheres of experience, and so on. Consider the acquisition of a language, which is one of the huge cognitive tasks of childhood. Now try to imagine what this would be like without any social context—nobody with whom to interact or on whom to model. If this thought experiment is too difficult, then try to imagine language acquisition absent the development of fine motor control in the tongue and lips. You will quickly find that development is holistic, not easily divided into separate areas of unrelated maturation.

Development Is Always Meaningful

Like the previous one, the final key factor for understanding development should come as no surprise given the approach to the topics covered in the preceding pages. While it is easy to view the meaningfulness of the problems that characterize the stage you currently occupy, it is not always easy to see the problems that mark earlier or later stages of development. In chapter 6 on a topic that wasn't exactly memory, I explained that many of my students looked back on their own endeavors in the past as "not doing anything." However, were we to investigate these people who are allegedly "up to nothing," we would hear quite a different story. This is because the situations that we face are *always* interpreted within the context of the development of a particular area of the life structure. In high school I would spend a great deal of time grooming and preening before going out into public. From the vantage point of the present this seems like a tremendous waste of time. The problem with this judgment is that it fails to take into consideration this behavior within the context of an adolescent male with particular problem spaces. When I retrospect on these experiences, I make the mistake that *my current vantage point, with its associated problem spaces, is the most informed perspective*. When I make this mistake, I ignore the meaningfulness that these experiences held at the time.

Erikson, whom we will be exploring later in some depth, has found it fit to characterize all developmental growth as *crises*. He explains, "Each stage becomes a *crisis* because incipient growth and awareness in a significant part function goes together with a shift in instinctual energy and yet causes specific vulnerability" (1990, 56). This means that persons are always caught in a specific tension—a tension that characterizes their particular stage of development: on one side is growth and on the other, comfort and security. It is a crisis because growth comes at the expense of vulnerability, whereas comfort and security come at the expense of a limited existence. Consider the experience of being born: an unborn child has all of her needs taken care of in the safe, comfortable, and secure environment of the womb. Why must she emerge? Few would argue that such an environment would be the best that one could aspire to: a world of independent and personal experience is waiting to be had just outside the womb. To explore this world—that is, to transition from the womb to the world—would come at the expense of certain safety, comfort, and security. So, is it worth it? Undoubtedly, yes. But can we appreciate the great cost at which this comes for the child? If you can earnestly answer yes to this second question, then you are prepared to explore the various *crises* that are found characterizing the lives of you and your loved ones. This means understanding that the problems encountered by a child who is struggling to master the will to choose are just as daunting as your struggle to find love, gain the respect of others, or see the meaning in your life's work. We will learn that "crisis" provides no exaggeration for expressing the meaning that development has.

I have outlined five key factors that characterize development: that it is not hierarchical; it is not linear, but more like a web; it is both continuous *and* discontinuous; it is holistic; and it is always meaningful. Once these key factors are understood, they may be applied to any developmental theory to yield insight. At no point do I assume that a particular experience has any single explanation or root cause, but that we may view experiences within the context of a greater life that gives them meaning. For the purposes of demonstrating the structure of developmental psychology, I will briefly outline Erik Erikson's (1990) psychosocial theory of development through early adulthood. This is not to say that Erikson's theory is the best or most insightful. He has, however, made it easy to apply the key factors previously outlined. This is because he emphasizes how his developmental stages overlap and that you are always, as it were, in the mire of human development.

ERIK ERIKSON'S STAGES OF PSYCHOSOCIAL DEVELOPMENT

Erikson outlines seven stages of life-span development. As mentioned above, these stages are not hierarchical: the importance of each stage is found only when one is in the midst of it; the stages are not linear: they are better understood as a web where each stage is in some way related to each of the others; they are both continuous and discontinuous: each of the stages overlaps others, yet a distinct and qualitative character separates one from the next; they are to be understood holistically: each stage is characterized by social, physical, cognitive, and other psychological constituents; and each stage is eminently meaningful: it is to be understood as a crisis or tension wherein one is pulled between poles of growth and comfort.

Basic Trust versus Basic Mistrust

Erikson's stages are titled by the very crisis that defines them. This serves as an important reminder that each stage is not merely the acquisition of new social, physical, and cognitive capacities but that it marks the struggle between the possibility of growth or the certainty of comfort. This first stage is the first, most basic crisis that characterizes human development. It is a question of belonging: Is this world for me?

Infants—in whom this stage first manifests—do not ask and answer questions the way that you or I might. For instance, we might ask the question "Is this psychology class for me?" by constructing a mental list of pros and cons and arriving at some rational conclusion. To be sure, this is not how infants answer this question. Consider also how physically helpless an infant is: she cannot gather her own food; she cannot distinguish safe food from unsafe food; she cannot protect herself from predators; and so on. Infants are supremely dependent because their social, physical, and cognitive faculties require this. They must trust that their needs will be taken care of. If infants are incapable of understanding what their needs are and are equally incapable of independently meeting their own needs, then what is the purpose of asking this question? This is why the addition of the adjective "basic" is so important.

By "basic," one could understand that this crisis is the simplest or most fundamental, but Erikson chooses this term to mark a different significance. By "basic," Erikson means that this question is not necessarily *conscious*. Infants have an unconscious sense of whether or not they belong in this world, and this is the question that defines the meaning of their experience. This is not as outlandish as it might seem from the outset. In fact, you or I have probably asked this question unconsciously in the past few days. When you walk into a new place—hair salon, shoe store, community center, classroom—you do not know what to expect. You start to develop a sense of whether or not you belong even before you open the door. Once inside you scan the area, looking at the type of people there, the way they are dressed, and how they respond to your entrance. You might even say: "I think I am in the wrong place," or "I think I made some mistake in coming here." We also ask this question whenever we start a new job, move to a new residence or city, or even settle into a new relationship or commitment level. It doesn't matter how nice your partner is in gesture and in words: what you gather is an unconscious sense of how genuine his commitment is. When you say that you and a prospective partner "clicked" while on a first date, there is nothing that you can point to and say, "This is how I know"—it is an unconscious sense you have about this. Hopefully these instances sufficiently demonstrate what is meant by "basic."

It is important that infants get a sense that this world *is* for them, or else they will not last very long. Harry Harlow (1958) has gathered a tremendous amount of evidence demonstrating how important the emotional needs of children are: the need for affection and love is every bit as important as the need for food and shelter. Indeed, if we could ask the infant, we would likely find that affection ranks higher than even food (as indicated by Harlow's experiments with infant rhesus macaques).

Autonomy versus Shame/Doubt

We have seen that in infancy, a person is supremely limited in physical, social, and cognitive faculties. These limitations frame a person's world. For example, before the development of a strong musculoskeletal system, children are basically limited to the environment and position in which they have been left. You can imagine that when these muscles begin to develop and, simultaneously, the child begins to master locomotion, then her world changes rather rapidly. This is the situation that emerges in Erikson's second stage of development, the stage he characterizes through the tension between autonomy and shame/doubt.

The question from the first stage of development is whether or not I belong in this world. With this first question, I have no power to influence how this question is answered: I am entirely dependent on my environmental surroundings. Throughout my life span, situations that I am powerless to influence will always arise, so the question of belonging will always be an important question. However, when a child enters the second stage of psychosocial development, she discovers that she *can* influence her environment. Erikson explains:

> The over-all significance of this stage lies in the maturation of the muscle system, the consequent ability (and doubly felt inability) to coordinate a number of highly conflicting action patterns such as "holding on" and "letting go," and the enormous value with which the still highly dependent child begins to endow his autonomous will. (1990, 68)

Autonomous will can be understood as the bourgeoning ability to practice *choice*. This can be as simple as choosing this environment over another: "I no longer want to be in this room but will wander into the hallway instead." The question that characterizes this stage of development is one of ability: "Can I . . . ?" Doing something by oneself means no longer relying absolutely on others to provide for one's needs. This is what we understand as "autonomy": What can *I* do?

And what a question this is. Every day a child adds many things to this list of what she can do. Yesterday I couldn't open the drawers in the kitchen, but *today* I might be able to; yesterday I couldn't push the dining room chairs over, but *today* I might be able to. Every day children learn more about what they can do, and this is exciting. But with the increase of ability comes the added recognition of things they cannot do: I can crawl upstairs, but I cannot crawl downstairs! The choice that is exercised in going upstairs is lost when it comes to returning downstairs. With the expansion of personal ability comes the recognition of *in*ability. The things that I still cannot do are highlighted by all that I *can* do. Autonomy, then, comes at a considerable cost.

As an infant, I must eat what I am given because I cannot choose to do otherwise. However, when my sphere of abilities expands, I learn that I can choose to take something or to leave it, eat something or throw it away. I learn to practice choice in every area of my life: my parents even insist that I choose when to eliminate my bowels. Now notice what happens to a child who has spent her entire life practicing her new ability to choose: she exercises this newfound choice on the selection of a particular brand of cereal. Her father, however, has different plans. Suddenly her choice is neglected. She is not incapable of choosing one cereal over another in the same way that she is incapable of moving the living-room furniture. Now her incapability stems from the will of another, more powerful person. The scene that unfolds is an insightful look at how it feels to learn that you are small and powerless.

It is important to emphasize that it is in this stage that shame is first understood. It is not, as some might suspect, that this is the most shameful age of life. Shame is the experience of *not* being able to do something that we should be able to do. I might be ashamed that I cannot start the lawn mower. After giving ten good pulls on the rip cord, I might be found giving a pretty good rendition of the cereal-aisle choice-thwarting dance. I am not, as it were, acting like a two-year-old. This is the mistake of assuming that a two-year-old is just a small adult, and an ashamed adult, a two-year-old. We may alternatively understand that shame is an important component of having the ability to make choices and exercise our abilities.

Initiative versus Guilt

In the stage where autonomy becomes increasingly evident, we also see a similar expansion of cognitive ability. Just as the development of the physicomotor system is important in facilitating a child's ability to make choices, a related development is occurring in cognitive abilities: namely, that I have more than a single choice for what I can be doing right now (hence the importance of the word "no"). The cognitive development that occurs at the third stage is more important in understanding the crisis that emerges here. We must first explore the emergence of this cognitive ability before we can understand what is meant by "initiative" *or* "guilt" for that matter.

It is in the third stage that a person's imagination is found developing. Like the developments that occur during the other stages, imagination is not limited to this third stage (however loath we might be to admit this). Children have mastered basic gross and fine motor skills and have spent a great deal of time practicing choice and exercising their autonomy. In stage two, their world grows a lot bigger: they are able to go places and see things, provided these places and things are close by and within their sphere of ability. It is difficult to think about how their world could expand any further—but it does. In this third stage of development, children learn how to imagine. Their world grows exponentially. Children may spend hours in spaceships made of cardboard and marker. They explore other galaxies and meet alien creatures. Children are not limited to the rooms in which they were left; they are not limited to where they can physically go; they are free to go wherever they can imagine themselves to go. It is also here where children can begin to imagine what they will be when they grow up. Erikson explains how in the third stage, a child's "learning is eminently intrusive and vigorous: it leads away from his own limitations and into future possibilities." I might not be able to eat Count Chocula cereal, but I can imagine an alternative scenario where I had an entire closet full of the cereal.

Here we can begin to understand *initiative*. Initiative is the ability to think about what you are going to do in advance of doing it. Deciding to cut my lawn is an example of initative. In choosing to do so, I am not weighted down by the fear that I am incapable of doing so—a stage-two crisis. However, when the motor is unyielding to my tugs on the rip cord, I find myself wallowing in pity over my inability. A child who first finds herself in the stage of initiative may be content to push a plastic lawn mower about the yard so that she can be like her uncle. She is imagining that she *is* cutting the lawn. It isn't until later that she grows concerned that she hasn't contributed a meaningful change to her environment (except for flattering her uncle, who is concerned with an entirely different developmental crisis—one of meaningful influence on the next generation).

It is also "at this stage," Erikson tells us, "that the great governor of initiative, namely, *conscience*, becomes firmly established" (1990, 84). Notice how this comes along. Once a child is capable of imagining alternative settings, then she is also capable of imagining alternative scenarios or choices that she could have made. Not only can she *choose* to cut the drapes in the living room with a pair of scissors, but she can also imagine a scenario where she chose *not* to cut the drapes or even that she *should not have* cut the drapes. "Guilt" is the experience that I have done something but imagine that I should have done something else. Shame, you will remember, is the experience of not being able to do what you wish to do. Shame is the experience of inability; guilt is the experience of having done the *wrong* thing. This is why Erikson has coupled "initiative" with "guilt."

Industry versus Inferiority

With initiative, we have seen the tendency of children to begin imitating their role models. Kids will bake fake cookies and cakes, imagining that they are pastry chefs; other kids will shout and throw things at the television set, imagining that they are devoted football fans. Eventually these kids will realize that the empty tray of cookies is only an empty tray and that the cookies that Dad makes taste really yummy. At a certain point, the child who was once content to push a plastic lawn mower will look down and see that the grass still needs to be cut. This is when the sense of industriousness begins to grow.

Erikson summarizes the path that we have just taken in order to get to industriousness:

One might say that the personality at the first stage crystallizes around the conviction "I am what I am given," and that of the second, "I am what I will." The third can be characterized by "I am what I can imagine I will be." We must now approach the fourth: "I am what I learn." The child wants to be shown how to get busy with something and how to be busy with others. (1990, 87)

It is at this point that the child will wish to participate in her father's baking session: "What can *I* do?" She is quite incapable of making cookies all by herself, but she earnestly wishes to play a meaningful role in *actually baking* cookies. Children understand that they can do a great deal more with the proper help and instruction. Notice how this is not somebody looking over her shoulder or doing everything for her; indeed, she is doing something with the help of another—something which she could not do on her own—but also not the work of somebody else that she has passed along as her own.

Erikson takes a great deal of time discussing the role that education plays here. We will do so briefly by looking back to our experience in elementary school. Ask a classroom of first-graders to complete the following sentence: "Learning is _____." It is funny to ask a classroom of college students to imagine how first-graders might fill in the blank: this is an example of retroactive interference. If you are having trouble remembering, elementary school children enjoy learning. And they should know. They are expert learners: mastering language and locomotion and developing a sense of independence all within the space of a few years. Somewhere along the line, this fun and exciting process is replaced with the lifeless and boring process of schooling. Erikson finds that the period of initiative gets *replaced* by industry: the relationship between initiative and industry is ignored. He writes,

Instead of pursuing, then, a course which merely avoids the extremes of easy play or hard work, it may be worthwhile to consider what play is and what work is, and then learn to dose and alternate each in such a way that they play into and work toward each other. (1990, 89)

Do we understand the importance that imagination has for work? Students will answer, "Yes, imagination is just as important as work," but then they will explain that this is because imagination makes it possible for them to complete boring tasks. In order to see where you place the value, on work or on imagination, consider the following: would you rather be a person who spends all her time *working* or all her time *imagining*?

A student of mine provided an exceptional example of the relationship between imagination and work: she was working as a nurse at a local hospital. She was given a list of six tasks to complete, ordered 1–6. This student decided that these would be most effectively accomplished if completed in a different order, maybe 1, 3, 4, 2, 5, 6. Such a move makes it possible to improve the efficiency of procedures in a hospital (provided this is an important goal).

Identity versus Role Confusion

In reviewing Erikson's first four stages of psychosocial development, we have found that these crises are still encountered well beyond the stage in which they were first experienced. Even though I am uniquely capable to understand the tension between autonomy and dependence as soon as I am able to reliably move myself from room to room, the problem of autonomy and dependence will continue to emerge even into adulthood. This is to say that the second stage of development is still important well after we initially become aware of it. The reverse may be said about the later stages—that is, even though we do not yet understand the crisis of identity, we still have some semblance of a stable identity in the stages that precede the identity crisis.

In the crisis of basic trust, my identity is fused with my environment: if my environment is happy, then I am happy; in the crisis of autonomy, I am defined by what I can do and what I cannot do; in the crisis of initiative, I am what I can imagine myself to be; and in the crisis of industry, I am the work that I can accomplish or the utility that I can demonstrate.

If I am already developing a sense of self, then how am I to understand the emergence of a crisis around this identity? Erikson explains how the previous four stages set us up for the crisis of identity:

> The sense of ego identity, then, is the accrued confidence that one's ability to maintain inner sameness and continuity (one's ego in the psychological sense) is matched by the sameness and continuity of one's meaning for others. Thus, self-esteem, confirmed at the end of each major crisis, grows to be a conviction that one is learning effective steps toward a tangible future, that one is developing a defined personality within a social reality which one understands. The growing child must, at every step, derive a sense of reality from the awareness that his individual way of mastering experience is a successful variant of the way other people around him master experience and recognize such mastery. (1990, 94–95)

We will begin by looking at the notion of "accrued confidence": we accrue confidence by successfully negotiating a particular crisis of development. To successfully negotiate a crisis does not mean that said crisis has been defeated or avoided but that it has been understood and accepted. Consider the crisis of autonomy: during this stage, I am defined by a widening sphere of capability. However, along with growing capability comes the recognition that there are things I cannot do. *To resolve this tension does not mean learning that I can do all things*; instead, it means accepting that there are some things I *can* do but also things I *cannot* do. This does not mean that I am happy with my weaknesses but that I have accepted them as part of me. This crisis is resolved when I accept my weaknesses and my strengths. I *am* my weaknesses and my strengths. This recognition is what Erikson means by "inner sameness and continuity." How, then, does the stabilization of an identity lead to a *crisis* in identity?

The crisis comes in the next sentence: does my inner sameness and continuity match the sense of sameness and continuity that others have of me? When I negotiate the crisis of my utility, I do so within the environment of my home. I derive a certain satisfaction from my utility when I wash the dishes and my family recognizes this. My family members shape what it means for me to be industrious. When I grow older and begin to socialize with others outside of this family structure, I learn that there are other definitions of industry. We can imagine two extremes with relation to washing dishes: in the first, a schoolmate of mine may get a sense of industriousness by simply clearing the contents of the plate into the trash and leaving his dish to be cleaned by an adult; for another schoolmate, washing the dishes is really nothing significant at all, and a sense of utility can be derived only from cleaning all of the dishes from dinner. Which child, then, has negotiated the crisis of industry the best? Individually, each child has developed a meaningful sense of utility in his or her household, but we find that there is a tremendous range of utility this entails. Children recognize the variety of this only when they begin to spend more time outside of the house in which they were raised: it is only here that they are confronted with the alternative ways of negotiating these crises. Suddenly, the resolution that *I* had found is not necessarily the resolution that my schoolmates had found. The schoolmate who only clears his plate is impressed that I should wash my own dish; yet the schoolmate who customarily does all the dishes is unimpressed by my lack of industriousness. Now I will begin to experiment with other ways of negotiating this former crisis—washing all or none of the dishes and seeing how this works out for me.

We can now see how the identity that has been in formulation all along begins to be drawn into question through comparisons with the identity structure of others. To this we may add the complication of puberty: the body begins to change in noticeable and unexpected ways; the voice changes; emotions become difficult to anticipate and sometimes understand; and physical attraction becomes increasingly common. What I *thought* I was yesterday has already changed in a radical sense. A twelve-inch growth spurt often turns the most capable athlete into an uncoordinated one. Finally, if the social, physical, and emotional changes were not already sufficient to upset any semblance of a fixed and unchanging self, we complicate the matter by demanding that teenagers begin to make definite plans about their careers, lifestyles, and life partners.

When we consider the crisis of identity from a developmental perspective, we cannot help but realize that there is no such thing as a definite resolution. Of course a person is going to make choices about her life when she does not yet have all the information—she cannot possibly have all the information; and of course these choices are going to have lasting consequences for her and those around her; and of course these choices are going to be scrutinized five years later when she has the benefit of hindsight; and of course she is going to wonder what would have happened had she chosen differently or if she had known then what she knows now. When we see the impossibility of navigating the developmental stage of development, we begin to see that each of the stages is somewhat impossible. Finally, we begin to realize that all people are doing the best they can in an impossible situation.

SUMMARY AND SUGGESTIONS: ADULTHOOD AND BEYOND

This chapter examined how a developmental perspective helps shape the way we understand ourselves and those around us. By making observations as a developmental psychologist, we have found that a person's experience always takes place within a historical and temporal context. That is to say that the time during which an experience occurs in life is an important factor to consider when trying to understand said experience. Moreover, this factor usually contributes a great deal of significance to the person concerned.

More specifically, we have learned that development is not hierarchical: there are not some periods of development that matter more than others. Indeed, every period is important to the person going through it. Also, we have seen that it is both continuous and discontinuous; that it is not a line but more like a web; that it is holistic; and, of course, that it is always meaningful.

To demonstrate these qualities of development, we have looked to Erikson's first five psychosocial stages of development. Unfortunately, this overview of development concludes here. The reader is directed to the texts covered if interested in considering development beyond the early adult years. The description of developmental crises and tensions, as they are experienced by adults now, continues in Erikson's analysis. Indeed, we find that development never ceases—our perspective simply changes. We do not emerge victorious over the developmental trials but merely find a happy medium somewhere in between resolution and no resolution. Erikson outlines three main crises that emerge between early adulthood and late adulthood, and he and his wife (1998) propose a fourth: the world as it is experienced in late, late adulthood.

Daniel Levinson (1986), whose approach to development was used to introduce this chapter, has also contributed a great deal to the understanding of adult development. To be sure, a great deal of time can be devoted to development as it is experienced at any given age. What is important is that the five factors of development remain as part of the analysis. In summary, we remember that development is not hierarchical; it is not linear; it is both continuous and discontinuous; it is holistic; and it is always meaningful. Armed with these factors, any region of human or nonhuman development may be investigated.

PSYCHOLOGIZING IN ACTION

A Glimpse at Early Adulthood

Richard Taylor was one of two Black novelists in our study. Following a long military service in World War II, he started college at 21, married a year later, and immediately started a family. His wife continued her work as a secretary to supplement his income from the GI Bill. Her aspiration was to have a secure life within the middle-class Black community. But he was already writing poetry and fiction, and his cultural interests pulled him to a world she could not share. His dreams were alien to her, and he could not provide the stability so essential to the life she wanted. For three years after college, he tried to maintain a steady job that would pay the bills and leave room for writing, but it didn't work.

At 28, he realized that he could not build a life containing both his aspirations and hers. The life they had was unsuitable for them and their children. He gave up the struggle, divorced and dismantled the fragile structure. Breaking up the family—and re-enacting the corrosive theme of the Black father abandoning his wife and children—caused him inner wounds that took years to heal. After the breakup, he worked harder at fatherhood than do most fathers in intact families.

Taylor's Age Thirty Transition, from age 28 to 34, was spent in a kind of limbo: moving around, often living from hand to mouth, working at transient jobs, hitting "rock bottom," nearly succeeding in killing himself, getting psychotherapy, starting a serious love relationship—and through it all finding time to write his novels. At about 34 his life took on some order and stability, and a new structure emerged. The central elements of this structure were writing novels and an enduring love relationship. The structure was made economically feasible by a hyphenated occupation: he earned money chiefly as journalist and writer on public affairs. Thus, the outcome of his Age Thirty Transition was a life structure that could contain the novel writing, but just barely. It took several years longer to make this structure secure and move his writing into the center of it.

Source: Levinson 1986.

Chapter Nine

Personality

Leave this to the human—to try and be something he is not—to have ideals
that cannot be reached, to be cursed with perfectionism so as to be safe from
criticism, and to open the road to unending mental torture. —Perls 1972, 8

The next few chapters will run together, beginning with a discussion of
personality. Personality, I maintain, is something that you *are* and not something that you *have*. After this discussion, you will most likely be able to
predict how motivation (chapter 10) might be understood as the actualization
of your potential as a person—that is, the most *you* you can be. The experience of anxiety will be viewed within the context of becoming a person and
what happens when you don't think you're doing a very good job with this.
And finally, the topics of mental disorders and health will be explored in
terms of their relationship to the self-actualization of persons (chapters 12
and 13, respectively). As it has been currently organized, this all begins with
personality.

If personality is where we must begin, then what is personality? Is this
something that is readily apparent, or is it more difficult to determine? Most
important, is personality something that we *have* or something that we *are*?
What is the difference between these two conceptions of personality? Let us
consider them in turn.

As something that you *have*, personality can be acquired or lost. This
means that you can become any kind of personality that you might wish to
become (or that others might wish for you to become); it might also be
brought about in other people: you can make people into the kind of people
you wish them to be. You might wake up in the morning in a lousy mood and
snap at your roommate or partner. You relax because you know that this is
not who you *have to be* and could be something different should you choose
to be so. For example, you might think, "I should probably be nicer in the

mornings," or "I think I will start being nicer in the mornings." In any event, there is little concern about morning mood because you can have whichever mood you choose to have that day. You can choose to be strong, assertive, quiet, and so on. It is as though you can choose your personality from an à la carte menu. This is possible if personality is something that you *have*; and it is this conception of personality that I will be arguing *against*.

As something that you *are*, personality is the best expression of your being. Since it is something that you are, you cannot "put on" a different personality. To be sure, you will try to cover up your morning temperament with a smile or a cup of coffee, and you might even do a good job of this. But your morning expression is what it is, and this is typically none other than selfish and pouty (okay, I'm drawing from my own experience). In this case, it is understood that your personality is the best expression of your being: it is who you are at this moment. You might even be surprised at this recognition. When it is understood that personality is what you *are*, then personality is something to be discovered, understood, and accepted. By doing so, it may be thought that understanding one's personality could be the ultimate goal in life: there is nothing more important for you than being yourself or, as Søren Kierkegaard (1989) has put it, "to be that self which one truly is." Think for a moment on what that would mean for you.

What if instead of spending your life trying to become some type of person you *think* you might like to be, you spent your life trying to discover who you *are*—trying to become more *you* and less *someone else*? That is what this chapter is about. To do this, I have consulted some of the names we have already explored in this book: Carl Rogers, Kurt Goldstein, and Fritz Perls. Rogers (1961) draws on his experience as a master therapist in his description of what it means to *be* a person(ality). Goldstein (1995) explains that each of us has a unique organismic (or biological) potential for becoming; he calls this a tendency toward self-actualization. And finally, Perls (1972) applies Goldstein's concept of self-actualization in his work as a therapist.

SELF-ACTUALIZATION VERSUS
SELF-CONCEPT ACTUALIZATION

Over the next few chapters you will see much talk of the "self." This is troubling because "self" is a problematic term in English. A "self" really isn't a thing you take along with you when you go about your day. It *is* you going about your day. To say it accompanies you is something extra. Freud introduces the term "ego" to refer to our personality structure. In German, "ego" is synonymous with the first-person pronoun "I." You do not *have* an I; you *are* an I. As such, "I" can only ever be engaged in some sort of activity—

some sort of process. But there is a complication when the word "ego" is used in the English language:

> In English, ego approaches the significance of the self-esteem system. We can translate "I want recognition" into "My ego needs recognition," but not "I want a piece of bread" into "my ego needs a piece of bread." To our ears this sounds absurd. (Perls 1972, 4)

The ego is intended to be the central "I" of the personality structure. But in English, this gets confused with some idea of what I might otherwise be. The "I" gets divided into a process and a thing. As a process, I am what I am what I am. As a thing, I am a list of character traits. The process is myself. I do not *have* a self; I *am* myself. On the other hand, my self-*concept* is a thing. My self-concept is my idea about who I am or who I might be. My self-concept is not me; it is what I want to be. If I would like to be a generous and selfless person but end up spending my time and money selfishly, then myself and my self-concept are at odds with each other. In this instance, I have actualized myself and ignored my self-concept. If I'm interested in actualizing my self-concept, then I might wag a finger of disapproval at myself and be more charitable in the future.

So we have two notions of self thus far: the process of being myself and the self-concept-thing. The process is what you *are*; the thing is what you have. Try going through a day while being nothing but yourself. This should be the easiest thing ever. You simply ask yourself, "What would I do in this situation?" and then you do it. Lionel Messi was voted FIFA player of the year (in football) in 2013; during the 2014 World Cup, it was interesting to watch him play in the midfield. He simply had to ask himself, "What would the best player in the world do?" and then do it. When you do this, some people will say "Good job!" while others will say "Shame on you." You take neither of these comments seriously because you couldn't have been any other way. But instead we often ask the question "What *should* I do?" and then we do this instead. However, something is different this time. In this case, we anxiously await the reactions of others: Will they give a standing ovation? Or will they throw rotten tomatoes? Depending on their reaction, we modify our self-concept accordingly.

We will return to this gap that forms between self and self-concept over the next few chapters. For now it is important to recognize that for many of us, the self that we are has become hidden under many layers of the self we hope to be. For example, we pretend that we're eminently intelligent and that everyone will hold us in the highest of esteem because of it.

If you have some idea of who you would like to be and hope that this chapter will help you get there, then you are reading the wrong chapter on personality. Many theories of personality exist that will help you shape *your-*

self into a dynamite, kick-ass self. This is not one of them. In this chapter, I explore what it means to *become* that self which you are—however boring that might be. Or so it will seem. You will actually find that it can be spontaneous and quite compelling. This has nothing to do with defining your self-concept and everything to do with realizing your own unique potential. It begins with the assumptions that you are what you are and that *this is wonderful*. You don't have a personality; you *are* a person. To avoid confusing personality with self-concept, I will refer to the process of being yourself as "person-ing." This discussion features Carl Rogers (1961).

PERSON-ING, OR BECOMING A PERSON WITH CARL ROGERS

Person-ing should strike you much like the title of this book—*Psychologizing*. Psychology, it has been argued, is not a thing but a process. By giving a noun (e.g., psychology, person) an "-ing" suffix, we transform it into a verb. Neither psychology nor persons are fixed like the subatomic particles electrons and protons—though these, too, on closer inspection, are not fixed either, but we will not wait for the rest of philosophy of science to catch up in order to begin understanding psychology as a process. With *psychologizing*, we recognize that as a method of inquiry and mode of understanding, psychology is always changing: it is always in the process of becoming. So it is with persons. We are all persons-in-becoming. So who are you?

Carl Rogers, drawing on several decades of experience as a psychotherapist, explains the process that his clients go through in therapy. He finds that the most meaningful developments that occur in life have to do with discovering and accepting our individual senses of self—that self which we truly are. How about that for a life goal? Becoming your own self. In the chapter on consciousness (chapter 15) we will explore some of the reasons why we have lost touch with ourselves and our experience.

Rogers authored a book called *On Becoming a Person*. Hopefully this kind of phrasing is becoming less and less peculiar. In his book Rogers emphasizes two main components of becoming your own self: a movement away from who you are *not* and a movement toward who you are. This would be a movement away from the self-concept and toward yourself. The result, then, is discovering that self which you truly are. Rogers explains that "this might sound so simple as to be absurd. To be what one is seems like a statement of an obvious fact rather than a goal" (1961, 166). But his understanding comes from several thousand people like you and me who have passed through his office—persons worried about their future, upset with their past, disappointed with their relationships, unenthusiastic about life, and so on. Throughout therapy, Rogers recognizes the continuing trend: the most important shift that occurs for each of these people is that they move away from some idea of a self they think they *ought* to be and toward the self that they are. We will consider each more closely below. Remember, we are not talking about personality as something that we have: we are discussing personality as *your own unique and individualized expression of being.*

Movement Away from What You're Not

How do you carve an elephant out of a block of marble? You cut away everything that is not an elephant. While this seems clever, it tells you nothing of the knowledge that the sculptor must have of his subject. In order to know those parts of the marble that *are* the elephant and those that *are not* requires a deep understanding of elephants (and of marble). How, then, do you become your own-most self? Eliminate all those things that are not your own-most expressions. The term "own-most" refers to those expressions that belong to you and nobody else. On the surface this sounds quite simple, but like the sculptor, this first requires great attention to your subject—yourself.

Rogers has noticed that the first important part of expressing your own unique self is avoiding the expressions that are not your own. You might be tempted to ask, "Well, wouldn't this just be another example of choosing the kind of personality that we want?" Not exactly. Finding out which expression is yours and which is alien or foreign to you requires careful attention. A few examples help demonstrate what Rogers means.

Rogers finds that in many instances his clients realize they have been *putting up a façade.* A façade is the front side of a building that has been built up more than the rest of the structure. Imagine that you're in an old western movie and you're riding into town. Each of the businesses on the main road has ornate detailing and a peaked roof. But if you were to walk around to the back, you would find that they're all the same rectangular boxes. The front view is only a façade and does not indicate what the building actually is. In one case, Rogers shares a client's recognition of his façade: "I know I'm not so hot, and I'm afraid they'll find it out. . . . I'm just trying to put that day off as long as possible" (1961, 167). In this case, the client recognizes that he puts out a false front for the public to see because he is afraid of not being accepted for who he actually is. This occurs because a person believes that the self-concept (in this case "being hot") is a better alternative to being one's own person. Rogers observes that by acknowledging his fear about being accepted, the client is *expressing himself.* That is, he has stopped *being a façade* and started *being himself,* if only for a moment. "Being hot" is an act that anybody can imitate, but the fear of being found out belongs to the client—it is the client's own-most feeling.

The next technique that people use to avoid being themselves is to *follow an ethical opinion of who they ought to be.* I ought to be nice, noble, dignified, neat, punctual, smart, talented, and so on. If you feel like you ought to be a certain way, then you will work at this endlessly, always finding that you could be *more* noble, *more* intelligent, and so on. This is the activity of building up a self-concept and trying to match yourself to it. The hope is that if you succeed in meeting these demands for your behavior, then you will be satisfied with who you are, and people will like you. Karen Horney (1950) explains that we feel as though if only we could have this or that, or be nicer, or be more charming, then everything would be okay. But we forget that we must always take ourselves along. If you hold up personality as an achievement to be reached, you will never reach it satisfactorily. This is not because we are incapable of reaching goals but because such goals are impossible. They are impossible because they ask you to be someone you are not. Fritz Perls provides an absurd example to demonstrate the futility of trying to become anything other than what we are:

> It is obvious that an eagle's potential will be actualized in roaming the sky, diving down on smaller animals for food, and in building nests.
> It is obvious that an elephant's potential will be actualized in size, power and clumsiness.
> No eagle will want to become an elephant, no elephant an eagle. They "accept" themselves. . . .
> How absurd it would be if they, like humans, had fantasies, dissatisfactions and self-deceptions! How absurd it would be if the elephant, tired of walking the earth, wanted to fly, eat rabbits and lay eggs. And the eagle wanted to have the strength and thick skin of the beast. (1972, 7–8)

Eagles become eagles and elephants become elephants; you'll become you and I will become me. If you work to actualize yourself as Patrick White-head, then you will have a terrible time because this ignores your potential.

Rogers explains a few other ways that we avoid becoming who we are: instead of discovering our own-most expressions, we meet expectations of groups and try to please those around us. With both, there is a privileging of what *others* think you should be rather than what you are. If you are motivated by pleasing somebody else, then is it really *you* with whom they are pleased? This is quite likely not the case. What they are pleased with is your self-concept. You might even be pleased with this self-concept, but you will have no idea what your own potential is. Let us now turn to what Rogers has discovered as the path to becoming the self one truly is.

Movement toward Being One's Self

By avoiding the various tendencies to become something other than yourself, you begin to discover who you are by eliminating those things which you are not. Another way of saying this is that we must first avoid actualizing our self-concept. Once we avoid the compulsion to become a particular brand of person, we begin to see who we are when nobody else is looking. That is, we begin to discover what our own potential is.

We have already used Perls to demonstrate what this might look like: an eagle becomes an eagle, and an elephant becomes an elephant. As the eagle soars, it actualizes its potential as an eagle. By being ourselves, we move "toward a process of potentialities being born, rather than being or becoming some fixed goal" (1972, 172). Do you see the difference? The fixed goal: "If only I could . . ." and fill in the blank with some self-concept ideal. The alternative is the process of becoming yourself. "I find that this desire to be *all* of oneself in each moment—all the richness and complexity, with nothing feared in oneself—this is a common desire in those who have seemed to show much movement in therapy" (1972, 172). This is what it means to accept yourself. Accepting yourself does not mean "I did a good job." This is a judgment that you make about what you once were—it is comparing your previous actions to your self-concept. Accepting yourself is more complicated. Perls struggles to find the words to describe what this means, exactly. He continues with the eagle/elephant example:

> No eagle will want to be an elephant, no elephant to be an eagle. They "accept" themselves; they accept them-"selves." No they don't even accept themselves, for this would mean possible rejection. They take themselves for granted. No, they don't even take themselves for granted, this would imply a possibility of otherness. They are what they are what they are. (1972, 7–8)

So how do you determine what/who/how you are? Rogers explains that this begins by "living in an open, friendly, close relationship to [your] own experience. This does not occur easily" (1961, 173). Rather than running your experiences through the sieve of public expectation ("Will I be applauded or will they throw rotten fruit?"), you simply express yourself: this is who I am in this situation. Self-accepting people, Roger explains,

> tend to move away from self-concealment, away from being the expectations of others. The characteristic movement, I have said, is for the client to permit himself freely to be the changing, fluid, process which he is. He moves also toward a friendly openness to what is going on within him—learning to listen sensitively to himself. . . . It means that as he moves toward acceptance of the "is-ness" of himself, he accepts others increasingly in the same listening, understanding way. He trusts and values the complex inner processes of himself, as they emerge toward expression. He is creatively realistic, and realistically creative. He finds that to be this process in himself is to maximize the rate of change and growth in himself. He is continually engaged in discovering that to be all of himself in this fluid sense is not synonymous with being evil or uncontrolled. (1961, 181)

You might even think, "How can I be the hell out of me?" Rogers reports a few examples of people who have really nailed themselves:

> El Greco, for example, must have realized as he looked at some of his early work, that "good artists do not paint like that." But somehow he trusted his own experiencing of life, the process of himself, sufficiently that he could go on expressing his own unique perceptions. It was as though he could say, "Good artists do not paint like this, but *I* paint like this." Or to move to another field, Ernest Hemingway was surely aware that "good writers do not write like this." But fortunately he moved toward being Hemingway, being himself, rather than toward some one else's conception of a good writer. Einstein seems to have been unusually oblivious to the fact that good physicists did not think his kind of thoughts. Rather than drawing back because of his inadequate academic preparation in physics, he simply moved toward being Einstein, toward thinking his own thoughts, toward being as truly and deeply himself as he could. This is not a phenomenon which occurs only in the artist or the genius. (1961, 175)

What would have happened had any of these creative thinkers given up their own unique being and had instead pursued the actualization of their self-concept? What if Einstein had set out to become a great physicist instead of becoming Albert Einstein? It is possible that he could have been a very good classical physicist (though we learn that he was not very enthusiastic about his studies while in the academy), but he certainly would not have been revolutionary.

SUMMARY

This chapter has looked at the topic of personality. It has been presented in a peculiar manner: instead of taking personality as that thing that you have which characterizes you, we have understood it to be the uniquely personal kind of being—the process of becoming yourself. We have introduced the notion of self-actualization: this is where an acorn turns into an oak tree. A particular tree is the potential of the acorn. As the tree grows, the acorn's potential is actualized. The acorn cannot actualize itself as an urban high-rise. Humans have a distinct ability to actualize potentials other than themselves. This is called self-concept actualization. When this happens, our personality is turned into a make-over project and we ignore our unique being.

In the following chapter, we will discuss motivation. As explained earlier, this will be closely related to personality. If compelled toward self-concept actualization, we are motivated from without: we have a particular person we wish to be and we rely on others to applaud us for this. Since this extrinsic motivation is aimed at making up for some deficiency in ourselves—making up for something that we lack—Maslow (1968) has called this *deficiency motivation*. If compelled toward self-actualization, we are motivated from within: we are what we are what we are, and this is reward enough. Since intrinsic motivation is aimed at being who/what/how we *are*—that is, being ourselves—Maslow calls this *being* motivation.

PSYCHOLOGIZING IN ACTION

Personal Things

We may with confidence affirm that our own possessions in most cases please us better [not because they are ours], but simply because we know them better, "realize" them more intimately, feel them more deeply. We learn to appreciate what is ours in all its details and shadings, whilst the goods of others appear to us in coarse outlines and rude averages. Here are some examples: A piece of music which one plays one's self is heard and understood better than when it is played by another. We get more exactly all the details, penetrate more deeply into the musical thought. We may meanwhile perceive perfectly well that the other person is the better performer, and yet nevertheless—at times get more enjoyment from our own playing because it brings the melody and harmony so much nearer home to us. This case may almost be taken as typical for the other cases of self-love. On close examination, we shall almost always find that a great part of our feeling about what is ours is due to the fact that we *live closer* to our own things, and so feel them more thoroughly and deeply. As a friend of mine was about to marry, he often bored me by the repeated and minute way in which he would discuss the details of his new household arrangements. I wondered that so intellectual a man should be so deeply interested in things of so external a nature. But as I entered, a few years later, the same condition myself, these matters acquired for me an entirely different interest, and it became my turn to turn them over and talk of them unceasingly. . . . The reason was simply this, that in the first instance I *understood* nothing of these things and their importance for domestic comfort, whilst in the latter case they came home to me with irresistible urgency, and vividly took possession of my fancy. . . . What greets our eyes is what we know best, most deeply understand; because we ourselves have felt it and lived through it.

Sources: James 2007, 1:326–27; Horwicz 1872, part 2, § 11.

Chapter Ten

Motivation

It would not occur to anyone to question the statement that we "need" iodine or vitamin C. I remind you that the evidence that we "need" love is of exactly the same type. —Maslow 1968, 23

In this chapter, I present two different forms of motivation that Abraham Maslow (1968) has supplied. These will follow nicely from the two forms of personality that were discussed in the previous chapter (the thing you have or the process that you are). These were the personality that you *are* and the personality that you *have*. When personality is something that you are, you accept yourself; when it is something that you have, then you try to mold it into something that you're not. So if you are motivated to become this person that you are, we call it *growth* motivation. If you are motivated to become something that you're not, then we call it *deficiency* motivation. *Growth* motivation begins with an acceptance of your own unique self-expression; *deficiency* motivation begins with a recognition that the person you are is missing something—that you could be better if only this or that were true as well.

If it is not obvious from the terms themselves what they mean, I will use Maslow to define each. Motivation can be understood as responding to two types of needs. A *deficiency need*, we will learn, is marked by the following:

1. its absence breeds illness,
2. its presence prevents disease,
3. its restoration cures illness,
4. under certain (very complex) free choice situations, it is preferred by the deprived person over other satisfactions,
5. it is found to be inactive, at a low ebb, or functionally absent in the healthy person. (Maslow 1968, 22)

131

Thirst may be understood as a deficiency of water, hunger as a deficiency of food, and so on. If we live too long in the absence of any of these things, the deficiency leads to disease or a general decrease in organismic functioning. Deficiency needs can be instinctive and basic. But they can also be of the "ought to" or "shouldism" variety (Horney 1950; Perls 1972). This is the (false) belief that we should always be more humble, more thoughtful, more considerate, and nicer than we are. That way we will be accepted, for how could somebody reject me if I were a good person? We *become* a generic, greeting-card personality—blameless yet superficial. After a while, we forget where the greeting card ends and we begin.

Deficiency needs may be compared to *growth needs*, whose satisfaction includes:

1. increased acceptance of self, of others, and of nature,
2. increased spontaneity,
3. increase in problem centering,
4. greater freshness of appreciation,
5. changed (the clinician would say "improved") interpersonal relations (Maslow 1968, 26).

The first need listed is at the heart of *growth* motivation: accepting yourself. There is no belief that "you might be a better person if only . . ." because you have already accepted who you are. Everything that flows from this first acceptance may be understood as *growth* motivation—as an expression of who you are. This is an important point because it seems as though Maslow is arguing that deficiency-need gratification must occur before one can address growth needs. For example, he writes how as "far as motivational status is concerned, healthy people have sufficiently gratified their basic needs for safety, belongingness, love, respect and self-esteem so that they are motivated primarily by trends to self-actualization" (1968, 25). This is where we find Maslow's "hierarchy of needs." The hierarchy is a food-pyramid-esque model for human motivation: the bottom or base layer comprises basic (deficiency) needs. Deficiency needs eventually build up higher and higher until you reach self-esteem and other growth needs such as self-actualization. However, since we understand where Maslow got his inspiration for his hierarchy of needs, we will not so easily concede that growth motivation must follow deficiency motivation.

Maslow was a close follower of Kurt Goldstein and from whom he borrowed the concept of "self-actualization." It is because of his relationship to Goldstein that I do not think Maslow intended to have his "hierarchy" interpreted this way. *We need not secure our basic needs before self-actualization may begin: securing these needs can itself be a self-actualizing expression.* Maslow explains that "the psychological life of the person . . . is lived out differently when he is deficiency-need-gratification-bent and when he is . . . growth motivated or self-actualizing" (1968, 27). This means that it doesn't matter whether my need is instinctual (or somehow "base") or transpersonal (or somehow more pure): both can be expressions of self-actualization. So forget about the needs that are being met and start thinking about the motivation you have for doing so.

Growth motivation comes about from within a person: this is the natural tendency to become yourself, and it happens without trying. Consider the example of running on a hot day. My goal from the outset is to run ten miles as quickly as possible. At mile six, I find that I am thirsty. Even though thirst may be considered a base or instinctual desire, it may be viewed as a *deficiency* need or as a *growth* need. *Growth*: when I am thirsty and I recognize that my entire being has conspired against the world to satisfy this physiological desire, I am recognizing that *I am thirsty*. My potential in this moment is in meeting the specific physiological demands that come about in my being. By satisfying this need, I distribute molecules of H_2O to my cells so that they may flourish—so that I may flourish. Drinking a glass of water can be powerfully self-actualizing. *Deficiency*: but it can also be an inconvenient need. I *want* to continue running, but I must stop for a drink of water. Until I get this drink of water, I cannot actualize my potential (as a runner). Indeed, I may run through the water stop so as to actualize what I imagine to be my potential as a runner, resisting the petty needs of my flesh. At this I may become severely dehydrated and collapse before I have finished. My imagined potential must be put on hold so that my entire being can participate in my actualization. When I believe that the negative state of "needing water" must first be brought up to normal before I may flourish, then my thirst is deficiency motivated. For example, "I had better put self-actualization on hold until I've had my glass of water." Here I am motivated to make up for deficits in my personality; only until I have done this may I move on to self-actualization, and so on. Do you see how this is different from the recognition that hydration is itself part of my self-actualization as a runner?

Deficiency motivation comes from without a person: this begins with the belief that you are *lacking* something, and to look for this from others, a glass of bourbon, a new haircut, a new job, a new partner, a renewed ethical conviction, and so on. *Growth* motivation comes from within: it begins with the recognition that you are what you are what you are, even this thirst, this disappointment with your sobriety or hairstyle, with your partner, or with your ethical apathy. It is understood that efforts made to address any of these disappointments do not fix or correct a problem: they are simply *new* expressions of self-actualization.

DISCERNING GROWTH MOTIVATION FROM DEFICIENCY MOTIVATION

Think about something that you did today. You got out of bed. You got dressed. You ate breakfast. You checked your e-mail. What motivated you to do these things? Were these instances of your personal and existential self-expression, or were they things that had to be taken care of *before* you could express your being? Were these actions based on a desire to grow as a person or out of a perceived lack within yourself? Eating when hungry and drinking when thirsty may be understood as motivated by deficiencies in your organism—emerging out of a sense of lack. But they may also be understood as your natural tendency toward health and wellness: actualizing the potential of who/what/how you are. It doesn't matter what your activity is—anything can be the vehicle for your self-actualization. It all depends on whether you relate to your existence as growth oriented or deficiency oriented. "Growth is seen then not only as progressive gratification of basic needs to the point where they 'disappear,' but also in the form of specific growth motivations over and above these basic needs, e.g., talents, capacities, creative tendencies, constitutional potentialities" (Maslow 1968, 26).

Maslow has gone to great lengths to differentiate growth motivation from deficiency motivation. He lists twelve differences that emerged throughout his investigations. We will review a few of them. Once again, these examples will be useful in helping us understand the difference between doing something as an expression of our being—that is, actions that are self-actualizing—and something that is deficiency motivated—that is, trying to make up for something that is missing in ourselves. The actual event itself might look the same in each case, but your relationship to it will be quite different, depending on how you understand yourself.

Rejecting or Accepting Impulses

The first example that Maslow gives in differentiating *deficiency* motivation from *growth* motivation is one's relationship to impulses: are impulses those things that should be endlessly managed or those things that are openly accepted? Take thirst, for example. It is difficult to pathologize thirst: we easily accept that drinking is an important part of healthy living. However, we seldom elevate drinking water to actualizing one's potential. This is because we accept that thirst is an important impulse to obey for one's health. Anger, on the other hand, is often rejected. "I do not wish to be an angry sort of individual; this interferes with my superstition that it is always best to be a nice person." Fritz Perls shares an example as it is lived by an angry man:

Two weeks ago I had a wonderful experience—not that it was a cure, but at least it was an opening up. This man was a stammerer, and I asked him to increase his stammer. As he stammered, I asked him what he feels in his throat, and he said, "I feel like choking myself." So, I gave him my arm, and said, "Now, choke me." "God damn, I could kill you!" he said. He got really in touch with his anger and spoke loudly, without any difficulties. So, I showed him he had an existential choice, to be an angry man or be a stutterer. And you know how a stutterer can torture you, and keep you on tenterhooks. Any anger that is not coming out, flowing freely, will turn into sadism, power drive, and other means of torturing. (1974, 80)

Do you share your anger? Do you accept it as an expression of your being, just like thirst and hunger, or do you squash it and hope to be something other than you are at this moment? In this instance, the need to express anger is a nuisance since it does not fit into my idea of who I would like to be. I manage it by screaming into a pillow, counting to ten, or taking some medication that makes such self-expression impossible. In each case I get to go on pretending that I'm someone other than I am—someone who doesn't get angry, upset, or excited. Maslow explains how "these people all find desire or impulse to be a nuisance or even a threat and therefore will try generally to get rid of it, to deny it or to avoid it" (1968, 28). The alternative is to give it expression: recognize that, just like being in an arid climate will demand of your organism that it drink, so too will being in a certain social setting demand anger. You can accept the anger as adequate to the setting in which you find yourself, or avoid said setting entirely. In each case you recognize that you are what you are what you are, and in this particular setting, you are angry. By expressing anger, you change both your setting and yourself. This is the same thing that occurs when you are hungry or thirsty: your environment provides need satisfaction or it does not. Anger is understandable at a death metal concert where the environment is ripe for producing anger and its expression occurs in the mosh pits. The potential of a death metal concert is anger expression. This is not the case at the symphony (unless the composer is Chopin, wherein the audience is likely to become frustrated).

Maslow (1968) continues his discussion about the differences between deficiency and growth motivations as they are lived in a variety of situations. He talks about the differential effects of gratification (30–31), species-wide goals and personal goals (33), the degree to which we rely on the environment or on others for meeting our needs (how self-sufficient we feel we are; 34–35), how these needs play out in personal relationships (36), and so on. His analyses are in his book if you wish to explore them. For now I would like to share an excerpt that I have found insightful. It is used as an example in his 1966 book, *Psychology of Science*, and it considers the motivations we have for loving another person. He writes,

If you love something or someone enough at the level of Being, then you can enjoy its actualization of itself, which means that you will not want to interfere with it, since you love it as it is in itself. . . . This in turn means that you will be able to see it as is, uncontaminated by your selfish wishes, hopes, demands, anxieties, or preconceptions . . . neither will you be prone to judge it, use it, improve it, or in any other way to project your own values into it. . . . It adds up to this: you may be fond enough of someone to dare to see him just as he is. (116–17)

For the remainder of the chapter, I'll examine the motivations we have for teaching and for learning. It is regularly argued that students will not learn if we do not reward them for doing so (or punish them for not doing so). This is something that we swallow piously as students. But might it be possible to learn for the sake of participating in the learning experience—might this be an honest expression of your being? That is, might we learn how to read without all of the free personal pan pizzas, ice cream cones, and public honors? In the final section, I compare and contrast two forms of motivation that we can have for learning: intrinsically motivated learning (I learn because I want to; or learning is what happens when I explore the things I wish to explore) and extrinsically motivated learning (it doesn't matter what I'm learning, I'm more interested in the goodies that come along with it, and without the goodies, I would learn nothing).

PERSONAL GOAL ORIENTATION OR IMPERSONAL GOAL ORIENTATION: MOTIVATION IN LEARNING

We can look at the role that motivation plays in the classroom. That is, how can we understand the work that students do every single day in terms of the motivation they have for doing so? Schoolwork, just like being a person, requires motivation. The motivation can come from three different places. It can come from inside: I can be motivated because of some intrinsic desire to take up or accomplish some task. This motivation belongs to me. I can be motivated to do something because of an extrinsic reward I might receive for doing so (or to avoid an extrinsic punishment). This motivation is external to me. Finally, I can do something and remain entirely unmotivated—that is, I am specifically not motivated but do it anyway. In this instance, I accomplish tasks not because of any motivation to do so but because the universe has acted upon me in such a way that tasks get accomplished through me. The cue ball is rather indifferent to the eight ball, yet the cue ball sinks the eight ball.

Motivation in the Classroom

We will consider the role that motivation plays in a learning activity and explore two types of motivation: intrinsic motivation and extrinsic motivation. Intrinsic motivation may be compared with *growth* motivation, and extrinsic, with *deficiency*. The learning scenario: we will imagine that the task for a classroom of sixth-graders is to find the area of a rectangle. Assuming the task is taken on at all, we are free to assume that there exists either intrinsic or extrinsic motivation for doing so. There is quite possibly a third—a passive motivational reason for doing so, which follows the decentering, mechanical procedure of operant conditioning—but we will ignore this for now. Were the problem-solving task completely ignored, we would then assume that the rectangular-area problem had not received the necessary motivation for students to begin working on it. Since they *are* working on it, from where does their motivation come?

Imagine yourself in this sixth-grade geometry classroom. See how each of the sixth-grade students begins working on the rectangular-area problem. This might include looking at the rectangle, calculating side lengths and angle measures, drawing a geometrical grid, or inserting measurements into equations. As a corollary to the two forms of possible motivation, the problem may be conceived in one of two ways. Furthermore, the role of the student is different in each. If problem solving is motivated intrinsically, then the student acknowledges her/his role as a problem solver: she or he *is* the solution to the problem. If the problem solving is motivated extrinsically, then the student is a passive participant in the problem's solution: the student must defer to this external cause (for example, checking with the teacher to see whether his solution is correct).

Intrinsically Motivated Learning

With intrinsically motivated learning, the rectangular-area problem presents as an uncertainty. With uncertainty, a problem is not yet recognized as solvable. It might seem familiar, but the verdict is still out. "Is it even a problem with a solution?" must be the student's first question. It could very well be the case that there *is* no solution. In order to perceive the problem as initially uncertain, the student must identify as the one not yet capable of understanding the problem's solution. Notice that the identity of the student is subject to change. There are many possibilities: there is no solution; there *is* a solution but not enough information; there is a solution and I am adequate to solve it. Here one must begin to play around with any means available in order to identify the details necessary for the problem's solution. After a necessary investment of time, the uncertainty will begin to dissipate, yielding either the solution or the impossibility of a solution. *In either case, the assertion that the problem is understood will belong to the student.* Once understood, the student may use the necessary equations or identify which element is missing if the problem is unsolvable. This approach to a problem has been related to intrinsic motivation because no extrinsically motivating impetus can improve this process; no amount of reinforcement can engender the identification of "self" as a "problem solver." Nobody can take this away.

One might even imagine a problem-solving continuum wherein the more harrowing the problem, the more elite the problem solver. Indeed, a student who has arrived at a solution in this manner would hardly require consultation with the answer key in the back of the textbook. The idea of being given the solution—by consulting the back of the book or looking it up online—would serve only to bypass the process of identifying as a problem solver. It would be like telling a woman who has been training for a marathon for the past six months: "Let's just say you've run it and give you the finisher's medal—no need to actually do it." Such an action misses the importance of the task. In the classroom, these actions are of the "answer-finding" ilk. *Cheating would not be inherently good or evil but would seem rather purposeless if the motivation is to identify and develop as a problem solver.* One might also imagine such a student working on additional problems encountered outside of class—something inconceivable in a contemporary classroom—because the motivations and subsequent solution would thus belong to the student in efforts more akin to play than to work. Note that intrinsically motivated problem solving may be likened to "productive thinking," mentioned in chapter 4.

Extrinsically Motivated Learning

The second approach to the rectangular-area problem, which relates to the extrinsic motivation, begins in a manner similar to the uncertainty of the earlier example. The difference is that the resolution of the uncertainty is the *means* to an end. The problem solving itself is arbitrary; its solution is currency for something better. Students would clap their hands if it gave them praise from the teacher and their parents and eventually led to a diploma.

Because students do not have a choice in their role as students, their circumstance is a forced one. In this manner, the setup is much like that of the behaviorist protocol: something external to the student decides what the latter must do. If the student meets the external expectations, she is rewarded; if she does not, she is punished. Regardless of their identification with the problems with which they are tasked, students are subjected to contingencies of punishment or reward. They are either punished with labels such as incompetent, failure, unintelligent, and unmotivated, or they are lauded with labels such as competent, successful, intelligent, and motivated. *Extrinsic motivation to solve the problem amounts to avoiding the contingent punishment or gaining the contingent reward for doing so.* In this manner, the problem has become incentivized; *it has been loaded with extrinsically moti-vating contingencies in an attempt to increase the desirability of arriving at a solution.* The solution, however, is a mere means to the incentive—more-over, an incentive chosen by someone other than the student. Indeed, the problem itself becomes an annoying impediment that keeps students from receiving more compelling promises of rewards or punishments. The prob-lem itself disappears into the background of "learning"—so too does the possibility of identifying as a problem solver. Indeed, it would be possible to take the reward without performing the behavior—that is, cheat—because it is the reward that is motivating, not the solution of a problem.

Extrinsically motivated learning, if this can indeed be called learning, is not the same as learning in behaviorism. For the purposes of comparison, what follows is an example of an instructional method that aptly portrays behaviorism. This will explain what a purely behaviorist protocol in educa-tion might look like, and it will also illustrate the ways in which contempo-rary schooling differs.

Passive or Amotivational Learning

For the subject learning to solve the rectangular-area problem in the third style—the passive or unmotivated style—no thinking is involved. No moti-vation is involved. The learner necessarily has no recognition that "if I do this, then I will get that." There is only behavior. Learning begins with "recognition." Recognition does not involve thinking; recognition simply means that the intended response behavior follows the presentation of a problem stimulus. In our rectangular-area problem, the presentation of the rectangle is the stimulus, and the multiplication of base measure by height measure would be the response. According to the principles of operant condi-tioning, this occurs due to the previous reinforcement of the aforementioned multiplication response. Thus, the solution is merely what happens after repeated exposures to the particular stimulus presentation. Notice, there is no identification of "self" and "problem solving." Indeed, the problem solution comes about—*is caused*—by the problem presentation; reinforcement is what keeps it there.

Inefficacy of Extrinsically Motivated Learning

The purpose of this final part of this chapter is to reconsider the effectiveness of the classroom that hinges on the extrinsic form of motivation. If it were the case that students are more likely to learn if they are promised something for their effort, then we would have an example of effective school reform. What we stumbled upon in the "extrinsically motivated" style of learning is a form of refurbished behaviorism. This is a behaviorism that grants organisms (and students) the ability to think about first- and second-order events. But does this refurbished form excel in ways that behaviorism has failed? In what seems to be the primary focus of his scholarship, Alfie Kohn argues that extrinsically motivated learning does not work. He writes:

> My premise here is that rewarding people for their compliance is not "the way the world works," as many insist. It is not a fundamental law of human nature. . . . I believe that it is long past time for us to [rethink this ideology]. The steep price we pay for our uncritical allegiance to the use of rewards is what makes this story not only intriguing but also deeply disconcerting. (1993, 4)

Kohn has an impressive résumé of scholarship that has been dedicated to the systematic evaluation of what he terms "pop behaviorism." This includes the counterintuitive yet robust finding that provisions of extrinsic reinforcement actually *decrease* motivation, effort, ability, and in some cases quantitative output. In *Punished by Rewards*, Kohn explains how the apparent contradiction in the title is not so contradictory. Rather than detail the sum of examples of this identity between rewards and punishment, we will consider a few of his broad conclusions.

To test the effectiveness of extrinsically motivated "learning" against that of the intrinsic ilk, Kohn designed experiments that would provide the experimental condition with an obvious incentive—for instance, money for college students and toys for children—and the control condition with no such incentive. Given the collective agreement that "the promise of reward will increase behavior," one might expect that students in the experimental condition would complete the task in order to get the reward, whereas students in the control group may or may not complete the task as there is obviously no purpose for doing so. Notice how any effort put forth by the control group would necessarily be self-motivated—even a null effort. Thus, if the control condition subjects did nothing, the explanation could be that they simply were not interested in the particularities of the target task. Despite the perfectly acceptable choice not to complete the target task, the control condition regularly and reliably outperformed the experimental—that is, incentivized—condition. Kohn explains:

> By the 1980s, anyone who kept up with this sort of research would have found it impossible to claim that the best way to get people to perform well is to dangle a reward in front of them. As the studies became more sophisticated, the same basic conclusion was repeatedly confirmed. College students exhibited "a lower level of intellectual functioning" when they were rewarded for their scores on the more creative portions of an intelligence test. In a separate study, third graders who were told they would get a toy for working on some "games" (i.e., IQ tests) didn't do as well as those who expected nothing. (1993, 44)

Study after study has continued to demonstrate the same result: the promise of a reward does not increase effort, accuracy, or interest. Indeed, Kohn cites McGraw (1978), who concludes,

> Incentives will have a detrimental effect on performance when two conditions are met: first . . . that the offer of incentives is a superfluous source of motivation; second, when the solution to the task is open-ended enough that the steps leading to a solution are not immediately obvious. (40)

These amount to the following: incentives increase student participation only when they are ignored. That is, they not only fail to increase participation, but they often *decrease* it. The second point sounds a little bit more like the intrinsic motivation discussed earlier. Here, the problem presents as ambiguous; there is some uncertainty as to whether or not a solution is even possible. Thus, with or without incentives, the student must identify as the source of the problem's incipient solution, thus circumventing the anonymity that extrinsic motivation requires.

The insistence on the efficacy of a "reward-dangling" procedure cannot be explained by its results. It seems as though *the only available explanation for the continued commitment to the idea that behaviorism* (and its "pop" form) *works is precisely the commitment to the idea that behaviorism* (and its "pop" form) *works*. This is manuals for the sake of still more manuals. It is not *behaviorism* that is being advertised as the solution to education; it is the *idea* of the solution to education that is being advertised—behaviorism is just the most contemporary form. Behaviorism is not the problem; the ideology that has governed the use of behaviorism is the problem. It is *this* ideology that Kohn has urged his readers to reconsider.

SUMMARY

This chapter looked at motivation—or why we do the things we do. As a continuation of the previous chapter, this can be viewed as the process of how we become who we are, or how we become a self.

We compared two types of motivation: deficiency and being. With deficiency motivation, it is understood that you are missing something. "If only I had . . . , then everything would be okay." We compared this with being motivation: the kind that accepts that who you are at any moment is good—that you are what you are what you are.

We also examined motivation in the classroom by describing three types. A student can be intrinsically or extrinsically motivated, or he can be completely unmotivated. With intrinsic motivation, we learn because doing so is enjoyable and we find it to be our best expression. This motivation is in tandem with the best expression of ourselves. With extrinsic motivation, our learning must be incentivized by rewards for doing a good job. It is not the learning itself we desire, but the reward. This learning alienates us from the learning process—as if the learning doesn't matter. Finally, the passive approach is the science of behaviorism: like a pigeon that learns to spin around in a circle, so, too, can you learn calculus.

PSYCHOLOGIZING IN ACTION

My Motivation to Start College

I've always known that I would have to start college somewhere down the line, but this experience gave me the motivation I needed to do so. I remember one day simply thinking to myself, "Where do I see myself about ten years from now?" Before then, I had already decided that I wanted to move to New York City to become an actor or something of that nature. I had already figured that New York City was a more expensive city to live in compared with where I live now. So I asked myself, "How will I be able to afford the cost of living there? How will I be able to shop as much as I want? Or live in the type of luxurious apartment I desire?" Later down the line, I discovered that I liked helping people and would make a great counselor; my dreams of becoming an actor vanished. Therefore, I started doing research on the career of a counseling psychologist. I discovered that they can make well over eighty-five thousand dollars per year in New York City, depending on their level of education. I could make enough money to live in my dream city comfortably by doing something I really enjoy doing. That would also mean I would have to spend the next six to ten years in college. Beginning then, my motivation to start college was based on building a brighter future for myself in one of the most expensive places in the country. I would also have to keep the same motivation and determination I had to start college and to pursue graduate school. I know this is what it will take to support my spending habits and survive in a city that I have long desired to be in.

Source: Bobby Knighton, Albany, GA.

Chapter Eleven

Emotion (Anxiety)

It is very difficult to appreciate from the outside what a person in severe anxiety is experiencing. [A patient of mine] rightly remarked about his friends "imploring a drowning man to swim when they don't know that under the water his hands and feet are tied." —May 1977, 208

Chapter 9 featured a discussion on the concept of personality. The personality that you *are* was discerned from the personality that you *have*. With the latter, we are tempted to construct a superlative personality that will garner the positive attention of others; with the former, we realize that there is only one person we can be—that is, the person we are at this very moment (that is, we are what we are what we are); we realize that we *are* our own unique person. In chapter 10, this discussion was carried into the topic of motivation. We found that we can be motivated to actualize ourselves or our self-concepts. Efforts made to develop the self-concept are built on a belief that "I need to be something other than I am at this moment." This is built on a sense of lack, and it is called *deficiency motivation*. This was discerned from *being motivation*, which refers to efforts made to actualize that person who I am since the goal is simply becoming myself.

As promised, you may read this chapter as a continuation of the previous two. The topic broadly concerns "emotion," which we will explore shortly. More specifically, this will include a close look at the experience of anxiety and how this differs from fear. Since Sigmund Freud, anxiety has been an important topic in psychology. Like all emotions, anxiety is a psychophysical phenomenon. If you recall from the introductory chapter, as psychologists we have made it our business to examine the intersection between the physical and the phenomenal—that is, between the physical world of objects (of which our bodies are a part) and our experience. Emotion is uniquely suited for this task because it always has physiological and psychological components, and in order understand them, we must consult both. That is, it is insufficient to explain anxiety or fear exclusively through their environmental context or physiological manifestations (though each of these are important). It is also insufficient to explain anxiety exclusively through subjective experiences—this emphasis also ignores important details about the body.

In this chapter, we will look more closely at what is going on during the experience of anxiety. In doing so, we will find that anxiety may be discerned from fear. This will begin with a look at the functionality of the autonomic nervous system in order to demonstrate how emotions manifest in your body. It is in the body that we will first consider the difference between anxiety and fear. In fear, your autonomic nervous system responds in a meaningful way to an environmental threat. With fear, we understand that the bodily response is proportionate to the imminent threat. With anxiety, the autonomic nervous system also responds to a threat, but this threat cannot be directly traced to the environment. Thus, anxiety is a response to nothing in particular. With fear, the environmental threat can be targeted and removed, which relieves the autonomic distress. With anxiety, this cannot be done: autonomic relief from anxiety is merely managed through avoidance tasks or substitute performances. These have the effect of distracting a person from the anxiety-provoking situation by decreasing a person's scope of behavior in a particular situation, with the consequence of limiting one's potential. This discussion will be carried over into the discussion of psychopathology in the next chapter.

THE EMOTIONAL BODY

As mentioned, our emotions are psychophysical phenomena. They are "physical" because the autonomic nervous system is implicated in emotional experiences. Consider: the autonomic nervous system has been called the "bridge between psyche and soma"—that is, the mind and the body (May 1977, 69). The first part of the word, "auto-," means that it functions autonomously. This is to say that the autonomic nervous system is not under direct conscious control. It is responsible for digestion, respiration, blood circulation, and everything included therein. These are tasks that continue without any conscious intervention on your part. These bodily changes also shape your experience quite dramatically. For example, imagine that you decide to introduce yourself to a fellow student: do you think this interaction would change at all if your heart rate were 160 beats per minute (which is considered a rate for intense aerobic exercise)?

Anxiety and fear are psychophysical responses to threats to your existence. When defined this way, it is understandable that these experiences are grave ones. Since they concern your very existence, you may consider them as existential threats. For the purpose of this discussion, threats to existence can take on two forms: fear and anxiety. With fear, the response can be traced to an environmental threat; here you know what you're reacting to and how to protect yourself. With anxiety, the response cannot be traced to an environmental threat; here you're not sure how to proceed since you don't know where the threat is coming from. Both experiences implicate the autonomic nervous system. With fear, the environment is sufficient to understand the autonomic response. For example, I'm about to get sideswiped by a semi, a gun has been drawn on me in an alley, a venomous snake has just crossed in front of me, and so on. In these instances, relief from the situation leads to relief from the autonomic nervous system distress: for example, the semi misses me, and eventually my heart rate returns to normal. This is different from the experience of anxiety. In anxiety, *I* am not in any imminent danger, but some aspect of my personality is. If it is a personality aspect that I am holding tightly to, then the self-concept threat is sufficient for arousing the autonomic nervous system: *I experience my life as in danger*. However, since my reaction cannot be traced to the environment, because my self-concept is not real, nothing can relieve my distress. This is the experience of a vague, nonspecific threat to my being, even though no such threat can easily be identified. Fear is a reaction to something from without; anxiety is a reaction to something from within. Kurt Goldstein, whose words will help us understand the psychophysical similarities and differences between anxiety and fear, explains:

> In the state of fear, we have an object in front of us that we can "meet," that we can attempt to remove, or from which we can flee. We are conscious of ourselves as well as of the object, we can deliberate how we shall behave toward it, and we can look at the cause of the fear that actually lies spatially before us. On the other hand, anxiety attacks us from the rear, so to speak. The only thing we can do is to attempt to flee from it without knowing where to go, because we experience it as coming from no particular place. (1995, 230)

Following the theme developed throughout this book, we will explore emotion as something that you *are* and not as something that you *have*. This is to say that emotion is a process and not a thing. "Thus it is not strictly accurate to speak of 'having anxiety'; rather one 'is' anxiety, or 'personifies' anxiety" (Goldstein 1995, 232). Since emotion plays out through your autonomic nervous system, which controls all the vital systems that make you up, we must understand and appreciate the gravity of the situations in which this is experienced. I should not be able to sit down and take a written exam if a mountain lion is pacing back and forth, eyes fixed on me. The blood vessels in my legs will begin to dilate; my irises will begin to expand, widening my field of vision yet also making focus more difficult; my heart rate will rapidly increase; and my breathing will increase. All of this will occur without conscious control. Indeed, no amount of conscious control will stall this process. How am I supposed to sit and write an exam? I am physiologically prepared to sprint flat-out for four hundred meters. So what happens when instead, I sit to take the written exam and my autonomic nervous system is behaving as though my life were being threatened? In the former scenario, my physiological response is proportionate to the environmental threat (fear of an incipient attack from a fearsome feline); in the latter, my response is disproportionate to the environmental threat (I am anxious about something in the context of a pencil-and-paper exam). Are you beginning to see the dilemma?

In both—fear and anxiety—emotions are something that you are. They are always an all-encompassing psychophysical experience. They demand all of you. Nothing escapes the impact of an emotion: your cardiovascular system, respiratory system, digestive system, nervous system, endocrine system, and so on. Each is implicated. A man or woman in love treats the entire world with warmth and open arms. Even psychological faculties such as cognition, perception, and emotion take on the tenor of the emotion while you are in it. To say that it affects everything that you are is to say that emotions are *pervasive*. Fear and anxiety *have* to be pervasive because they are the response to the threat to some value that you hold essential to your existence as a person (May 1977, 205). In fear, your ability to continue living is at risk; in anxiety, your ability to continue *being your self-concept* is at risk. *Neurologically, however, there is no difference.* We will look first to what is occurring at the neurological level during the experience of fear and anxiety.

The Neurophysiology of Anxiety and Fear

There is no experience of fear or of anxiety without a body. Only in the context of a body is an experience fear evoking or anxiety provoking. However, a discussion of the physiology of anxiety is troubling because it suggests that what is happening is *merely* physiological. This is to suggest that the only important factor during an emotional experience is what is occurring in a person's body. May reports how

> in most discussions of the neurophysiological aspects of anxiety, the procedure is to describe the functioning of the autonomic nervous system, and the bodily changes for which this division is the medium, and then to assume implicitly or explicitly that this adequately takes care of the problem. (1977, 67)

For now, suffice it to say that a powerful psychological component determines whether the "*merely* physiological" response is a damaging one or a helpful one. With that disclaimer, consider the role of the autonomic nervous system.

As mentioned earlier, the autonomic nervous system is so-named because it has been understood to operate autonomously. Indeed, it is exceedingly difficult to consciously influence the variety of functions operated by the autonomic nervous system: heart rate, blood pressure, digestion, peristalsis, vascular dilation or contraction, and so on. We have since learned that certain practices can be used to influence these functions (such as controlled breathing to lower one's heart rate), but we will cover that more thoroughly in the chapter on health psychology (chapter 13). The autonomic nervous system, May tells us, has been called "the bridge between psyche and soma"—or between mind and body. Once again we see the appropriateness of this topic for psychological investigation.

The autonomic nervous system is divided into two parts: the sympathetic and parasympathetic divisions. The *parasympathetic* division "stimulates digestive, vegetative, and other 'upbuilding' functions of the organism. The affects [or emotions] connected with these activities are of the comfortable, pleasurable relaxing sort" (May 1977, 69). The parasympathetic division is *enervating*, which means that it decreases nervous system excitement. Think about the sorts of activities that initiate parasympathetic nervous system activation: the period after eating a large meal, heavy exercise, or sex, dusk, overcast skies, and so on. The other division is the *sympathetic*. The sympathetic division "is the medium for accelerating heartbeat, raising blood pressure, releasing adrenalin into the blood, and the other phases of mobilizing the energies of the organism for fighting or fleeing from danger" (May 1977, 69). The affects associated with sympathetic division activation are "typically some form of anger, anxiety, or fear" (69). The sympathetic division is *invigorating*, which means that it arouses nervous system excitement. Consider some of the activities that excite the sympathetic nervous system: nearly getting hit by a car, driving in unsafe conditions, being surprised by a poisonous snake or spider, meeting a potential lover. . . . For now, it is important only that you recognize the difference between the parasympathetic and sympathetic divisions of the autonomic nervous system.

Another important detail about the autonomic nervous system is that the divisions work in opposition to each other. This means that when one is active, the other is inhibited (and vice versa). In the midst of a fear response, blood and gastric juices evacuate your stomach so that you cannot digest food and, as a result of this, your appetite wanes. This is why Rollo May gives the example of the "speaker" who "finds his appetite strangely absent at the dinner after which he must make an important and crucial address" (1977, 69). This is also why people do not eat when they are stressed out or worried about the future (or the past). However, the same oppositional quality between these divisions makes it possible to inhibit one with the other. Perhaps you have *overeaten* when worried or you know of someone who has. In this instance, by eating, one activates the division responsible for digestion (and relaxation), and as a result this enervates the nervous system. The oppositional relationship between the divisions of the autonomic nervous system makes it difficult to try to predict or control what will occur when you become anxious. Moreover, efforts to control the anxiety response will prove only to exacerbate the problem. This is when a change occurs in your awareness about a potential problem in your environment. For example, this is why you suddenly have to pee when the "fasten seat belt" sign lights up in the airplane or the lengthy class period has begun. The closed door or seat-belt light indicates a change in the environment that makes bladder relief a limited possibility. Ironically, the conscious effort to relax makes relaxation impossible. The paradox of anxiety amounts to this: your kidneys evacuate because time has run out for using the lavatory.

So far we have explained the two components of the autonomic nervous system that are implicated in the experiences of anxiety and fear. In doing so, we have discussed which division is directly implicated in anxiety/fear responses (the sympathetic) and which is indirectly implicated (the parasympathetic). Also, we have learned that these two divisions have an oppositional relationship to each other. In so doing, we have seen how emotions are always accompanied by nervous system excitement.

This section considered the "what" of the emotions of fear and anxiety. From a physiological perspective, the emotions of fear and anxiety are virtually identical. Each results in sympathetic division excitation and parasympathetic inhibition. Moreover, both seem to be evolutionarily developed responses to a threat to one's existence. So what is it that differentiates these two emotions? Certainly we are correct when we say that anxiety has a different character from the experience of fear. Indeed, these are distinct. But we must explore them from the experiential or subjective side in order to understand this distinction. This is to say that we must consult the person who is experiencing them. We will now turn our attention to understanding the importance of these emotions—that is, the "why."

Anxiety and Fear as Meaningful Responses to Potentially Catastrophic Situations

Anxiety and fear are both the experience of a threat to one's existence: they are physiological responses to potential catastrophes. The major difference between anxiety and fear lies in the location from which one perceives the threat to be coming. With fear, the threat may be found in one's environment; with anxiety, the threat doesn't seem to be coming from anywhere in particular.

Consider fear. We have talked about a few of these life-threatening situations: venomous snakes, car accidents, and dangerous mountain ranges among others. These are the situations in which a fear response is likely. This is not to say that venomous snakes cause autonomic arousal. The situation in which a venomous snake is encountered is important to consider in determining whether or not the body will initiate a fear response. If invited to touch a venomous snake by a zoo attendant, the fear response would be less severe than if challenged to touch one in the wild. The sympathetic nervous system response is an evolutionary adaptation, and it initiates the unconscious preparation for fighting or fleeing, both of which require nervous system excitation. Thus, the degree to which the autonomic nervous system is aroused must be determined by the subjective experience of a threatening situation. If the subjective experience is one of imminent peril, then the fight-or-flight response is initiated. The alternative is to remain vulnerable to a potential threat on your life. In situations of fear, it is also understood that the autonomic nervous system response is proportional to the environmental threat: a fear response can be understood in terms of a direct and imminent threat in the environment. One wrong step and you could fall several hundred feet into a rock bed or take a fatal pair of fangs on the ankle. Thus, the rapid heart rate and pupil dilation make sense, given the objectively dangerous environmental situation. Finally, since the threat to your existence may be traced directly to the environmental threat, then eliminating this threat will end the fear response (initiate parasympathetic activity). For example, once the snake is back in its cage or is at a safe distance, your heart rate will return to normal.

But how about those situations where *I* am not in any imminent danger and the physiological response is the same? Taking a written exam—the Graduate Records Exam (GRE)—for instance. In this situation I sit before a pencil and paper (or computer monitor, as the case may be). What, in this environment, puts me in a life-threatening situation such that I might understand the reason behind my increased pulse, restlessness, and heightened attention to sensations? Many of you have had a similar experience when sitting to take an important exam—college exam, aptitude test, driving exam, and so on. Indeed, we seldom have fear-evoking, life-threatening situations in the industrialized world. They might happen only a couple of times a year. But we regularly have situations that initiate the physiological fear response. For example, we might drive cars around at fifty to seventy miles per hour, which is awfully fast for a human being to be moving. If this is not terrifying enough, many drivers also distract themselves by listening to music and talking or texting on their mobile phones. For many, *even this* threat to life is insufficient to warrant autonomic nervous system excitation. But here I am in an exam, and I cannot sit still or concentrate: what is the threat I am experiencing?

In the experience of anxiety, the autonomic nervous system response is similar to that of the fear response. The difference is that it seems to issue from nowhere in particular. With fear, I know the object of my fear: I can locate it within my environment. The object of fear comes from without—it is outside myself and somewhere in my environment. With anxiety, I have no apparent object of fear. The fear comes from within. It is "an emotional state which does not refer to anything definite, that the source of anxiety is nothing and nowhere. Anxiety deals with nothingness. It is the inner experience of being faced with nothingness" (Goldstein 1966, 92). Moreover, with fear there is a meaningful response to an external stimulus viewed within a particularly catastrophic context. A fear response is meaningfully directed toward a threat in the environment: the snake *right there* is threatening my continued existence. With anxiety, "we find a meaningless frenzy, with rigid or distorted expression, accompanied by withdrawal from the world, a shut-off affectivity, in the light of which the world appears irrelevant, and any reference to the world, any useful perception and action, is suspended" (Goldstein 1995, 231). Fear leads to action whereas anxiety leads to inaction or freezing; fear leads to heightening of the senses whereas anxiety leads to the dulling of the senses. After all, if one cannot identify the object of anxiety, how is one to face it or avoid it? Before exploring the ways that anxiety is mitigated, we will look at the examination example in more detail. Such an account will hopefully demonstrate how an anxiety response might come from nowhere in particular.

In my GRE anxiety, I *am* experiencing a threat to myself. But we cannot understand this in the same objective manner as we have understood fear. Fear may be traced to a threat to my continued existence: a threat to myself; anxiety is a threat to my self-concept. If you remember the discussion on personality, we have an existential option to actualize ourselves or our self-concepts. Ourselves are the organic beings that we are: the meaningful organization of cells, tissue, experiences, and history. Actualizing myself is becoming the me that is most like myself; it occurs simply by *being*. Self-concept actualization, you will recall, stems from an idea of *who I would like to be*. Self-concept actualization relies on the impression of others and begins with the assumption that I can become anybody that I wish to be. This difference is extremely important in understanding the experience of anxiety. In fear, myself is at risk; in anxiety, my self-concept is at risk.

While sitting down to take the GRE, the threat that I experience is to my identity as a scholar/academic/scientist. The person whose life is at risk is Patrick-the-scholar. The latter has been frequenting urban coffee shops and wine bars with stacks of existentialist literature, playing the role of the intellectualist and scholar. Part of this role, I think at the time, is admission to graduate school. The GRE determines how qualified I am to continue into graduate school—and by extension, how legitimate my identity as an intellectual is. The determination might be that I am unqualified, so my identity is currently under attack: there is an imminent threat to the life of Patrick-the-scholar. *If I identify as Patrick-the-scholar*, then *the subjective threat that I experience*—and the associated excitation of my nervous system—*is no dif-*

ferent than if my objective life were in danger. This is because there are two parts of an emotional response: the objective situation and my subjective understanding of the situation. We might otherwise offer Patrick-the-scholar the following advice: just give up your unreasonable identity as a scholar; who cares whether or not you fit some definition of being a scholar; or, relax, your definition of scholar is the best scholar that you can be anyhow. If I identify with and take great pride in this particular self-concept, then giving up this identity is akin to giving up on my life. Or at least this is how it seems. In any event, my subjective experience of the threat to my identity as a scholar is the same as the threat to my continued existence. Thus, in order to understand anxiety as a meaningful response to a potentially catastrophic situation, we must understand that an emotional experience has two components: objective experience and subjective understanding of this experience. The objective experience (including my physiological response, which is autonomic nervous system arousal) is the same in both; but the subjective understanding is different. For a long time in the history of psychology, it was believed that the objective response caused the subjective understanding or vice versa. Stanley Schacter and Jerome Singer (1962) have demonstrated that these two are both important in the experience of an emotion.

Schacter and Singer's Two-Factor Theory of Emotion

Schacter and Singer conducted a variety of experiments that challenged the way emotion had long been understood. Before their work, emotion was understood as a reasonable biological (neurophysiological) response to an environmental situation. Now look back at the description of sympathetic functions and their associated effects: increased heart rate, increased blood pressure, flushing of the face, pupil dilation, and so on. What emotion does this sound like? Is it love or fear? Anxiety or anger? Schacter and Singer reasoned that the physiological response isn't alone responsible for our experience of emotion. The physiological response must be understood *in light of a cognitive appraisal of the environment.* The following example considers the "actual" experiential difference between sexual arousal and fear.

To test Schacter and Singer's theory, two psychologists at University of British Columbia put male college students in an objectively terrifying situation (Dutton and Aron 1974). The objectively terrifying situation was in the middle of a suspension bridge that spanned a deep ravine on campus. Then they added an attractive female researcher to the mix. When college students met this attractive researcher in the middle of the bridge, they were *over four times more likely to call her and ask her about the results of the experiment than when they met her on the control (read: nondangerous) bridge.* The only difference in the two conditions was where the students were meeting the researcher (dangerous bridge or nondangerous bridge).

Schacter and Singer, and the experiments that would follow, demonstrate that the bodily response is not alone in determining the subjective experience—the latter includes a cognitive appraisal of what is happening. If, for instance, I come up against a mountain lion who is pacing back and forth, eyes on me, then I understand that my temporary physical paralysis is the expression of my fear. The autonomic arousal becomes fear *only when I understand it in the context of the objectively threatening situation*. In the absence of the attractive researcher, we can imagine that the UBC students would have attributed their arousal to the dangerous suspension bridge. Subsequently, I manage this fear by avoiding the threat to my life (if the cat walks away or if I safely cross the bridge).

Being Afraid, Being Anxious

With fear, the response is proportionate to the environmental threat; fear may be understood as a reaction to an objective threat of a catastrophic situation. This is certainly the case with the mountain lion, but it can even be understood in the case of the potential loss of an idealized opinion of who I am as a person. When viewing the GRE example from a distance, we might understand that what concerned me was the loss of an important aspect of who I wish to be—namely, Patrick-the-scholar. In this instance, the threat to myself is a subjective one. Indeed, it needn't be the case that a poor GRE score will "kill" my identity as a scholar, but this is how I understand it. How am I to resolve the threat in *this* situation?

According to Goldstein (1995, 1966) and the subsequent analysis by May (1977), the experience of anxiety is accompanied by an *inability* to respond. "Fear sharpens the senses, whereas anxiety renders them unusable; fear drives to action, anxiety paralyzes" (Goldstein 1966, 94). In anxiety, awareness actually becomes less acute. There is an important reason why awareness narrows during the experience of anxiety, which we will get to in a moment. For now, we will ensure that we understand what is occurring during this experience. The situation is an important examination, and my body is responding as though my life is in danger: my heart is racing, I'm having some difficulty catching my breath, and it has become difficult to focus. In the case of fear—like a run-in with a venomous snake—I can trace my autonomic nervous system arousal to a specific object in my environment. If I can negotiate this one object (moving to safer ground), then I can reverse the autonomic distress. This is what is meant when we have said that fear is in response to something in particular. But with anxiety, the response cannot be linked to anything in the environment, so there is nothing from which I can flee. The examination itself doesn't pose any direct threat, but it is something about the event of the examination that creates the possibility of a threat. The response is toward the *anticipation* of a disaster: "What if I fail?" The possibility of failure is what threatens, even though the possibility is nothing in itself. Since there is no thing in the environment to face when one is anxious, this leads to paralysis. The next movement may be the one that actualizes the threat against my existence, so I cannot act: I cannot think, I lose fine motor control, I forget what I am doing, or I cannot move.

As it is experienced, the inability to react during anxiety is counterintuitive. This was mentioned before in the paradox of kidney evacuation as soon as it becomes too late to use the lavatory. For another example, if I am giving a speech but I am anxious about forgetting one of my lines (or of forgetting an important word, or slurring my speech, or so on—the examples are endless among college students), then this very concern is what prevents me from remembering my lines. It is the fear of possibly forgetting my lines that leads me to freeze during my speech and forget my lines. The fear of speaking publicly is that anxiety will set in: "What we fear is the impending anxiety" (Goldstein 1995, 233). The fear is in the face of a possible catastrophe: anxiety is the breakdown of any ability to react in a situation.

Now is a good time to recall the quotation that began this chapter: May reminds us that "it is difficult to appreciate from the outside what a person in severe anxiety is experiencing" (1977, 208). We might want to remind the graduate student that she should just relax and that she will remember each of the points she wishes to make. But doing so is like reminding a drowning man to swim when under the water his hands and feet are tied.

To move forward in a meaningful way with the treatment of an anxiety issue, we must first understand the importance of the narrowing of locomotor, cognitive, and sensory abilities. Earlier I mentioned that the decreased awareness that occurs during anxiety is important, and now it is time to explain why. Remember how with fear, a definite object is in my environment that threatens my existence, but with anxiety, this threat comes from nowhere in particular? This means that the only way to prevent anxiety is to avoid situations in which anxiety might present. This begins quite simply by a decrease in the range of perceptions. The sensory field has a lot to take in: anybody walking in a crowded street (or forest) might be overwhelmed by sensory stimulation. When faced with a potential anxiety-inducing situation, these perceptions narrow: "rather than make eye-contact with everybody, I am just going to go my own way and ignore everything else." In a classroom, students report that they did not answer a question out loud or raise their hand because they didn't want to be incorrect; I didn't tell my lover what my fantasies were because I was afraid she would be disgusted with me. In each example, the possibilities of self-expression are limited in order to avoid the potentially catastrophic situation. Moreover, these are not merely cognitive computations of probabilities: I do not think that I have a 40 percent chance of being incorrect and thus decide not to answer. Instead, my sympathetic nervous system makes it nearly impossible to raise my hand and speak up in any clear or unencumbered manner. Hopefully these less pathological examples are helpful for understanding the role that anxiety plays in *reducing my field of awareness* and the cognitions and physical expressions that accompany this reduction.

So let's look to some more pathological cases. Can you imagine a scenario in which a person cannot even speak? Think back to one of the first few times that you got into any trouble with your parents or guardians (or more recently, your management): "Did you lie to me?" "Why did you hit her?" "Why did you send that e-mail?" What's the answer? "I don't know." These are avoidance behaviors wherein one limits the field of awareness so as to mitigate the incipient catastrophe that comes with a complete admission of guilt. Admitting that I hit my sister is what I am incapable of doing. Instead I just stare. If I were paying attention, I would notice how my fields of vision and audition are getting narrow. I would also have trouble carrying on a basic conversation since focus would be completely lost. What I fear is the catastrophe that might befall me were I to admit to hitting my sister. Instead, I play dead. This, like most expressions of anxiety, is the worst thing that I can do.

Do you think this could be taken even a step further? Perhaps to the point where I am incapable of even understanding the question or I don't even hear it? For instance, you might wake up the day after making a horrible blunder and feel like all is well. But then the consciousness of it slowly creeps in from the back, and you are slowly overcome by this paralyzing sense of doom. You can't quite place it. So it lurks. The avoidance tasks help—alcohol, drugs, hobbies, new friends, old friends, or shopping—but the dread remains. Perhaps this is a stretch from the embarrassed young boy who hit his sister, but perhaps it's not.

A Reasonable Case for Pathological Anxiety

I conclude this discussion on anxiety with a simple argument that it is perfectly reasonable to experience pathological anxiety in the present-day Western world. I will use Erich Fromm's *Sane Society* (1990) to demonstrate that our world is anxiety provoking.

From the outset, the argument that our luxurious, affluent, and excessive first-world lifestyles are anxiety provoking is palpably absurd. Certainly we have come a long way from the conspicuous inequality of medieval feudalism. In feudalism, inequality is the norm; in contemporary capitalism, everybody has an equal shot at becoming the feudal lord. In the twentieth century, as Fromm explains, the "working class . . . has an increasing share in the national wealth." Moreover, "[h]e cannot be ordered around, fired, abused, as he was even thirty years ago. He certainly does not look up any more to the 'boss' as if he were a higher and superior being" (1990, 101). Indeed, when viewed beside the sixteenth through nineteenth centuries, the twentieth and twenty-first seem quite grand; we have come a long way. Why, then, might pathological anxiety ensue? Fromm explains:

> In fact, it seems that in spite of material prosperity, political and sexual free-dom, the world in the middle of the twentieth century is mentally sicker than it was in the nineteenth century. . . . We do not submit to anyone personally; we do not go through conflicts with authority, but we have also no convictions of our own, almost no individuality, almost no sense of self. (1990, 102)

The individualized sense of self is an important part of development. R. D. Laing (1990) calls this "ontological security," by which he means we have a sense that we are "real, alive, whole; . . . as having an inner consistency, substantiality, genuineness, and worth," and so on (41). We might also call this establishment of an individualized sense of self the process of becoming a person, a central theme throughout this book. Remember how in each chapter I have continually reminded you that you are a process and not a thing? A personality is something that you are and not something that you have; motivation is an expression of your own-most being and not a motto or slogan by which you live; emotion is something you are and not something you have; and so on. In instances where we focus on what we *have*—for example, we *have* a body, a mind, a perception, a thought, a memory—we are in effect dissociating a part of ourselves: we separate a piece of ourselves away from who/what we are, and in so doing we pretend that we are not these things (or at least we are free to make the decision to keep them or discard them). In clinical psychology, this is called dissociation. But in our experience, this is the feeling of alienation. It is lived as though we are aliens in our own body or aliens to our own experience. Alienation is the conse-quence of having no sense of self. Fromm continues,

> He has become, one might say, estranged from himself. He does not experi-ence himself as the center of his world, as the creator of his own acts—but his acts and their consequences have become his masters, whom he obeys, or whom he may even worship. The alienated person is out of touch with himself as he is out of touch with any other person. He, like the others, are experienced as things are experienced; with the senses and with common sense but at the same time without being related to oneself and to the world outside. (1990, 120–21)

Anxiety is the psychological illness of the twentieth and twenty-first cen-tury because of the very luxurious and presumptuous notion that we can be a better person if we work at it or that we can become whatever we wish: that we can be happy. As a result, the person you are gets turned into a self-improvement project. Psychology has colluded with you in this alienation and has worked at turning every aspect of your person into a thing (body, mind, memory, emotion, thinking, perceiving, and so on). Why is it that I can fear for my life while sitting down to a written examination? Because I am completely out of touch with my own experience. This has been replaced by my imagination of what my experience might be. That experience which, if I work hard enough at it, can be mine. Fritz Perls explains,

> Anxiety is the excitement, the *élan vital* which we carry with us, and which becomes stagnated if we are unsure about the role we have to play. If we don't know if we will get applause or tomatoes, we hesitate, so the heart begins to race and all the excitement can't flow into activity, and we have stage fright. So the formula of anxiety is very simple: anxiety is the gap between the *now* and the then. If you are in the now, you can't be anxious, because the excitement flows immediately into ongoing spontaneous activity. (1974, 2–3)

Pathological anxiety is the consequence of turning our experience, which is a process, into a thing. We protect ourselves from this by remembering that what we are is this continual process of becoming.

SUMMARY

We have explored the phenomenon of emotion. This featured the emotions of fear and anxiety. Both of these, as with all emotions, have physiological and psychological components—that is, they are psychophysical. The physiological component includes the autonomic nervous system arousal (sympathetic or parasympathetic, as the case may be). The psychological component includes the cognitive appraisal of the situation. We call this the subjective understanding of the situation. This is when we understand the meaning behind the change in our nervous system and body. With fear and anxiety, the autonomic nervous system excitation is identical. The difference is the subjective evaluation of the experience. With fear, the sympathetic arousal can be traced to an objective threat in the environment (e.g., a venomous snake). With anxiety, the arousal cannot be traced to anything in particular: it is a fear of no thing at all or the fear of becoming anxious. Since fear may be meaningfully understood in a context, it leads to increased awareness and attention (fight-or-flight response). Since anxiety issues from nowhere in particular, we can manage it only through avoidance techniques. These avoidance techniques manifest in a shrinking of the fields of motor, cognitive, and sensory awareness (which, incidentally, is the event that one has feared all along).

In the following chapter, we will see how the invention of the terms "normal" and "psychopathological" have contributed to the neurotic experience of anxiety. According to popular psychological opinion, the experience of anxiety would fall beneath the umbrella of psychopathology because it is specifically unhelpful and should be treated (that is, made normal). Fear, on the other hand, would fall beneath the umbrella of normalcy because it is helpful and should thus remain intact. We will challenge this distinction between normal and pathological and use Goldstein's (1995, 1966) case studies to demonstrate this with patients who exhibit anxiety. We will consult Georges Canguilhem, philosopher and historian of medicine, in the discussion of normal and psychopathological.

PSYCHOLOGIZING IN ACTION

Loneliness

I first began to awaken to the meaning of loneliness, to feel loneliness in the center of my consciousness, one terrible day when my wife and I were confronted with the necessity of making a decision. We were told that our five-year-old daughter, Kerry, who had a congenital heart defect, must have immediate surgery. We were warned, gently but firmly, by the cardiologist that failure to operate would cause continual heart deterioration and premature death. At the same time he informed us that there were many unknown factors in heart surgery and that with Kerry's particular defect, there was about twenty per cent chance that she would not survive the operation.

What were we to do? We experienced a state of acute worry, followed by a paralyzing indecision that lasted several days.

There was no peace or rest for me, anywhere, at this time. I, who had known Kerry as a vigorous, active child, bursting with energy, whether on roller skates, a two-wheel bike, or in the pool, was suddenly forced to view her as handicapped. In spite of her exuberance and her seemingly inexhaustible energy, there in my mind was the report of the X-rays and the catheterization showing a significant perforation and enlargement of her heart.

Visions of my daughter were constantly before me. I roamed the streets at night searching for some means, some resource in the universe which would guide me to take the right step. It was during these desperate days and nights that I first began to think seriously of the inevitable loneliness of life. I was overcome with the pain of having to make a decision, as a parent, which had potentially devastating consequences either way. . . . This awful feeling, this overwhelming sense of responsibility, I could not share with anyone. I felt utterly alone, entirely lost, and frightened; my existence was absorbed in this crisis. No one fully understood my terror or how this terror gave impetus to deep feelings of loneliness and isolation which had lain dormant within me. There at the center of my being, loneliness aroused me to a self-aware-ness I had never known before.

Source: Moustakas 1972, 1–2.

Chapter Twelve

The Normal and the Psychopathological

In this chapter, I advance the argument that the categories "normal" and "psychopathological" are unhelpful to our efforts to try to better understand persons and their experience. This is first because the two concepts are highly ambiguous, so in using them one isn't being very clear about the intent in using them. These terms are also unhelpful because of the way they position healthy and unhealthy, or psychologically well and unwell, as opposites to each other. Both problems will be considered in turn, beginning with the first. I follow this with a revision to this entire category: a positive emphasis on health, which will be the topic of chapter 13.

The ambiguity of the terms "normal" and "psychopathological" stems from the fact that each term has more than one definition. Incidentally, these definitions follow the two styles of psychology that have been discussed throughout this book. You will recall: psychology can be understood as a fixed set of facts that concern what it means to be human (which it is the business of psychologists to discover), or it can be understood as an examination of personal experiences through which psychology is created. The same can be said about trying to understand normality or psychopathology in a person. That is, should "normal" refer to all persons: "What is normal for everyone?" or should it refer to a single person: "What is normal for you or normal for me?" In the first instance, what is normal for me is also what is normal for you because normal applies to everyone. In the second case, what is normal for you is not necessarily normal for me because we are different persons with different personalities and potentials.

In the introduction to this book, I argued that the first definition of psychology, which would rely on a universal definition of "normal," is impossible. Not only is it impossible, but it actually interferes with any meaningful projects in psychology. The dangers of treating everybody as a general psychological subject have been observed in each chapter, most recently including the prevalence of anxiety in a world where we become alienated from our own experience while we instead follow some generic pursuit of happiness. The "norm" we follow has nothing to do with us; it is not our own. The concluding thesis of this chapter is that "normal" and "psychopathological" can be understood only within the context of a single person and that both are meaningful expressions of being. That is, what is normal for me might in fact be psychopathological for you (or the reverse), and both may be understood in terms of our entire beings (and not isolated to specifically diseased regions, for example).

The first section looks at the way that modern science has defined "normal" and, by negation, "psychopathological." I argue that these do not mean anything in particular. We have no confidence about what either one looks like on its own. This is because we must understand them within the context of a living person; viewed in this way, we find that normalcy and pathology are both working in the same direction: toward self-actualization. This means that they are not working against each other (as if a battle of healthy against unhealthy is being waged within each of us). Doing this will require that we revise how health is often conceived. This is the focus of the second section: looking at the history of the health polemic. "Polemic" means that one concept stands opposed to another one: health and disease, normal and psychopathological, and so on. I will argue that the polemic needs to be replaced with a more fitting model of what health means.

NORMAL

The concept of "normality" is a peculiar one. The act of asserting it does two things: it first presupposes a state of optimal functioning and, by negation, a state of specifically nonoptimal functioning. There is allegedly a difference between normal and abnormal (which may be read as a synonym for pathological in this discussion; we will later see that abnormal does not necessarily mean "pathological"), and it is assumed that normal is the better of the two. Thus, the definition of normal is consequential to what is considered desirable and what is considered undesirable. So what does "normal" mean?

For its consideration within the field of psychology, normal can mean one of two things. First, it can refer to the statistical average that has been calculated within a particular population. For example, we might understand what is normal for the height of college men. If the heights of all men are measured, then we can discern the average height by dividing this number (in inches) by the number of men measured. The "normal" height would fall right in the middle of this distribution, with "abnormally tall" falling to the right and "abnormally short" falling to the left. In this case, there does not have to be a single person who is actually this exact height (6 feet, 0.011253 inches, for example). This conception of "normal" refers to all people but nobody in particular. The second conception of normal deals with a case-by-case basis. In this instance, normal refers to an individual person: what is normal for me is not necessarily normal for you. In my particular world of relationships, coordination, perspective, and wardrobe, it is normal for me to be five feet ten. If I woke up two inches taller, then my clothes would not fit well; I might have difficulty coordinating movements due to a slightly longer torso or legs; the people whom I customarily look up to see might be at eye level; the branches I normally don't duck for would hit the top of my head; and so on. As such, the six-foot average height would be *abnormal* for me. This second conception of normal refers to the particular: it deals with an actual person. Both of these will be discussed with greater detail in the sections that follow.

Statistical Approximation of Normal

When viewed within a psychology that is fixed and unerring, "normal" refers to the statistical approximation of *the* average person. This refers to nobody in particular but to everyone in general. We use this reference to the normal every time we talk about intelligence. With intelligence, as gathered by the Binet-Simon IQ test, an average score corresponds to 100. This means that an IQ of 100 is normal. All persons may be compared to this number and labeled normal, above average, or below average, depending on the score she gets on the intelligence test. The 100-point IQ score does not refer to an actual person who has the definitive measure of intelligence; it refers to all persons and the amount of intelligence that persons most typically have. Thus, the score refers to a general scale of intelligence to which we may compare ourselves. A score of 100 on an IQ test means that your score most closely resembles the score most common for people your age and from your particular social/political/economic background (assuming these factors have been controlled).

The "statistical approximation" conception of normal can be demonstrated by a Gaussian statistical distribution as shown in figure 12.1—that is, the "normal bell curve." In this curve, we might imagine that some psychological characteristic is being measured (say, intelligence). The *x* axis (horizontal axis) refers to the measurement of the psychological characteristic—your score on an IQ test. Since we already know that the average score on these tests is 100, we can put a score of 100 at the centermost point along the *x* axis. The *y* axis (vertical axis) refers to the number of people who have this characteristic (or score). As we can see in this normal curve, a score of 100 has the highest number of people. This frequency tapers off to the left and to the right, demonstrating that these scores are less common. The uppermost limit we know is 140, whereas the lowermost is 60. Moreover, we understand that a score of 140 is *better* than 100; these people are geniuses (which we understand is a good thing). However, a score of 60 is *worse* than 100; these people are nincompoops, imbeciles, idiots, and so on (these were clinical terms that have been used throughout the years to describe the people with lower scores on an intelligence test; this, we understand, is not a good thing).

Intelligence is only one example of the "statistical approximation" conception of "normal." But this chapter is concerned with psychological illness or psychopathology. So what are some of the illnesses we can plot to understand what it means to be normal in this sense? How about sexual illness? What is a normal weekly number of sexual encounters? Should this number change with age? With relationship status? Gender? Other problems? How about normal sleep patterns: How many hours per night is normal? What is a normal bedtime? A normal waking time? If people get *more* sleep, is this preferable, like a higher IQ? If people get less sleep, is this pathological, like being an idiot?

We could plot normal distributions for emotions such as happiness (can there be too much or too little?), sadness/depression, loneliness, fear or anxiety, and so on. In each case, we assume that there is an amount of each emotion that is normal and an amount (deficiency or excess) that is abnormal (or pathological). From this vantage point, the goal is to try to get everybody as close to normal as is possible. For example, it would be best if everyone were never lonely, always happy, and had sex no more or less than three or four times per week.

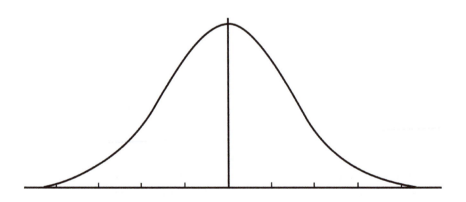

Figure 12.1. Normal Distribution

Problems with the Statistical Approximation Conception of "Normal"

The first conception of "normal" has two chief problems: the first, mentioned earlier, is that "normal" doesn't refer to any actual person. We'll use philosopher of medicine Georges Canguilhem to explain this first problem. In the second, we find that the statistical approximation conception of "normal" cannot in principle do justice to an individual person. This is because it fails to consider differences in person, circumstance, and context of the normative characteristic. We'll use biologist Kurt Goldstein to explain the second problem.

For his philosophy dissertation, Georges Canguilhem wrote a comprehensive critique of modern medicine titled *The Normal and the Pathological*. I have borrowed his attitude and his title for this chapter. Canguilhem argues against the continued reliance on the disease model for understanding illness in the twentieth century. He specifically problematizes the ambiguous use of the concept "normal" for defining the healthy organism (1991, 155–79). Like this section has argued, Canguilhem observes how "normal" is supposed to be in reference to a statistical average expressed by the bell curve, pictured earlier. But this, he argues, is impossible when considering a biological being. To say that my average heart rate is sixty beats per minute does not require that my heartbeats distribute themselves evenly across a sixty-second period. There is considerable variability of time between beats in a pulse. The first might be one second, the next 1.2 seconds, then 1.2, 0.7, 1.1, 1.4, and so on. Indeed, saying "sixty beats per minute" does not mean that the heart beats once per second: it is understood that the statistical approximation is not exactly what the organism follows. That is, we understand that this definition of normal does not refer to any actual heart. Canguilhem concludes that "we shall limit ourselves to maintaining that . . . the normal is defined as an ideal type in determined experimental conditions rather than as an arithmetical average or statistical frequency" (1991, 152).

What, then, might it mean for a normative guide for mental wellness if the ideal form cannot, in principle, represent an actual person? The ambiguity of what normal means is impressive. This leads Goldstein to say the following about "normal": "Even if the idealistic norm concept would do justice to the 'constants' of the species, by forming the ideal according to these constants, it may nevertheless fail with respect to the individual" (1995, 325). What he means is that even though the majority of North Americans might have a heart rate of sixty beats per minute, it doesn't mean anything for my heart that is beating right now. How much more might this be true for a complicated problem, such as psychological distress or anxiety? If the ideal norm is to have zero psychological distress and zero anxiety (which is not the point I am advancing), what does this mean if it tells us nothing about an individual case that averages out to zero? Indeed, a statistical norm concept "cannot be used to determine whether a given individual is to be regarded as normal or abnormal. The statistical norm concept cannot do justice to the individual" (Goldstein 1995, 326).

When we use the term "normal" to refer to the standard baseline that is ideal for a population (for all college students, for example), then this standard needn't apply to anybody in particular. That is, even though the number might be derived from an average that includes each of us, this doesn't actually tell us anything about any one of us by ourselves. As an ideal average, "normal" doesn't tell me anything about you. The next definition of "normal" will come from Goldstein and will emphasize normality as a case-by-case definition. This is to say that it will deal specifically with our individual selves.

Self-Actualization Conception of "Normal"

The second conception of "normal" should sound familiar; it has been a central theme in this book. As burgeoning psychologists, we have made it our business to try to understand persons and their experience. In the past few chapters, we have talked about what it means to become your own person. In the chapter on personality, this means discovering and becoming the person(ality) you are. We do not have the potential to be some generic definition of normal—that is, a regression to the mean. We have only the potential to be ourselves. Motivation, we saw, is the energy to actualize this potential. If the motivation comes from within, you can be somewhat certain that it is my own self-expression; if the motivation comes from without, then you can be somewhat certain that I am trying to become what somebody else wishes of me. And so on.

So what does this mean for the concept "normal"? In the second conceptualization of "normal," we have in mind the actualization of a single individual: an acorn, for example. An acorn has the potential to become a giant oak tree. It is never in the potential of an acorn to become a pine tree, even though the forest in which it is growing might feature a majority of pine trees. This statistical average has no bearing on the potential of the acorn in question. No matter how tall and narrow the rest of the trees are in the forest, tall and narrow would be *abnormal* for the oak tree. To understand what normal is for the acorn, we have to consider the acorn itself.

But what if we were to look at the potential of acorns in general? Could we not simply limit our averaging to all acorns? By no means. This is because the potential does not begin and end with the generic acorn; the oak-tree-potential is also contingent on its environment: the self is not limited to the boundary of one's skin. How big and how strong the oak will become depends on the soil, sun, water, and surrounding landscape (heavy winds or rains; cold temperatures or hot; and so on). A big and beautiful oak tree might be a possibility in the middle of a forest where there is shelter from heavy winds, but not alone in the middle of a field. Indeed, we might expect a shorter, stockier oak in the latter scenario. A tall, slender oak tree would face problems if situated all alone. *We could not label a tree normal or abnormal unless we are prepared to consider the context in which it is found.* Are you beginning to see the importance of reviewing each individual instance in determining what "normal" means? Carl Rogers provides a striking example of how even a pale and sickly plant can be seen as strong and courageous when viewed within its context. He writes:

> I remember that in my boyhood home the potato bin in which we stored our winter's supply of potatoes was in the basement, several feet below a small window. The conditions were unfavorable, but the potatoes would begin to sprout—pale white sprouts, so unlike the healthy green shoots they sent up when planted in the soil in the spring. But these sad, spindly sprouts would grow two or three feet in length as they reached toward the distant light of the window. The sprouts were, in their bizarre, futile growth, a sort of desperate expression of the directional tendency I have been describing [that is, self-actualization]. They would never become plants, never mature, never fulfill their real potentiality. But under the most adverse circumstances they were striving to become. Life would not give up even if it could not flourish. In dealing with clients whose lives have been terribly warped, in working with men and women on the back wards of state hospitals, I often think of those potato sprouts. So unfavorable have been the conditions in which these people have developed that their lives often seem abnormal, twisted, scarcely human. Yet the directional tendency in them is to be trusted. The clue to understanding their behavior is that they are striving, in the only ways that they perceive as available to them, to move toward growth, toward becoming. To us the results may seem bizarre and futile, but they are life's desperate attempt to become itself. This is the potent tendency. (1980, 7–8)

What might it take to transform a sickly potato sprout into a strong, green shoot? To suggest that the sickly appearance is the *problem* completely ignores the extraordinary strength the plant exhibits. The pale, spindly shoot is an expression of strength: this potato plant has beaten the odds. When viewed within the context of its environment and milieu, we can see this as a healthy expression of growth and not an abnormality.

In this case, we can see that what is normal for the plant is the sunlight toward which it is growing: if we can recognize and acknowledge it, we can shape the environment to be more supportive of this plant's life. *But the plant itself is not expressing disease; it is capable of expressing its needs and an impressive directional tendency for growth.* Goldstein explains that we may understand this expression as normal for the organism. Is it normal for a potato plant to grow weak, pale, and spindly? It is impossible to answer this question for a generic plant. We must look to a particular one, and in the case of Rogers's plant in the basement, yes. Normal and pathological make sense only when viewed within the contexts out of which they emerge.

> An organism that actualizes its essential peculiarities, or—what really means the same thing—meets its adequate milieu and the tasks arising from it, is "normal." Since this realization occurs in a specific milieu in an ordered behavioral way, one may denote ordered behavior under this condition as normal behavior. (Goldstein 1995, 325)

Here Goldstein combines individual potential with environmental constraints to define what is meant by "normal." We know that an acorn does not have the potential to become a pine tree. But we also understand that the environment is important for understanding the actualization of this potential. A weak, pale, and sickly potato sprout doesn't seem very healthy, whereas a big, strong, expansive potato plant seems self-actualized. Certainly the former would be better off if it looked like the latter. But this is to ignore the role of the environment. The first plant's growth is truly remarkable, even admirable if viewed within the context of a dark and dank basement. Indeed, it was reaching up toward the light; this doesn't seem like pathological behavior at all. We see this too in plants whose roots will grow outward and toward nutrients; this doesn't seem optimal in terms of developing a strong structural foundation. Roots also grow differently in the sand or between rocks than they do in soil. The sickly potato plant is the strongest that it can be; were it any bigger, it would wither and die because the sunlight and nutrition are insufficient to support it. Also, we would be inaccurate to argue that the plant would be better off as a bigger, stronger, and more impressive plant.

In the self-actualization conception, "normal" indicates ordered behavior toward growth, and this cannot be identified without considering both organism *and* environment. I will have more to say about Goldstein's definition of normality within the context of psychological health later. For now we need to talk about part two of what happens when one uses the term "normal": one also asserts abnormal. As you might have expected, what is meant by abnormal depends on what one means by normal. If one uses the first (statistical approximation) definition, then not-normal pertains to anybody who falls outside the center of the normal distribution. In the second (self-actualization) definition, not-normal refers to anything that inhibits a particular person's actualization within a particular setting or milieu. Since contemporary medicine and psychology have used the term "pathology" to refer to these abnormal deviations from the mean within medicine, we will use the term "psychopathology" to indicate abnormality.

PSYCHOPATHOLOGY

As mentioned previously, the concept of "normal" presupposes an abnormal. With the disease model of medicine, abnormal is understood to be a pathological state: normal + pathogen. In this section we look at what this means in psychology—that is, psychopathology. In the disease model of medicine, psychopathology is something you have that can be fixed. We will examine what this means exactly. In conclusion, we will find that "normal" and "psychopathological" both refer to a person trying to make the most of a situation—trying to flourish. As such, they are both seen to be in the service of health and wellness. This is why I propose that these two categories be replaced by the one category of health—the topic of chapter 13.

For the purposes of connecting this discussion with the previous chapter, we will specifically consider psychopathological anxiety. Therefore, whenever an example would be helpful, I will use anxiety. Anxiety, you will be reminded, is the physiological fear response in the face of nothing in particular; that is, it is physiologically identical to fear, but with nothing in the environment that is sufficient for understanding the response.

The term "pathology" comes from the disease (or pathogenic) model in modern medicine. In the eighteenth and nineteenth centuries, it was still common for people to die from infectious diseases. It was understood that a normal person and a diseased person differed in a very particular way: the diseased person had something that the normal person did not have (namely, a virus, bacteria, parasite, disease, and so on). This model proved eminently helpful because based on this assumption, scientists could look for the cellular or infectious aberration and treat that. If the treatment made the aberration reduce or disappear, then the person was restored to normal health. Georges Canguilhem notes how decidedly convenient this is. He speaks of the "germ theory," which is the basis of the disease model:

> [T]he germ theory of contagious disease has certainly owed much of its success to the fact that it embodies an ontological representation of sickness. After all, a germ can be seen, even if this requires the complicated mediation of a microscope, stains and cultures. (1991, 40)

The confusing term "ontological representation" means that a concept is taking on a definite form (takes up space in the material world). Canguilhem observes how the disease model treats unwellness as a *thing*, which is precisely the modern scientific temperament we've been busily guarding ourselves *against* throughout this book: turning processes into things. Notice what this kind of relationship to wellness and unwellness brings: it is as though health and disease are opposed to each other. Canguilhem says that they "envision a polemical situation: either a battle between the organism and a foreign substance, or an internal struggle between opposing forces. Disease differs from a state of health, the pathological from the normal" (1991, 41). It is as though a battle is waged within us, and it is our responsibility to help the good guys. This separates our body from our own experience—making it a thing that we have. It makes it impossible to experience health and disease as meaningful expressions of our being in the world. And Canguilhem is arguing against this conception in *medicine*; we're talking about psychology. Psychology is not medical biology; it deals with life, relationships, perception, meaning, and so on. How much more so must we argue for this alternative in psychology? Are we really ready to concede that the "germ theory" is how we should understand relationships?

Have you ever met somebody who was toxic? Whenever you greet them or carry on a brief conversation with them, you feel like wanting to run headfirst into a brick wall? Fritz Perls (1972) explains that when you encounter toxic people, you leave feeling like your energy has been drained. This is different from encountering nurturing people, whose company leaves you feeling energized and enthusiastic. Try to think of someone you know who is toxic and someone you know who is nurturing. It is actually quite simple to do. Indeed, if you pay attention to your intuition in this matter, you will avoid much turmoil down the road. Consider this: is the solution to take toxic people with a cup of coffee and nurturing people with alcohol? That way you can fight off the infection and remain normal, right? By no means. You recognize that different company engages you in different ways, because you are a whole person with meaningful experiences. When you interact with someone or something, your entire person is engaged. Feeling drained is not a pathological response: it is a warning. Your person cannot handle the toxic environment and it begins to disengage, to shut down. We cannot view the lethargy as a problem; it is a solution. It becomes a problem only when you have in mind a particular and normal way of feeling (like "happy") all the time. Instead, we may view even pathology as an expression of self-actualization in the context of another person. Toxic people make you want to take on very little and nurturing people, very much. Avoid toxic people; keep nurturing people around. Neither should be treated as though a battle is being waged in your person. Toxicity does not make me diseased; it initiates a health response, which is one of disengagement. The "disease" of wanting to run headfirst into a brick wall is actually the solution. This means that you would be better served if you were unconscious than remaining conscious and in the company of a toxic person. Try it sometime.

Disease (and psychopathology) may be seen as a good thing—as an expression of health—instead of being viewed as a germ that needs to be sprayed with disinfectant. Since infectious diseases have gone from the leading cause to an unlikely cause of death, we can understand how successful this model has been. But contemporary ailments don't fit quite as neatly into the disease/pathogen model as the ones of two centuries ago. We'll address this theme once more in the subsequent chapter on health.

If Normal Is Good, Is Psychopathology Evil?

For now, we will focus on the assumption that stems from the first conception of normal: that a generic norm exists that we would do best to meet. This is to say that "mental health" for a particular individual looks exactly like that for everybody else. It also says that what's good for you is also good for me. So what might pathology look like in this instance? It would be any*thing* that stands in the way of my being normal (that is, most closely representing the average person). In the case of anxiety, where might I find the *thing*, that bit of disease, that stands in the way of my normal functioning? If seated for an exam, would the increased heart rate and narrowing of senses be the things that are preventing the normal exam-taking scenario? That is, would I be a normally functioning person except for this misplaced autonomic arousal? If so, then the pathology model could fix the problem by enervating the autonomic nervous system. This could be done with drugs that target my nervous system—something that keeps it functioning at a low level so that I cannot be overcome or upset by its arousal.

In this example, do pharmaceutical drugs cure me of my anxiety? If viewed through the disease model, then anxiety *is* a problem and, moreover, it is a thing. In this case, it could be argued that the problem-thing of anxiety is limited to the nervous system, and drugs provide the solution (curing your body of anxiety disease). But am I diseased in this scenario? To say this another way, is my autonomic arousal in the context of an exam pathological? Or can it be meaningfully understood as a solution—is it a meaningful response that aptly expresses my relationship to this particular exam? If you can remember from the previous chapter's discussion, then it seems like the anxiety *is* an important response: *my identity as an intellectual is at stake.* My life is at risk. So when I take the drugs, I am able to relax for the exam (or at least it seems like that). What becomes of my relationship with sitting for this exam? *I no longer know how this makes me feel.* I might assume that it means precious little to me since it fails to excite my nerves. Moreover, I am able to maintain the delusion that I am my self-concept (intellectual) regardless of what I actually am (namely, nervous about keeping up the act of an intellectual).

In sum, the isolation and elimination of the presumed pathological manifestation of anxiety gives the impression that a problem is being solved. But upon review, it does little to address the problem that is my deluded belief that I am my self-concept. Instead, when under threat to my self-concept I no longer feel anything. The disease model of psychopathology always leaves something out because it wishes to reduce the issue to a single *thing* (pathogen, disease, germ, and so on). But in the second analysis, we see that problems do not lend themselves to such simple reduction.

So far in this discussion of pathology, we see that even when this pathological *thing* can be isolated and eliminated, we are not really sure any "fix" has been supplied. Furthermore, this begins with a problematic assumption that the *thing* that has been isolated is indicative of disease and not of health. This, it seems, can never be perfectly clear. In the anxiety example, we understand the importance of my anxiety as a response to a legitimate threat to my self-concept existence (as an intellectual). But it can also be interpreted as an out-of-place physiological response that I would be healthier not having. The question arises: how are we to discern whether an isolated content (thing, reaction, thought, feeling, and so on) is indicative of a *disease* or of *health*?

To conclude, Goldstein argues that it is not so simple to differentiate normal from pathological when we are looking only at the symptoms. He writes how "not every deviation from the norm, as to contents, appears as disease. It actually becomes a disease only when . . . it carries with it impairment of and danger for the whole organism" (1995, 328). And he continues, "Strictly as to contents, there is, on this basis, no far-reaching fundamental differences between the healthy and the diseased organism" (327). We may instead lump "normal" and "psychopathological" into the same category of "being toward health." This recognizes the tendency within each of us to self-actualize. Since this perspective begins with the assumption that we are always striving toward health, it will be called "positive." That is, we will focus on the ways in which we actualize psychological (and physiological, since these cannot be easily separated) health and not on the ways in which we avoid psychological disease or psychopathology.

In sum, I hoped to demonstrate how the conversation of psychological wellness and unwellness should not begin with a differentiation between normal and psychopathological. This doesn't accomplish very much in terms of understanding one another. The terms themselves are ambiguous, and they allow us to continue thinking about our own health and well-being in terms of things that we have (and not processes that we are). In the next chapter I will propose my alternative to "psychopathology": "health psychology." I do not think health psychology should be some extra appendage of psychopathology or abnormal psychology; I think health psychology should replace these. This is primarily because our *most natural* tendency is *not* toward survival or self-preservation (as we often expect) but toward flourishing or self-actualization.

ADDITIONAL ROUTES TO A HUMANIZING CLINICAL PSYCHOLOGY

In this chapter, we have already examined how the categories of "normal" and "psychopathological" present problems that are difficult to resolve. Chief among them is the common assumption that we ought to avoid psychopathology and strive to be normal. But when we consider these more closely, we see that both categories demonstrate the quality of self-actualization. By demonstrating that these categories are more similar than dissimilar, we avoid thinking of health in terms of a battle being waged inside of us and may instead begin thinking about health in holistic and meaningful terms. However, this is not the only way of avoiding a dialectic conception of health and illness. In what follows, I briefly summarize a few alternative routes that psychologists have taken in efforts to humanize the treatment of suffering individuals. That is, the categories of normal and psychopathological can be used in a way that still validates the experience of the person going through them.

The Phenomenological Psychopathology of van den Berg

Given the objectives of this psychology text—namely, an observation of the meaningful ways in which the disciplines of psychology are experienced—the topic of psychopathology could easily have emphasized the phenomenological approach of J. H. van den Berg (1972).

Van den Berg tells of a single case study—a client who suffers from severe anxiety. Despite his being tested by a variety of specialists, none of them could find evidence that some*thing* was the matter with the client. In the traditional medical model, this means that nothing is wrong and the client is fine. But this was not his experience. Van den Berg chooses to begin with his client's experience—very similar to the approach taken up in this book.

"All patients," van den Berg writes, "share the same human existence. Thus, I hope, by discussing my single patient, to create understanding of other patients, in principle of all patients" (1972, 4). Like all experiences, the experience of psychopathology can be understood only within the lived context. It is only from this context that it derives its meaning. By looking at psychopathologies this way, van den Berg is arguing that even *these* experiences make sense. As clinicians, our task is to understand the world from the vantage point of the client. Listen to what this sounds like:

> The patient's description of [his world] was so convincing that one wondered whether he lived in another world—a world just as real as the ordinary, sound world. The impression that the patient was talking about something that was real to him became even stronger when one realized how much he suffered as a result of his observations. . . . The objects of his world were frightening and

ominous, and when he tried to establish that the house, the street, the square and the fields would reasonably have retained their former shape and nature, and that, therefore, his perceptions must have provided him with a falsification of reality, this correction, in which he wanted to believe, if only for a moment, seemed unreal and artificial to him. It was more unreal than the direct, incorrect observation which was so frightening that it drove him back to his room. What he perceived was a reality, just as he described it. (1972, 9–10).

By beginning with the assumption that a client's experience is a meaningful one, clinicians treat it as they might treat their own experience: granting it validity and importance. This, to van den Berg and other phenomenological psychotherapists, is an integral first step in understanding a client.

Existential Psychotherapies

While phenomenological clinicians humanize their clients by validating their experience, existential clinicians humanize their clients by recognizing the basic concerns of all humans—that is, the existential concerns. By "existential concerns" I mean the necessary boundaries that serve as limits for all human beings. Existentialists argue that these boundaries provide backgrounds upon which all basic problems can be understood. For example, the existential fact that all living things will eventually die is one such boundary. Death provides a backdrop for all decisions that we make since it presents the possibility that we might not have another moment like the present one to accomplish a task or repeat a particular experience. In this face of the possibility that this will be our last experience or opportunity, it makes the importance of our decisions all the more salient.

Master storyteller and psychotherapist Irvin Yalom (1980) has constructed a psychotherapeutic method around these existential boundaries. He argues that the problems that clients bring with them can be understood within the context of four ultimate concerns: death, freedom, isolation, and meaninglessness.

The background of death has already been summarized above, but it receives more in-depth attention from the likes of Martin Heidegger (2008) and Medard Boss (1963). The background of freedom is another element of existence that is often ignored. Our ability to choose is understandably beneficial, but we seldom fully recognize the weight of the consequences that accompany this: by choosing a psychology degree over a physics degree, *we are responsible for the consequences of this choice.* Nobody else can choose for us, and nobody can absorb the responsibility that accompanies this. When the weight of responsibility attaches to any of us, it can be enormous. Yalom also recognizes the existential problem of isolation—one that can even be seen with the increasing connectivity afforded by social networking: even if we are surrounded by lots of people, each of us is profoundly and utterly alone. Despite efforts made by others to help us feel like we belong and are accepted, only we can accept this for ourselves. And finally, in the context of these other existential boundaries, each of us must reconcile the relative meaninglessness of our own lives in the cosmos. "What impact will we make on others without limiting their own freedoms?" "What change will we bring about in the world?" Try asking yourself these questions before ordering your lunch at a fast-food drive-through. These are questions that are debilitating, and they require that you consider the totality of your existence within a single frame of life.

Yalom (1980) provides a variety of stories and vignettes that demonstrate how the majority of problems that clients bring with them can be understood within the context of one of these four existential concerns.

Antipsychiatry with R. D. Laing

The position that I have taken in the main body of this chapter may be understood as an antipsychiatric position. This is because I challenged the fundamental categories of affliction (psychopathology) and wellness (normal) in modern medicine—categories upon which the practice of psychiatry is based. I used Goldstein and Canguilhem to accomplish this, but I could just as easily have used R. D. Laing.

Laing was an exceptional psychiatrist because, like Goldstein, he was not too bound by the categories that were supplied by his field. Goldstein was given brain-damaged patients who were supposed to represent all manner of pathology, but he was always able to see meaningful comportment of brain-damaged persons in their environment. In the kinds of mental institutions where Laing was working, it was customary to assume that schizophrenic patients were impossible to understand—that their behavior was random and meaningless. Laing was unperturbed by this restriction: he assumed that all behavior, regardless of how apparently ridiculous it was, could be understood. To demonstrate this, he provides the medical community with a series of vignettes—stories of schizophrenic patients who from the outset seem crazy and incapable of being helped. Laing is able to spend enough time with each of these patients to understand their problems more deeply—usually by viewing them within the context of the patients' family homes. The pages of his books are filled with illustrative examples of this, and I highly recommend looking up a few of these. In the meantime, I offer a brief summary of one of the vignettes: it is "the ghost of the weed garden."

The story begins with Julie, a twenty-seven-year-old schizophrenic patient who has been in the psychiatry ward for ten years. She speaks in incoherent sentences, has trouble determining whether ideas belong to her or to others, and believes that her mother has murdered her or someone like her. The last part is what landed her in the psych ward to begin with. I like this story because Laing tells it to us chronologically, and that helps those of us who are unfamiliar with schizophrenia better understand how it comes about.

Laing (1990) explains that Julie was a *good* little girl and that her parents and relatives loved her. Then, during late childhood and adolescence, she became a *bad* girl—arguing with her mother and saying some terribly awful things that she couldn't possibly have intended. This upset her parents greatly. Finally, Julie went *mad*. She accused her mother of murder, which was obviously false. At this her parents were relieved because they realized that she was crazy and that this couldn't be helped.

While Julie's story sounds like a perfectly legitimate one about how a person goes crazy, Laing tried to understand it more deeply: what did her parents mean by the terms "good," "bad," and "mad"? After interviewing Julie's parents, siblings, and relatives, Laing realizes that "good" Julie was actually emotionally impoverished and existentially dead. Her parents praised her for this. Next, when she tried to express her own unique personality and perspective, this was sanctioned as "bad behavior." Unable to identify an identity that was separate from her mother's wishes, Julie experiences her "self" as being smothered and eventually murdered. At this, the entire family (and medical community, save Laing), stopped taking what she said seriously. Is it any surprise that she has seen no improvement in ten years? Indeed, can you blame her?

Ethical Imperative of Clinicians

Steen Halling, clinical psychologist and emeritus professor at Seattle University, views clinical work in a manner that is different from but still related to the examples we have seen. To begin with, Halling maintains that clients who seek the counsel of therapists must be humanized. To humanize them means that clients can never be understood merely in terms of their symptoms. This, of course, has been the argument throughout this book. But in his practice, Halling takes this much further: he recognizes that such humanization is an ethical obligation that we all have as persons.

Halling describes the difficulty that accompanies trying to understand the experience of another person. Following the philosophy of Emmanual Levinas, of whom Halling is a great scholar, Halling maintains that we can never know the perspective of the other: we cannot understand their depression, their anxiety, their loneliness, or their frustration. "I cannot 'empathically,' 'imaginatively,' or in some other way place myself in the Other's position, or take a genuinely exterior point of view on myself and on my interaction with the other" (Halling 1975, 208). As soon as he assumes that he understands his client, then he does violence to him or her, ultimately removing him or her from participating in the process of psychotherapy. Halling explains how this is an ethical decision:

> What Levinas wants to emphasize is that ethics is a relationship with someone exterior to me, in other words, ethics arises in a genuine relationship, not in a pseudo-relationship where there is a meeting of two parts already belonging to a larger whole. (1975, 216)

Understanding another person's experience is difficult. But notice what happens when a therapist begins with the assumption that he or she cannot, in principle, "figure out" the client: this leads to a genuine interaction and, if both are interested in working through the problems of the client, they may pool resources and work together. Here one finds no hierarchy where the client always submits to the therapist. Instead, both learn a great deal about themselves and about each other. Halling concludes, "Therapy is in some sense possible, but it is possible only because everything does not depend on the therapist, because there is another whom each of us can meet" (223).

SUMMARY

This chapter examined psychopathology from the opposite perspective: if psychopathology is being *abnormal*, what does it mean to be normal? Our inquiry left us thinking that "normal" is an ambiguous concept and is not very helpful in trying to understand another person.

In considering these categories of mental well-being, we see how influential the disease model has been on clinical psychologists. When someone is mentally "diseased"—they have depression, for example—it is assumed that there was once a normal and healthy person who now has a depression infection of some sort. The attending physician must isolate and treat this depression so that the person may return to normal. We are again reminded that the body is not a machine with independent parts but a coordinated system of processes. Depression is not inside a person: depression *is* this person.

As soon as the division between normal and pathological begins to dissolve, it allows us to try to understand and help people in new ways. We reviewed a handful of these approaches: phenomenological, existential, antipsychiatric, and ethically grounded psychotherapies.

PSYCHOLOGIZING IN ACTION

"A Patient Appears at the Psychiatrist's Office"

A few years ago, unusually late in the evening, I was called on the telephone by a man, evidently nervous by the sound of his voice, who asked to consult me about his personal difficulties. . . . We agreed on the next evening, and at the appointed hour I greeted my caller, a young man of about 25 years. At first he seemed undecided, but eventually he explained the reason for his visit.

Even the first moments showed that he was in great difficulties. He looked at me with a mixture of distrust and shyness, and when he shook my extended hand, I felt a soft, weak hand, the hand of a person who doesn't know a way out and, not being in control of himself, lets himself drift. Stooping uncertainly, he sat down in the chair which I had invited him to take.

He did not relax, but sat on the edge of the chair as if preparing to get up and leave. His right hand, which he had held under his unbuttoned vest when he entered, and which he had removed from there in order to greet me so unconvincingly, was immediately replaced in its original position. With his left hand, he drummed the armrest of the chair uneasily. He did not cross his legs. His behavior created the impression of a man who has been tortured for a long time.

His story confirmed this impression entirely. He said he was a student but for many months had not attended courses because he had been unable to go into the streets during the day. The one occasion on which he had compelled himself to do so had stayed in his memory as a nightmare. He had had the feeling that the houses he passed were about to fall on him. They had seemed grey and decayed. The street had been fearfully wide and empty, and the people he had met had seemed unreal and far away. Even when someone passed him closely, he had had an impression of the distance between them. He had felt immeasurably lonely and increasingly afraid. Fear had compelled him to return to his room, and he would certainly have run if he had not been seized by such palpitations that he could only go step by step.

Source: Van den Berg 1972.

Chapter Thirteen

Health Psychology

The previous chapter began the discussion of clinical psychology. This is the area of applied psychology that deals with the mental wellness of persons. When wellness is divided into "normal" and "psychopathological," then the conversation of wellness takes on a negative tenor. This means that it deals in terms of only normal wellness (an ideal or average wellness) or some deficit to normal wellness. From that perspective, "normal" is what we're after. Not only does this ignore anything "better" than normal, but normal itself doesn't mean anything to anyone in particular. Unfortunately, this negative approach is the most common in clinical psychology. The previous chapter outlined a number of problems with this approach. The most troubling of these problems is that we have no way of knowing whether or not a "symptom" is an expression of *disease* or *health*. For example, is a rapid heart rate a *healthy* response or an *unhealthy* one? To determine this, we cannot look to what is "normal" because normal doesn't refer to anyone in particular; we also cannot simply look at how it manifests in a particular person because this also neglects the context in which it appears.

In this chapter, we are not going to look at mental illness (in the negative) but mental wellness. Instead of beginning with the assumption that persons are normal unless something is wrong with them (disease model of wellness), we will begin with the assumption that persons are always *being-toward-health*: everything that a person does is in service to her or his self-actualization and can be seen as a meaningful, healthy activity. This is called a salutogenic model. Pathogenesis understands wellness as the termination of disease or pathogens; salutogenesis understands that wellness is always in the capacity of persons. Pathogenesis emphasizes illness; salutogenesis emphasizes health.

The salutogenic model runs against the common assumption that the strongest biological tendency is toward survival. Goldstein (1995) argues that this doesn't seem true at all. *The survival instinct is not the strongest biological motivator.* The need to survive is what emerges only when the organism is under direct threat: when continued existence is at stake. When we look only to the persons whose existence is under threat (that is, they are anxious, fearful, and so on), then we see what looks like self-preservation activity. For example, under the stress of fear, the autonomic response is one of fighting or fleeing. If this activity is viewed in a manner that segregates it from the life of the person experiencing it, then it seems like the fighting and fleeing is in support of self-survival. Goldstein argues that this is only one way of looking at this example.

We may also look at self-preservation as though the person is trying to effect the optimal circumstance. "If the biologist rests his theory on observations of such [pathological] conditions," Goldstein explains, "then a drive toward self-preservation may appear as an essential trait of the organism, whereas, actually, the tendency toward self-preservation is a phenomenon of disease, of 'decadence of life'" (1995, 337). If we are under direct threat, then the optimal change will be in the safety of our environment: moving from unsafety to safety. If these are the only scenarios that we analyze, then we will naturally conclude that the chief tendency of life is "self-preservation." But we might also see "self-preservation" within another category of "self-actualization." Indeed, we must do so in order to understand clinical psychology from a health perspective. This means that we can understand that all biological behavior moves toward optimal functioning (and not simply survival). How else would we make sense of the rapid rehabilitation of persons with severe cardiac disease or the survival of persons whose basic needs have been deprived for years? There is a biological tendency that exceeds the tendency toward self-preservation, and it is making the most of life; it is self-actualization; it is health.

"PATHOLOGICAL AND DISEASED" OR "SALUTARY AND HEALTHY"?

A pathogenic model makes sense when we assume that the most natural tendency in persons is the survival instinct. This is a compelling thesis, but it fails in understanding a person. Along with our shift from a negative conception of mental health to a positive one, we will be replacing a *pathological model* with a *salutogenic* model. Something that is pathological gets in the way of health: it is an ailment to health. Something that is *salutary*, on the other hand, contributes *to* health: it is *healthy*. When psychological wellness is considered from the position of psychopathology, the procedure is to focus on outliers in the direction of pathology: observing persons with profound schizophrenia, anxiety, depression, and so on. In a salutogenic model, we will look at the outliers who are uncharacteristically healthy and happy. We will look at the people who have the worst prognosis medically—those people we would expect to be the *least* healthy, and we will look for those who have managed to flourish—to find wellness even here.

Tired of the question "Why do people get sick?" or "Why do people feel depressed?" Aron Antonovsky wishes to ask the question "Why are people located toward the positive end of the health ease/dis-ease continuum, or why do they move toward this end, whatever their location at any given time?" (1987, xii). He does this in his book *Unraveling the Mystery of Health*. We all know that stress is positively correlated with heart disease. Indeed, our medical textbooks are full of such correlations between lifestyle choices and various types of cardiac diseases. As a result, we eat low-sodium diets, exercise regularly, eliminate red meats and cigarettes, and think happy thoughts. Each of these is a little defense against disease in the health-versus-disease battle that we discussed in the previous chapter. Instead of fighting *against* disease, Antonovsky wants to ask a positive question: what is to be said of those people who defy the odds in the direction of health? Antonovsky uses the well-known example of stress as a likely predictive element in the precipitation of illness and disease. Indeed, myriad studies have reported the ill effects of stress on persons. But rather than focus on the strength of the positive correlation between stress and illness, why not also focus inquiry at the elements present that have a relationship to wellness despite the presence of stress? After all, not everyone who loses her job will suffer coronary heart disease. "The study of factors determining tension management, then, becomes the key question of the health sciences" (Antonovsky 1987, xii). Instead of eliminating all the little contributors to stress like a germ-obsessed Spartacus of Sanitization, we can recognize that disease is an expression toward wellness and not the reverse. We can go to those people who have gone through those experiences in which we would expect disease to develop but in whom it hasn't. What about those people who are at high risk for coronary heart disease who *don't* develop it? What is different about them? And moreover, what does this teach us about health?

FROM PATHOLOGICAL TO SALUTARY

In shifting from a negatively valenced, pathological model of psychological illness to a positively valenced, salutogenic model of psychological wellness, we must first give up the "health versus disease" conception of wellness. I argued against this conception at the conclusion of the previous chapter. By looking at wellness as a battle being waged within each of us, we are allowing ourselves to be divided into little pieces—some of them healthy, some unhealthy. Then we eliminate the unhealthy bits and try to add more healthy bits. We forget that all of these are bits of the persons we are. Finally, when we dissociate each bit from the whole (ourselves), then we have no way of telling whether that bit is a *good* bit or a *bad* bit. So let us give up this dissociative nonsense.

Instead, we will look at health and illness as a continuum. Antonovsky provides the following helpful reminder: "We are all terminal cases. And we all are, so long as there is a breath of life in us, in some measure healthy. The salutogenic orientation proposes that we study the location of each person, at any time, on this continuum" (1987, 3–4). Sorry to burst your bubble, but today you are dying. As mortals, we all face an inevitable existential limit. This needn't be cause for concern, however. Indeed, a generation of existentialist philosophers, some of whom helped us understand the experience of anxiety earlier, have argued that this very existential limit reminds us of the richness and uniqueness of our lives. Antonovsky notes that we are not *only* terminal cases, but we are also *living* ones. Every one of us has some life in us as well. We are both living and dying; we are on a continuum between health and disease. So how are we to understand this continuum?

In the pathological model, the game of medicine is played by isolating those things that push us toward disease. Once these are isolated, they are eviscerated. "The pathogenic orientation invariably sees stressors as pathogenic, as risk factors, which at best can be reduced, inoculated against, or buffered" (Antonovsky 1987, 7). This positions life as up against us: we must forever be on the lookout against possible stressors. Avoid marriage because some of the biggest stressors begin in marriage (death of a spouse and divorce). Antonovsky argues that it doesn't have to be this way.

We don't have to ignore the disease model of wellness in order to consider the latter from a positive, health-oriented perspective. That is, we can accept that stress often leads to cardiac disease and that the death of a spouse is a big stressor. But this doesn't mean that we should focus on only those things that correlate with disease. Antonovsky explains that "the salutogenecist, without disdaining the importance of what has been learned, looks at the deviant case. . . . Who are the type A's who do not get coronary disease? Who are the smokers who do not get lung cancer?" (1987, 11). Instead of focusing on the problems (which, we learned earlier, are not as clearly defined as they might seem), we can focus on the outlier instances where health is achieved despite the existence of stressors that predict disease. That is, we will not try to dissociate health or disease away from the people who experience them, but we will try to understand them within the context of the people who are living them.

SALUTOGENIC ORIENTATION

Antonovsky explains the salutogenic orientation through six postulates (1987, 12–13). We will briefly discuss these before reviewing his analysis on persons who suffered from a single cardiac episode. These are the people at the highest risk for a(nother) cardiac episode. Thus, it is most impressive when they do *not* have a repeat experience. We will examine what might be different about them and how that can help us understand a bit more about health.

First, Antonovsky explains that the salutogenic orientation views each of us on an ease/dis-ease continuum and not caught in a battle between the two. This has already been discussed at length, so we will move onto postulate two. The salutogenic orientation "keeps us from falling into the trap of focusing solely on the etiology of a given disease rather than always searching for the total story of a human being, including his or her sickness" (1987, 12). This one should sound familiar given the aim and scope of this book: we are interested in understanding persons and their experience, thus we can understand health and disease only insofar as they are experienced by whole persons.

In postulate three, the salutogenic orientation moves away from asking the question of "What caused a disease?" and instead toward asking, "What are the factors involved in . . . moving toward the healthy pole?" (1987, 12). Notice how stressors are viewed. These are no longer viewed as taboo—the great list of things to avoid or things that your significant other repeatedly bothers you about.

Postulate four removes "stressors" from the list of naughty words, steeped in a strong moral ethic that suggests that people who do not smoke are better persons than those who do. We are *all* terminal cases, remember? Each of our lives has a great variety of stressors. A salutogenic model is not interested in systematically eliminating these from your life as an exterminator might go about your infestation problem. Indeed, "the consequences of stressors are viewed not as necessarily pathological but as quite possibly salutary, contingent on the character of the stressor and the successful resolution of tension" (1987,13).

In postulate five, Antonovsky explains that the salutogenic orientation looks not for a magic cure but for understanding how a person makes the most or worst of a difficult situation (be reorganizing her/his environment). Losing vision in one or both eyes does not put a person one or two eyes below a full-sighted person. The one with the visual impairment learns how to navigate the world in a new way—finding vision through the alternative sense modalities (such as through the hand with aid of a walking stick, fingers with braille, or the tongue with Bach-y-Rita's tactile-visual-sensory-substitution machines; 1967).

Finally, Antonovsky explains that the salutogenic orientation will move forward by looking at deviant cases: finding wellness where we least expect it.

Sense of Coherence

In his study, Antonovsky looked at the rehabilitation of posttrauma recovery patients. These were people who had suffered major cardiac episodes and whose prognoses looked grim. These patients were told that rehabilitation would take four to six weeks of bed rest, but even then the results were uncertain. Antonovsky was interested in the difference between those patients who were ready to walk out of their hospital room at the shorter end of the estimated timeline (or even early). That is, he was interested in those who recovered most quickly. Everyone had suffered a traumatic cardiac episode, so what is it about those people that got them back on their feet despite a dramatic threat to their lives?

Antonovsky spent many hours with these trauma patients, asking them a variety of questions about what happened and how they were doing during the whole medical drama. He was trying to better understand them, and what he discovered when doing so was very impressive. Antonovsky noted that two groups emerged that could be discerned in terms of their ability to cope with their circumstances. Some coped considerably well, making it through rehabilitation more quickly than expected; others coped poorly, taking much longer to get through rehabilitation than expected. Antonovsky labeled this difference in coping "sense of coherence," which I will define in more detail later. For now, consider the difference: for the patient with a *low* sense of coherence, the belief was that life happened *to* one and that this was invariably unfortunate. It didn't matter what these people did; it was life that would mercilessly dole out random punishment. Can you think of any people in your life who interpret their experience this way? Antonovsky calls them the "sad sack" or "*schlimazl*"—"the one upon whom the soup always gets spilled" (1987, 17). *Of course that would happen to me*, says the patient with a low sense of coherence.

Can you imagine what a patient with a high sense of coherence might think? "At the other extreme," Antonovsky begins, "events in life are seen as experiences that can be coped with, challenges that can be met. At worst— and recall that these are people who have undergone very difficult experiences—the event or its consequences are bearable" (1987, 17). Both groups have met with considerable misfortune. The difference is how these misfortunes are experienced. For the patient with a *high* sense of coherence, these misfortunes are experienced as challenges to be overcome—not as one more roadblock to success. Notice how the objective life event doesn't change at all; sense of coherence has everything to do with how one relates *to* the events in one's life.

Antonovsky divides sense of coherence into three characteristics. Persons with a high sense of coherence experience their problems as comprehensible, manageable, and meaningful. The words themselves strongly suggest what is intended, but let us look at each one in turn, giving helpful examples of each.

Comprehensibility

The first of the three elements of Antonovsky's sense of coherence is comprehensibility. This is the extent to which one finds that the problems that confront one make cognitive sense. Is it even understandable? Have you ever experienced a car accident or traumatic incident during which you lost focus and began to be confused about what was even happening? This could be called a state of shock. The impact of what just happened hasn't set in yet. It is not yet comprehensible. Antonovsky explains that with comprehensibility, we encounter an event clearly, one "that is ordered, consistent, structured and clear, rather than as noise—chaotic, disordered, random, accidental, inexplicable" (1987, 17). Does the problem situation make sense? Do you understand the long-term consequences, and what rehabilitation might be required? Sometimes doctors wait to tell their patients the severity of damage until the patients have demonstrated that they understand the situation—for example, telling a recent spinal cord injury patient that he will never walk again is likely to be met with confusion. A patient with a sense of comprehensibility will be prepared to understand the extent of a problem and not overwhelmed. We can also see that the more a patient understands the problem, the more the patient accepts it.

Manageability

The second sense of coherence component is manageability. This is the degree to which one believes that the resources at one's disposal are sufficient to meet demands imposed upon one. This is the belief that one has what it takes to tackle the problems that lay before him—the sense that "I can do that" or "I am adequate to handle that." When the doctor says you must complete all sorts of tedious rehabilitation exercises, you say, "No problem, doctor." You perceive your experiences as within your control. This does not mean that you micromanage everything around you but that you are capable of handling even the worst scenario that might befall you. "To the extent that one has a high sense of manageability," Antonovsky explains, "one will not feel victimized by events or feel that life treats one unfairly" (1987, 18). This does not mean that one will not be upset by upsetting events. The difference is that upsetting events are still manageable, albeit undesirable.

Meaningfulness

And finally, the third component is meaningfulness. In meaningfulness, we return to the argument that began this chapter: that the "survival instinct" is not the strongest biological tendency. The problems that you face might be daunting, but do you experience them as meaning*ful* or meaning*less*? If you can see them as meaningful, then you may accept them as part of the narrative of your life. If an experience is meaningful, then one sees it as fitting in with the rest of one's experiences—that life has been leading up to it so that one can handle it, or that life will no longer be the same but that this is okay.

Antonovsky gives the example of Victor Frankl's story, *Man's Search for Meaning*. Frankl was a well-respected psychiatrist in Austria before the Second World War. He was also a Jew. As the anti-Semitic sentiments were getting stronger in Nazi Germany, Frankl was encouraged to leave Austria. He declined, uninterested in leaving and upsetting the home he had made in his community and with his family. As the problems got worse, he was eventually given a last resort: "Dr. Frankl, it is time to go. We have a seat left for you but you have to leave now." Frankl agreed under the condition that his father be able to join him. His condition was declined, so he stayed. Frankl spent the next two years being shipped between some of Poland's most notorious death camps. He began as an esteemed psychiatrist. He witnessed man at his worst, both in terms of *evil*—subjecting other men to dehumanizing forms of torture and murder—and in terms of *having nothing*—he witnessed men who were profoundly malnourished, emotionally abused, and physically abused. Whatever might a psychiatrist conclude after witnessing man at his worst in both senses of the term? I would be curious to know, wouldn't you?

Frankl concludes that it is of tantamount importance psychologically that man be able to experience life as meaningful. Meaningful? What an absurd conclusion! To survive Auschwitz and Dachau, camps that claimed the lives of his father and wife, and arrive at the importance of meaning. Frankl credits his survival to his ability to experience this terrible existence as meaningful: he dreamed that he would once again embrace his wife, even though he knew the probability was exceedingly slim. Frankl observed a noticeable change in his companions before they died; something would fade from their eyes. It wasn't malnourishment, because nobody had had a nourishing meal in eighteen months; everyone was dangerously below any healthy body weight. It was something different. Something happened, and they would no longer get out of bed, and they would stop eating what menial meal they were served. They stopped following the officers' orders. They had given up.

He explains that eight men can be served their four ounces of chicken broth with bits of wood and the occasional vegetable, and their two hundred calories of bread. One man looks to his neighbor and sees that he is not doing well and splits his bread in half. Who survives until the next day? If you started counting calories, then the person with more bread will be physically stronger than the one with less and will thus have a higher probability of surviving. But this assumes that the strongest biological motivation is self-preservation—the survival instinct. Frankl watched this unfold in person: the man who gave up his bread was the stronger of the two—he found meaning in being among a group of emaciated men sitting in the dirt, eating stale bread and miserable soup. This man was not merely surviving, he was actualizing his potential for being in that moment.

In recounting Frankl's story, Antonovsky reminds us that unhappy experiences may befall one, but "when these . . . are imposed on such a person, he or she will willingly take up the challenge, will be determined to seek meaning in it, and will do his or her best to overcome it with dignity" (1987, 18–19). Combining meaningfulness with comprehensibility and manageability, we see that the events that occur to us in our lives tell only part of the story. Indeed, this doesn't even end up being the most important part. Our health and wellness has more to do with the way that we experience these. How about sense of coherence as a starting point for a psychology of health?

SUMMARY

This chapter considered the role that psychology might play as a health science. Health, it seems, is not simply about ensuring that the bodily processes are each in working order or that stressors are limited as much as possible. To be sure, stress is an important factor in many of the leading causes of death today, but trying to get rid of them fails to recognize the benefits that stress provides.

The body is incredibly resilient. Stress challenges the body to change in order to become stronger. This is why lifting weights makes your muscles stronger. But between weight lifting and the strengthening of your muscles, the fibers in these muscles break down, and they are actually weaker than when you started. The weight stress kills your muscle fibers. But then your body recovers, and does so stronger than when you started. It is not stress that we must eliminate, but our negative relationship to stressors as taboo.

Antonovsky explains that medical specialists must pay attention to the sense of coherence a person's life has. This includes an experience's comprehensibility, manageability, and meaningfulness. These mean, in order, does a stressor (or trauma) make sense? Do you know that you have what it takes to do what is necessary to rehabilitate? And do you understand that this experience is a meaningful one—that is, that it happened for a reason?

PSYCHOLOGIZING IN ACTION

Restorative Effects of Nature

Our hike had started the night before, when my friend had said, "The moon is out, let's walk." We met at three o'clock that morning and began hiking up through the redwood-covered canyon to the coast ridge of Big Sur. My young heart was hurting from the breakup of a long-term relationship. Even though I had spent a good amount of time working with the pain, I felt shut down and separate from everything in my life.

We struck a leisurely pace, following whatever seemed to arise in the moment. Sometimes I found myself in tears, other times stopping to drink water from the creek or investigate a new plant, sometimes talking, other times quiet. We followed exactly what was before us, and as the day wore on I found myself softening to and accepting whatever emerged inside. My heart and belly felt expansive, and gradually I was overcome by the strangest sensation of webs connecting me with all that was around. I could sense webs of light extending out of me to every living thing and from them to me. I was sustained by all that surrounded me. The experience slowly dissipated as we climbed to the summit of the ridge, where I stood smiling, sweat in my eyes. And although I still had more grieving to do, the experience stands out as a clear turning point in my healing process, as well as in my life.

People have always turned to wilderness to become whole again. We need only think of the many primary cultures that use intensified wilderness experience as a rite of passage to see these healing qualities at work. The "civilized" person, however, has approached wilderness from a very different place. Our society is unique in the degree to which we have tried to split ourselves off from nature. We have lost touch with many basic, yet quite mature, ways of knowing nature that were commonplace to our ancestors. But we may also be unique in our potential for accessing far more modes of being and knowing than our ancestors could. . . . When we embrace that which is most wholesome of both "old" and "new," we may find that wilderness holds the potential for transformative experiences that were perhaps never possible before.

Source: Harper 1995.

Chapter Fourteen

Dream Analysis

I typically reserve a few class periods toward the end of the semester for special-interest topics that don't get covered in a normal course. I provide a list of ten or fifteen possible topics, including sports psychology, cyberpsychology, criminal profiling, psychology of music or acting, psychology of religion, and so on. I'm surprised by the lack of interest among student athletes and musicians for some of these topics. But students always express interest in hearing more about the psychology of dreams and dream interpretation. Since my approach to dream analysis closely follows the themes covered in this book, I include it here as a special-interest chapter.

About a week before I plan to cover dream analysis, I ask students to begin keeping a dream journal (if they had not done so already). I also give them a few pointers about how to remember their dreams if they have trouble doing so. For example, you don't need to be able to reproduce an entire narrative in order to "remember your dream." As Perls (1974) maintains, all that is important is the residual felt sense. Do you wake up feeling peculiar? Hungry? Tired? Afraid? Nauseous? And so on. Key into the feeling you have upon waking, and get into the habit of describing this. After a few trials, bits of dream material will attach themselves to the felt sense. After all, we do not have dreams that simply produce a felt sense, but our dreams *are* that felt sense as well as the reverse.

Based on my own experience with dream analysis, I teach an approach that focuses on Perls's method of embodiment and psychotherapy, though it quite certainly includes others who have influenced me along the way. This emphasizes the holistic and personal nature of dreams, emphases that will be outlined as the chapter progresses. It begins with the assumption that everything in the dream belongs to the dreamer and nothing is superfluous: this means that everything in the dream is meaningful and important. Be sure to include even those things that make you think "Oh, this doesn't really matter at all," or "I'm not sure why I even included that." Actually, those things are especially important.

It is best to work with a partner, but chances are that neither of you is prepared to do honest dream work. This is because dreams are the manifestations of those things (those parts of your personality, those bits of you) that we have not yet allowed ourselves to think openly. Since they are a part of us, they stick around and eventually show themselves when our guard is down (such as when we're sleeping). So when we bring them into the open, we either experience shame about them or alienation from them. Shame, you will gather, is the more honest of the two responses. If a dream seems impersonal and distant—as if you're talking about something that happened to your cousin's neighbor—then you are a long way from assimilating it back into yourself. That's what we do with dream work. We recognize that dreams contain personal baggage that we refuse to accept as part of ourselves. Since they're here to stay, they occasionally rear their head but only do so in safe places (such as our dreams). When we do dream work, we identify with these dissociated bits of our self and accept them back into our entire person. This is a very emotional and often upsetting task. Indeed, few of us are prepared for such an undertaking. In class, most students begin by saying something like this: "*A* happened, then *B* happened, and then I did *C*, which was just weird. Then I woke up. What's it mean, doc?" And then they follow my instructions and identify with some part of *B* and realize its significance. Their entire demeanor changes and they wonder whether they need therapy. In one case, a student realized that he resented others when they asked him for help; another identified with a seemingly meaningless hole of death and decay. I assure them, and you, that if they are able to identify with the bits of dissociated self, then they're in good shape—well on the road to becoming a whole person. This is because the bits of dissociated self are not so far gone that people no longer recognize them. The people who remain indifferent to their unconscious are the ones who need to spend some time on the therapeutic couch, provided they are interested in being a whole person.

From this chapter we will be moving to the topic of consciousness. There I maintain that with consciousness, we are aware of and present to our experiences. We *are* our consciousness. We identify with our feelings, recognize our impact on others and others' impact on ourselves. With dreams, we *are* our unconscious. When we are aware that we are what we are, we are our consciousness; when we are unaware that we are what we are, we are our unconscious. This chapter might also be called "Unconsciousness." We quite often do things without thinking about them—have conversations, hum melodies, or drive to school. When we do things without being aware of them, we are doing them unconsciously. This does not mean that we're knocked out and acting like a robot or zombie, only that we're not aware of our experience as it is unfolding. We still respond meaningfully to our environment: slowing for a yellow light, yielding to a pedestrian, even sneering at a person whose company we do not enjoy, but these are not under our conscious control. What we don't have is the superego filter on each of our behaviors. This is the person looking over your shoulder saying, "What will others think?" or "You *should* be nice, charming, and compassionate." This is present only when you're consciously aware of what you're doing and are interested in micromanaging it. We are our consciousness and our unconsciousness. These are not opposites, though it might seem they are. It is only that we will admit we are our consciousness but we are not yet prepared to admit that we are our unconsciousness. So it remains below the surface of our awareness.

DREAMS AND THE UNCONSCIOUS

For the psychology of dreams and dream analysis, we begin with the assumption that our dreams are our unconscious thoughts, feelings, expressions—that is, our unconscious self. This simply means that it is the collection of all those attributes of ourselves that we are not yet prepared to bring into the light and accept. If these things were meaningless, then we would have no reason to conjure them while sleeping. But they are meaning*ful*, and they require expression, like the conscious parts of us do. For instance, I might fancy myself an intellectual type but really hate the idea of reading a book cover to cover. Since the latter interferes with my role playing as an intellectual, I am not yet prepared to admit this. This is actually a bit of repressed personality that I discovered in graduate school. When I picked up a book, I felt like I had to conquer it by reading every last page from beginning to end. I often hated doing this but felt like I had to. It would be understandable that I would share how "natural" it was for me to read a book cover to cover because this supported my role as an intellectual. So where does my distaste go? It remains, emerging only when I'm not preoccupied with that role. So while I sleep, I have these vivid dreams that I start a four-hundred-page book, but then some intellectual authority—like my academic adviser—tells me, "You only have to read the first and last ten pages." This is what I do in my dream. Notice that I don't have to take ownership of taking a shortcut: I project this onto someone who takes responsibility for my laziness so that I don't have to. But then I wake up and realize that I must own this desire for intellectual shortcuts, so I think, "How strange that she would give me the green light to take a shortcut for reading," and I don't give it a second thought. In other iterations of this scenario, I dream that my bookshelf is simply full of books that I have "read" where in fact I haven't read any of them. But in my dream I had. This means that I can have the intellectual credential without doing any of the actual work in my dream. So when I wake up, I realize that I've read only six or seven books. If I analyze this, I eventually have to ask myself the question: "Do I wish that I didn't have to read any books?" I might try out this phrase: "I wish I didn't have to read an entire book." Since this is what actually happened, I can tell you that such a phrase will make me feel a bit more alive than I had moments before saying it: I simply expressed a truth about myself that I hadn't accepted earlier. It was always there, only now it is out in the open.

Why This Works: Growth by Skillful Frustration

Imagine that a child, we will call her Evelyn, wishes to put on her shoes. She sits down beside the door and begins to pout. Her family is busily getting their shoes on because they are preparing to go to the zoo for the day. She picks up her shoes and brings them to her mom and looks at her with big, puppy-dog eyes. Her mom asks, "Yes, Evelyn?" Evelyn responds, "Can you put *your* shoes on?"

"I can, thank you!"

"But my shoes are not on."

"No, they're not." At this, Evelyn begins to cry, playing the role of the absolutely helpless child. At this, most parents capitulate, but Evelyn's mother has a few options. First, she can fix Evelyn's problem and put her shoes on for her. This, however, assumes that the problem is limited to the shoes and not some bigger issue of Evelyn recognizing and having confidence that she can do things herself. So at best, this puts off the problem until later, and at worst it fails to respond to the actual problem. Second, her mother can recognize the frustration that Evelyn is experiencing and try to make *that* better: "Aww, I don't want you to ever feel frustrated." This might assuage the despair that Evelyn currently faces, but it does nothing to resolve her shoelessness. Finally, Evelyn's mother can exacerbate the problem as it is experienced: "The rest of us have our shoes on, and now it's time to go."

"By my shoes are *not* on!" Evelyn says, hoping that her mother will take on the responsibility of her problem. Mother lets Evelyn own her problem: "No, they are not."

Evelyn has an existential choice: admit that the problem is *hers* and face the frustrating and difficult task of putting on her shoes, which will likely include much effort and determination, or maintain that the problem is her mother's, or father's, or that of the stupid zoo that requires guests to wear shoes. We recognize that Evelyn is developmentally in a place where the question of what she can and cannot do is of chief importance: what does it do for her if we remove this problem from her?

"People have to grow by skillful frustration," Perls tells us. "Otherwise they have no incentive to develop their own means and ways of coping with the world" (1974, 77). Dreams are one more opportunity to do so, but they work even better because you're already beginning with unowned material. If the dreamer owns the dream as part of herself, then she has taken responsibility for a bit of herself.

Okay, so on to the method of analysis. With the help of Perls, I will outline six elements of dream analysis and follow with a dream of my own, on which I will perform this analysis.

First, when you read over a dream, you have to remember that all the little parts of the dreams are experiences (processes) and not things. As things, they don't belong to you; as processes, you have to acknowledge your participation in them. This means that you cannot think, "Oh, I know what *that* symbol means" because you can't. It's not a symbol; it's your self-expression. But this bit of self-expression hasn't found an outlet in your conscious life. This is why it can find its expression only in your unconscious—in your dream. Dream analysis involves making your unconscious conscious.

Also, don't get lost talking about the dream, listing facts endlessly. Perls calls this a word that is inappropriate for this book. For now, we'll call it BS. This is the "beating around the bush" behavior. We can talk around and around and around and around and never have an actual experience. But we don't call it "beating around the bush" because this phrase also beats around the bush. When we call it "BS," we realize that we are keeping the conversation on an intellectual level and not having any real experience. Perls reminds us that "everything deals with the present. All talking *about* is out, all interpretation, all [BS] is discouraged. What is, is. A rose is a rose is a rose" (1974, 95).

When we imagine that our dream is full of symbols, then we place our dream content opposite ourselves. It begins with the assumption that the dream content is *impersonal* and that anybody can look at it and determine its meaning. This involves the process of determining what all the symbols mean and why this is the best explanation. Notice how such a dream analysis doesn't even require the participation of a dreamer? This is not how the present dream analysis will go.

Second, you will recognize that all the material in the dream *is you*. "I believe we are all fractionalized," writes Perls. "We are divided. We are split up in many parts, and the beauty of working with a dream is that in a dream every part—not only every person, but every part is yourself" (1974, 95).

The symbols are not from somebody else or caused by some other event. Everything in your dream belongs to you. The purpose of dream analysis/ interpretation is the same as the purpose of psychotherapy: for taking responsibility for yourself. If I were to tell you that you were irresponsible or that for the most part you are a phony, you would likely respond with indignation. We pride ourselves in being responsible, honest, and authentic. If this were true, then our dreams would be completely obvious from the outset. But since they seem obscure and uncertain, we are under the influence of some delusion. So their subsequent analysis allows us to take responsibility for them. This does not mean heroically taking on some burden for the betterment of humanity: it simply means the process of being yourself. Perls explains:

> Responsibility means the ability to respond: the ability to be alive, to feel, to be sensitive. Now we often have made of this responsibility the idea of obligation, which is identical with being a megalomaniac, omnipotent. We take over responsibility for somebody else. But responsibility simply means "I am I; I have taken and developed in myself what I can be." In other words, responsibility is the ability to respond and be fully responsible for oneself and for *nobody else*. (1974, 107)

Third, since everything in your dream is a part of you, a specific feeling accompanies each of the dream elements. This is to say that everything in your dream is personal. This is easy since you already acknowledge that they're a part of you. You experience them *in* the dream as separate from you even though they are a part of you: this is called projection.

> The *it*, the noun, goes into the projection. It's been externalized. So first it's been killed and then it's been put outside of our organism. So it seems as if we have lost *it*, or this bit of life, completely. And once a projection has occurred, or once we have projected some potential, then this potential turns against us. (1974, 106)

Fourth, as a corollary to the third point, everything in the dream is important, *especially those things that you think are not important*. If you are tempted to say, "Oh, that? That's not important at all," then you should be clued into the fact that it *is* important. Deflection is a common defense mechanism that prevents you from identifying with problematic elements of your personality.

No matter what the object, person, setting, or event might be, it has personal significance to the dreamer. It might also have personal significance to the dreamer's lover, friend, or therapist, but the meaning it has for the dreamer is what matters. Perls explains this at length:

> But if you realize, "this is my dream. I'm responsible for the dream. I painted this picture. Every part is me," then things begin to function and to come together, instead of being incomplete and fragmented. And very often the projection is not even visible, but it's obvious. If I have a staircase without railings it's obvious that the railings are somewhere in the dream but they're missing. They're not there. So where railings should be, there's a hole. Where warmth and color should be, there's a hole. So we find here a very brave, maybe stubborn person who can make it. (1974, 105–6)

Fifth, you learn the significance of the dream imagery, symbolism, events, and material by *identifying with them*. This is where the significance lies: by assimilating the unconscious projections. This is where it is helpful to have an analyst: the analyst can watch you, the dreamer, as you describe your dream. The analyst can see where the defenses are the strongest, she can see where the blockages to self-expression are, and she can make sure that you confront them entirely. This is the purpose of dream analysis: to reintegrate those parts of yourself that have become repressed—things that haven't been allowed expression in conscious life. For instance, I may secretly wish to punch a colleague in the face. Instead, I dream that another colleague has punched *me* in the face. I express the collegial altercation, but only after it has become transformed into something I am prepared to admit. I have alienated myself from my desire to punch my colleague. This works for the moment, because now I get to avoid the consequences that follow such an action. But after time, I begin to experience less and less when I am around my colleagues. The person I am around my colleagues—not just the aggressively angry person, but also the interested, enthusiastic, and concerned person—becomes less and less available.

> If we alienate something that is really our own—my own potential, my life—then we become impoverished: Excitement, living, becomes less and less until we are walking corpses, robots, zombies. And I'm sure you know plenty of people who identify with their duty rather than their needs, with their business rather than with their family. (1974, 107)

In order to start feeling real again, we need to identify those parts of ourselves that haven't been able to be expressed—those parts that have died. As we do so, we become alive again.

> So, we have to see whether you can re-identify this alienated part, and the means is playing that part which we have alienated. This wall is part of the self-alienation, of the disowning of something, of some potential, and we have to do the opposite of alienation—identification. The more you really become this thing again, the easier it is to assimilate and make our own again what we have thrown out. (1974, 107–8)

Sixth, read the dream to yourself or to another person and try to see where something important occurs. Importance is measured by how strongly it makes you feel. Happy, frustrated, confused, upset, aroused, childish, and so on. Any feeling is important. Even the feeling of nothing (a peculiar feeling to have, indeed).

When you find an important detail, you have to identify with said detail and act it out to its fullest. This is awkward because we think, "I'm not this part." Then we remember that it had to emerge in a dream state as something other than us because we are loath to admit that this is a part of ourselves. By acting it out—becoming this dream image—we get to own our projection and assimilate it into our personality. This is very powerful and cathartic. I will give an example from a dream I had in youth. I can use it because I'm still effectively weirded out by it. I have never analyzed this before but have always felt like I should; I'm not sure what will come up. I will stop it if it isn't going anywhere (which means I've reached a blockage that I'm either afraid of what comes next or what you'll think of me, or that there really isn't any significance. I highly doubt the latter). I will explain the dream as I remember it, being careful not to edit it as it comes. This is in line with the free-flowing unconsciousness promoted by free association. I will put commentary of insights of psychological significance in parentheses.

Many of you will recall a dream of your own that has occurred more than once. This should tell you something. This means that there is an unresolved part of yourself—something you have shut out but that demands expression. These kinds of dreams are a great place to start. "So if anything, it's an attempt to become alive, to come to grips with things. And very often these repetitive dreams are nightmares" (Perls 1974, 95–96).

A GIANT SPIDER AT GRANDMA'S HOUSE:
A SAMPLE DREAM ANALYSIS

To demonstrate the previous dream-analysis discussion, I have decided to provide an analysis I have performed on a recurring dream of my own. I will write the dialogue of the dreamer, including the description of the dream, in *italics*, and all commentary will appear in the normal font. This was a dream that I first started having in elementary school, but it continued through college. Even in graduate school I could still recall the feeling it gave me upon waking.

At the risk of sharing my dark, unconscious material, here goes my dream analysis of my recurring "giant spider" dream:

I was wandering around my grandmother's home where I used to play in a rock garden. The rock garden had great big rocks that I could climb up and down. The garden was between the garage and the front entrance, situated in a corner. The corner was poorly lit and had a few large trees that covered it. In my dream there was a giant spiderweb that spanned the entire corner, and upon it sat a giant spider. The spider had a leg span of eight to ten feet and looked like a tarantula (hairy and with greenish eyes). It never moved. It just sat there. It wasn't really looking at me, but I was afraid that if I moved, then it would get me. I couldn't run away because I knew it could move much faster than I. Because of its size and the acrobatic ability of spiders, I knew it could probably jump thirty to forty yards. I still attribute my arachnophobia to this dream.

So what do you see? The first tendency is to analyze a part of it: "Well, the childlike size is a fear of weakness and impotence, whereas the spider . . ." Forget the intellectual analysis. You cannot analyze *my* dream without *me*. So ask me to associate with part of it. Since it is the most ridiculous part of the dream, you ask me to identify with the giant spider. You ask: "What can you tell me about giant spiders? Pretend you are the giant spider and describe yourself. Begin, 'I am a giant spider and I . . .'"

I am a giant spider: I am dangerous if I bite you, but I could also jump on you and crush you. I sit very quietly and stoically until something weaker comes along, and then I pounce. My nest is beside a nice rock garden and you will want to play, but you had better not because I will pounce on you.

If you're watching my body and expression, you will see that I don't seem to be getting anywhere because I'm not having any trouble identifying with the spider. Then you have an insight (which I just had). Maybe there is something about the spider I won't admit out loud. That is, I can "BS" about spiders for hours without ever getting to that part that terrifies me so much. This time you ask me to describe the spider at a comfortable distance: "Will you describe giant spiders in giant webs?" By asking this question, you hope that I will include something that I left out of the earlier description, something with which I was afraid to identify when I was pretending that I was the spider.

Giant spiders are (notice, now I am describing a spider that is separate from me and not a spider that I am) *terrifying. They are hairy and gross. If you see one, the hair stands up on your neck and you freeze—you cannot move* (this is important to me, because I'm beginning to have the experience of feeling frozen, and the hair on my neck is beginning to stand on end). *They trap you in their spell. If you get caught in their web, you're a goner; you're helpless. Once you get stuck, there is no getting free. But you're stuck anyway because they can get you even if you try to run away.*

There's a quality that I cannot get at here. This is where an analyst would be helpful. What is it about the spider that means you're trapped if you get too close? *You are trapped by fear and powerless to save yourself.* Okay, I've reached another blockage—there is a term I cannot come up with or that I am afraid to admit out loud. The felt sense is dissipating, and I'm beginning to concede that I will always be arachnophobic. To get through this impasse, I will employ another method from Perls's toolbox: the empty-chair dialogue.

The Empty-Chair Assimilation Dialogue

Perls's empty-chair dialogue provides a simple way of trying out different forms of assimilating unconscious material. Imagine that two chairs face each other and that I am in one of them. I put the bit of unconscious material in the other chair and have a conversation. Notice how I am able to "pretend" that I am the bit of unconscious material without actually admitting that it belongs to me? It is a clever tactic. Now I can act out the conversation between dreamer and spider; moreover, I am acting out both parts. (After all, I *am* both parts of the dream.) Now I will write a dialogue between myself and the spider.

> Spider: *You are caught by me. You are powerless to get away. If you move, I will get you; if you don't move, you will wither away and die.*

> Me: *I am caught. I am powerless to get away. You are too powerful. People get close to you and they are stuck forever, and they slowly wither away because they cannot move.* (I think I might be onto something here, but the associations aren't coming.) *They are trapped by fear.*

> Spider: *I trap people by fear. I do not eat them; I do not even harm them, but they are so afraid to make the wrong move that they trap themselves.*

> (Is that me? I will try it out to see whether it fits.)

> Me: *I am trapped by my own fear*(?). *Why can't I just walk away? I am afraid that what . . .* (and I've got it. Can you see the insight?)

I have had an insight about what it is about myself that I find so terrifying—so petrifying. I see that I am afraid to act; I am afraid to make a move. I want something but I cannot go for it because I won't admit what I want. I'm afraid that people will think that I'm gross, prickly, and so on. So instead I stay put. But this doesn't work either because inaction leads to death. So I have an existential choice: admit my desire and face the ensuing judgment, or do nothing and wither away. In the dream and in my past, I usually stay put.

You might be able to see my insight in the dream imagery, but you must remember that it is *my* dream and *my* meaningful insight. I know it is accurate because admitting it out loud is accompanied by a felt sense of relief (and dread). In the future I may acknowledge that the spider is not going to "get me"—the spider is my own superstition that being honest about my desires means that I am a nasty person.

Time to perform your own analysis. Write down a few of your dreams and see whether you can analyze them through Perls's method of assimilation the way that I have shown you.

PSYCHOLOGIZING IN ACTION

Jean's Dream

I think it first started in the—sort of like the New York subway, and kind of paying—putting a token in, and going to the turnstile, and walking a little way down the corridors, and then kind of turning a corner and I realize that some way or other in here uh . . . instead of being a subway, it seemed like there were sort of like inclines that started going down into the earth. And it seemed to turn and I realized what was going on, and some way or another just about this point as I discovered this incline, my mother was with me, or maybe she was when I started—I can't remember.

It was this incline—it was sort of muddy, sort of slippery, and I thought, Oh! We can go down this! And well, sort of on the side, I picked up a left-over carton—or maybe it was just flattened out or I flattened it out. At any rate, I said, "Let's sit down on this." I sat down on the edge, kind of made a toboggan out of it, and I said, "Mom, you sit down behind me," and we started going down. And it sort of went around and around (quickly) and there were other people it seemed like, waiting in line, but then they kind of disappeared, and we were (happily) just going down and around and it just kept on going down and down and down, and I was sort of realizing that I was going down kind of into the bowels of the earth.

And every once in awhile I'd turn around and say, "Isn't this fun?"—it seems, although maybe I'll discover I didn't have that attitude either. But it seemed like fun. And yet I wondered what would be down at the bottom of this—going, turn and turn, and then finally it leveled out and we got up and I was just astounded, because here I thought, "Oh my God, the bowels of the earth!" and yet, instead of being dark, it was like there was sunlight coming from somewhere. . . . And I don't remember saying anything particularly, except maybe something like, "Who would ever have expected this!"

Source: Perls 1972, 158–59.

Chapter Fifteen

Consciousness

A look at consciousness concludes this book. Consciousness makes an appropriate ending point because it could easily be argued that each chapter has been directed toward it all along. Indeed, all of the preceding discussions, themes, and problems find their genesis in the way we have historically understood consciousness. Consciousness brings this discussion full circle. The question we have faced this entire time may be framed as follows: is consciousness something that you *are* or something that you *have*? You probably even knew that this question was coming before you read it. Like every topic reviewed thus far, consciousness has long been understood as something that we *have* (or do not have, as the generational temperament might have it). If we can understand that consciousness is something that we *are*, then everything else falls into place: this includes our experiences, our pathologies, our emotions, our perceptions—everything can be understood as an expression of what we are. We will no longer be forced to perform ontological surgery on ourselves, dissecting away parts of ourselves that we don't want. Instead, we get to remain as whole persons. Moreover, when we look at experience more carefully, we see that our bodies and our minds are wrapped up in one big, interconnected web. We then see that this includes other people along with the world and that each of these comes together in making us who we are. We are all of these things: we do not have relationships; we participate *in* them and they transform us. We do not have perceptions; we live them. And so on. But as soon as we start to believe that consciousness is a thing that we have, this entire process of being is lost. It is replaced with a collection of things. Suddenly the richness of our experiences becomes a collection of interchangeable items in the buffet line that is our life.

In the previous chapter we looked at dream analysis. This began with the assumption that you *are* your dream: that everything that occurs within your dream is a little bit of unexpressed "you." These bits of "you" are pieces with which you have not reconciled yourself, so they can emerge only when your guard is down (when you're sleeping). Dreams are a safe place because we can just say, "Oh, those are my dreams—they don't mean anything in particular." Or sometimes we analyze them from a safe distance as if they are some*thing* that has happened to us and have some transcendent meaning; they could have happened to *anyone*. Instead we looked at dreams as necessarily *meaningful* and *personal*. If you and I had the same dream, it could not have the same interpretation (indeed, it could hardly be considered the same dream). In dream analysis, we recognize that we are what we are. We admit that our dreams do not happen to us; they are *us happening*. One is a process and the other is a thing. The purpose of dream analysis, then, is to identify with these bits and to accept them, assimilating them back into our being.

When we *are* consciousness, then our dreams are an expression of what we are. When we *have* consciousness, then dreams are things that happen to us. Do you see how everything rests on how we understand consciousness? Dreams don't have to mean anything at all. We can keep dreams at a safe distance and remain alienated from certain aspects of ourselves that require expression. In this way we inhibit our self-actualization and become alienated from our energies. So we feel upset and think: "Why am I upset?" Or we feel aroused and think, "Why am I aroused?" And we end up taking medications to modify our experiences and end up modifying ourselves.

To aptly bring this project full circle, I would like to link the present consideration of consciousness with the process of *psychologizing* that I described in the introduction. Psychologizing, you will recall, comprises three interconnected elements: (1) adopting a different attitude in relation to psychological phenomena, (2) emphasizing first-person and subjective knowledge, and (3) paying scrupulous attention to the meaning of experience.

The first element—adopting a different attitude toward psychological phenomena—is the primary focus of this chapter. This is because consciousness has been historically filed away as a thing that we all have, and neuroscientists and philosophers have been busily trying to locate its whereabouts. But we have been practicing the avoidance of such conclusions. We recognize that experience seldom organizes itself neatly into boxes. This is also the case with consciousness. If we begin with the assumption that consciousness is a thing located somewhere in particular, then we will ignore its manifestations elsewhere and ultimately miss out on its significance. Thus, as with each topic in psychology, we will suspend the assumption that consciousness is some*thing* and start looking to the experiences in which it manifests. After all, our interest is in *persons* and not in parts of persons. If my consciousness is a thing that is in my brain, then it is not affected when my left leg is lopped off. But this, of course, is not the case.

Also remember: since the three elements of psychologizing are interconnected, we recognize that we cannot adopt a different attitude toward consciousness without also emphasizing personal, subjective knowledge and carefully examining experience. We will first look at two of the main theories of consciousness: materialist and intellectualist. These definitions will be supplied by one of the leading scholars in consciousness theory—Christof Koch (2012). Materialist theories of consciousness begin with the assumption that the latter may be understood entirely in terms of matter—for example, the nerves in our brain: somewhere in the ten million billion neural synapses that make up your nervous system, there is consciousness. Intellectualist theories of consciousness begin with the reverse assertion: that consciousness can never, in principle, be reduced to bits of matter (no matter how complex that matter might be). A line has been drawn between body and mind, so where might we find consciousness? As you might have expected, the thesis of this chapter is that consciousness is both mind *and* body: *minding body* or *embodied mind.*

CONSCIOUSNESS DIVIDED

Two theories support the thesis that consciousness is something we *have*. To say that we "have" consciousness means that we are a person who is in some sort of possession of a consciousness. Here one assumes that there might be a person without it (like a zombie), or a consciousness without a body (like a brain in a vat). It is almost as if our understanding of consciousness demands that it be considered as a thing. The argument that consciousness is a thing stems from the way we understand the world. If it has become our habit to divide the world of experience into individual parts that bounce into one another like billiard balls on a pool table—that is, the modern scientific assumption about reality—then consciousness *must* fit into this narrative or we have to revise the narrative. Since our project has specifically required that we *avoid* fitting elements like consciousness into boxes, we don't need to begin with the assumption that there is a box labeled "consciousness."

Nonetheless, two assumptions about the world pigeonhole consciousness. The first follows many of the trends we have examined in psychology: that there must be a neural correlate of consciousness. This is the material theory of consciousness: it states that something in the body is the cause of consciousness. The assumption is that we can understand consciousness by understanding whatever physiological or neurological elements *cause* it. This is an objective definition of consciousness. It means that anybody, provided the proper training, could look at it and understand what my consciousness or your consciousness looks like. The other theory begins with the opposite assumption: consciousness is something that specifically *cannot* be reduced to any physiological or biological mechanism. This is to say that it is always something just beyond any materialist theory. The brain might be necessary, but it is insufficient for understanding consciousness. This is the intellectualist theory of consciousness. Since the intellectualist theory maintains that a material definition of consciousness necessarily leaves something out, the focus is on the manifestation of consciousness in subjective experiences. So is consciousness *objective*, or is it *subjective*?

Both theories posit that there is a definite place to look if one is interested in understanding consciousness. The materialist looks to the brain; the intellectualist to the mind. So where will we look? As psychologists, you will recall, we are interested in the intersection between mind and body: we must understand the reciprocal relationship between mind *and* brain. Once again, consciousness does not demand that it be placed in a box; this is just the way we have historically divided up our world in Western thinking. Even the term "consciousness" suggests that it is a thing. Henri Ey explains the difficulty that stems from referring to the process (*being conscious*) as a thing (*consciousness*):

> The expression "conscious being" more strongly indicates that "consciousness" is not a simple "function of being but is instead its organization insofar as it is constituted at the same time as both *object* and *subject*. Conscious being . . . can exist neither as a pure subject nor as a simple object. . . . It is understandable why so many writers prefer to deny consciousness so as not to have to define it. (1978, 4)

Conscious Matter, Conscious Thought

In this book we have looked at experience. Experience is the vehicle through which one encounters the world. Experience puts a single subjectivity into a place—body, social setting, history; it is here that meaning may be found (constructed, encountered, and so on). This has already been shown in the following: psychological methods, learning, intelligence and thinking, biological psychology, sensation and perception, memory, development, personality, motivation, emotion, psychopathology, health, and dreams. The manifestation of meaning in experience, which we have observed in each of these domains, does not occur in vacant space: the domains are occupied by individuals and through the things with which these individuals are concerned. This occupation, which could be read as a noun and a verb, *is* consciousness. In this chapter I will show that the both/and unification of consciousness may be maintained despite centuries of their separation.

Christof Koch, a scientist who has daringly committed his life's work to its study, defines consciousness as follows:

> Without consciousness there is nothing. The only way you experience your body and the world of mountains and people, trees and dogs, stars and music is through your subjective experiences, thoughts, and memories. You act and move, see and hear, love and hate, remember the past and imagine the future. But ultimately, you only encounter the world in all of its manifestations via consciousness. And when consciousness ceases, this world ceases as well. (2012, 23)

Following Koch's lead, we will take for granted that the ambiguous interface between person and world is consciousness. In keeping with the dichotomy from Descartes onward, any transformation that seems to occur between world (*res extensa*) and mind (*res cogitans*), including no apparent transformation, has come about via consciousness. Consciousness is the world meeting the mind. It constitutes both. Indeed, their separation is only a consequence of their being conceived as independent from each other in the first place. In dualism, consciousness is *either* body *or* it is mind; nondualism suggests that consciousness is *both* body *and* mind. Thus, in the latter conception, consciousness must be considered as a minding body or an embodied mind.

However, as our project has maintained, Western metaphysics has been marked by the tendency to turn processes into things. As a thing, consciousness is conceptually limited to intellectuality or materiality. This is what has happened in contemporary consciousness theory. Consciousness has been caught between the Scylla of intellectual things and the Charybdis of material things.

Intellectualist Theories of Consciousness

At no point in an intellectualist account of consciousness may a material cause be cited. One is limited to intellectual things in its discussion. This can include thoughts, cognitions, feelings, and so on. Since the first few chapters of this book have examined the justification for the objective and subjective ways of thinking, we may skip right to the pithy definitions of the intellectualist theories of consciousness that Koch (2012) has provided in his survey of the state of the field. He notes that the intellectualist conception could be taken one of two ways: the first, a "commonsense definition," which may presumably be found on the street; and second, a "philosophical definition."

"A *commonsense definition*," Koch writes,

> equates consciousness with our inner, mental life. Consciousness begins when we wake up in the morning and continues throughout the day until we fall into a dreamless sleep. Consciousness is present when we dream but is exiled during deep sleep, anesthesia, and coma. And it is permanently gone in death. (2012, 33)

The lack of structure in this intellectualist conception of consciousness throws the sum of experience into a jumble of uncertainty. Consciousness simply becomes the arbitrary designation of all things mental. Also, the world of the unconscious—inattention, apperception, intuition, and dream states, is ignored completely. The unconscious must be considered if a theory of consciousness is to be developed in earnest—a belief shared by the reductionist theorists (Koch 2012) and the holistic theorists (Ey 1978), both of whom provide chapters on the subject (their co-consideration of the subject would make for an interesting analysis).

The intellectualists focus their investigation on the indivisible qualitative unit of experience: the *quale*. The *quale*, the intellectualists maintain, cannot be reduced to a material bit: it is that which resists such reduction. Merleau-Ponty beautifully defines the *quale* as follows: "a pellicle of being without thickness, a message at the same time indecipherable and evident, which one has or has not received, but of which, if one has received it, one knows all there is to know, and of which in the end there is nothing to say" (1968, 131). As such, the *quale* stands well beyond the reach of any objective scientist, but it also stands at a distance from anyone who wishes to understand it. It amounts to the argument that we can really never know about the *quale*. I agree with Merleau-Ponty that consciousness is too interesting and important to give up on so easily. After all, are we really prepared to accept the idea that something can tell us all there is to know?

In the second intellectualist conception, the *"philosophical definition,"* consciousness has been defined as the "what-it-feels-like-from-within perspective," that is, "the principal, irreducible trait of phenomenal awareness—to experience something, anything" (Koch 2012, 34). Since phenomenal awareness has been the method of exploring experiences throughout this book, its analysis will wait for the end of this chapter. Here we will be combining the analysis of the body along with an analysis of phenomenal awareness—recognizing that consciousness is physical and phenomenal and that we cannot understand one without also considering the other.

Materialist Theories of Consciousness

Like intellectualist accounts, materialist accounts of consciousness are similarly strict regarding what may be included; at no point in a materialist account are thoughts, feelings, intuitions, or perceptions consulted. Indeed, everything that is of use to understanding consciousness is understood to have material reality. This is the same as saying that it has mass (or takes up space for those of you who haven't seen the inside of a physics classroom in a while). Koch (2012), an unapologetic materialist, defines two types of materialist theories of consciousness: *behavioral* and *neural*; these, he admits, are the most useful for understanding consciousness (34).

For the *behaviorist theory*, consciousness amounts to "a checklist of actions or behaviors that would certify as conscious any organism that could do one or more of them" (33). The *behaviorist theory* answers all of the "simple problems" of consciousness—those that deal exclusively with physical and verbal behavior. This, however, does nothing to touch what has been termed the "hard problems" of consciousness—namely, why there is an accompanying "feeling" to conscious experience that exceeds such behavioral explanations. Taken without the "hard problem," human consciousness is no different from zombie consciousness (Chalmers 1995), that is, exact replicas of humans but no accompanying and presumably superfluous feelings.

And finally, defined with the care that betrays it as his favorite, Koch explains that a "*neuronal definition* of consciousness specifies the minimal physiological mechanisms required for any one conscious sensation" (2012, 34). Any experience, thought, feeling, intuition, or perception may be explained with specificity and concision provided the scientist knows where and with what instruments to look for it. Even the indefinable unit of phenomenology—the *quale*—is understood to be the "consequence of unknown laws" which, furthermore, materialist theorists make it their business to discover (28). With enough diligence and care, it is believed that the neural bases of consciousness—hard problem and all—may be discovered eventually.

Indeed, Koch is quite confident that soon consciousness will no longer be a mystery. He makes quick work dissipating the aforementioned enigma of ontological certainty that has plagued the intellectualists: "Humanity is not condemned to wander forever in an epistemological fog, knowing only the surface appearance of things but never their true nature. We can see something; and the longer we gaze, the better we comprehend" (2012, 12). And it is in this fashion that Koch has directed his focus inward, gazing long and hard so as to better understand that material thing called consciousness.

Unsurprisingly, the logical conclusion of consciousness, hard problem and all, precedes its actual investigation. The thesis of Koch's work runs as follows:

> The take-home message is that small chunks of the cerebral cortex are responsible for specific conscious content. This bit of the cortex endows phenomenal experience with the vividness of faces, that part provides the feeling of novelty, and the other one over there mediates the sound of voices. The linkage between cortical location and function is a hallmark of nervous systems. (Koch 2012, 62)

Once the cortical locations of all conscious phenomena (experience) have been cataloged, the science of consciousness will be complete, and the latter will be understood in its entirety—even down to the particular neuron. For instance, one may isolate the "Jennifer Aniston" neuron (Koch 2012); the "snake" neuron (Lauwereyns 2011); and the "45-degree angle neuron"—which is not to be confused with the "~45-degree angle neuron" (Watanabe 2010). The neural correlate of consciousness explanation runs something like this: if a possibly snake-shaped figure is detected amid a background of mushrooms, then the snake neuron will begin to fire. That is, the action potential of the neuron will increase through the process of coming into visual contact with a curved snakelike shape. If the shape resembles "snake" more than "stick," then the snake-neuron will fire at a frequency directly proportional to its resemblance to the former.

Assuming that the neural-correlate hypothesis has some legitimacy, what has really been discovered concerning consciousness? The perception of "snake" may now be identified with the activation of a particular cortical region. For example, seeing snake = firing of the "snake neuron." After all, this sort of statement—an identity statement—has been vilified by Wittgenstein (2001) as the most deplorable. For example, what is gained by explaining that Indiana Jones has a "paralyzing fear neuron" that fires in conjunction with the activation of the "snake neuron"? Have we thus made sense of Indy's ophidiophobia? This explanation provides no novel information regarding consciousness save a new vernacular for its discussion. (By the way, I trust that your "Indiana Jones" neuron has begun firing.)

Few doubt that naturalistic, reductive explanations for scientific phenomena are exceedingly popular. We can see the evidence of this in contemporary cognitive neuroscience literature. As is common with abstract representation, this system is not without its anomalies. Neural plasticity, or the capacity for cortical matter to develop and adapt, draws into question the end point of the "neural correlates of consciousness" hypothesis. If damage to the cortical area that is home to the "snake neuron" occurs, then perception of a snake—which has been identified with the firing of this neuron—would be impossible. But the phenomenon of cortical neuroplasticity challenges this assumption. Indeed, the plasticity of cortical matter allows for the absorption of the now lost "snake perception" task by another neuron. This would suggest that experience does not begin and end with particularized cortical matter of the brain. It also suggests that a neural correlate to a conscious state is an incomplete picture—that certainly much more is going on.

By historical standards, the hunt for neural correlates of consciousness is still in its infancy. As such, there is much agreement—and money—surrounding its laboratory investigation. Specializations in affective neuroscience, behavioral neuroscience, cognitive neuroscience, developmental neuroscience, and so on throughout the alphabet, have been erected. With this hunt is a shared collective assumption regarding the ontological allegiance to the neural bases of being. Note, however, that this mass proliferation is not without its dissidents.

For example, Alva Noë (2009) has argued against the neural correlates of consciousness on the grounds of its limitations. By restricting the investigation of consciousness to the human's biological composition, not only has one ignored its additional manifestations, but the investigation itself is proceeding backwards. That is, in developing a science of consciousness that includes the brain, one must not start with the brain and attempt to discern consciousness; *instead, one must begin with conscious experience and attempt to understand its relationship to the brain* (Noë 2009, 9).

Owen Flanagan (2007) also emphasizes the limit of scope that a neuronal definition of consciousness requires. He explains that it is the naturalist who "must accept the burden of showing how, *using only natural resources*, he proposes to explain phenomenal consciousness" (27, emphasis added). A more comprehensive investigation of consciousness should emphasize its interdisciplinarity, which would require input from art, science, technology, ethics, religion, and politics, that is, the sextet of which the space of meaning in the early twenty-first century is composed. The argument is one in favor of context: there is no consciousness that exists independently of the space of meaning in the early twenty-first century—that is, there is no consciousness that is independent of a person with a particular identity that lives in a particular culture, at a particular time, and so on.

Noë explains that in order to "understand consciousness in humans and animals,"

> we must look not inward, into the recesses of our insides; rather, we need to look to the ways in which each of us, as a whole animal, carries on the processes of living in and with and in response to the world around us. The subject of experience is not a bit of your body. You are not your brain. The brain, rather, is a part of what you are. (2009, 7)

He defends this claim first by illustrating that mental states are not reducible to brain states and secondly by demonstrating that consciousness often exceeds the boundaries of the skin—an argument that has been articulated by Merleau-Ponty (1962) and as far back as James (2007; who, incidentally, admits that the idea did not begin with him). Together, these examples suggest that a *neuronal definition* of consciousness is insufficient. Furthermore, they lay a rudimentary framework for an alternative and more comprehensive system of explanation.

YOU *ARE* CONSCIOUSNESS: CONSCIOUSNESS AS A PROCESS

The point that has been emphasized throughout this entire book has been that you are a process and not a thing. The same goes for consciousness. You are consciousness, and this is not a thing but a process. The multidimensional and complicated network of experiences is your conscious being. We have been examining this throughout a variety of topics. So what is it that we're looking at? What is consciousness?

Well, since it has already been argued that consciousness cannot be reduced to "mind" and cannot be reduced to "body," then it must include both. Merleau-Ponty calls consciousness "what the perceiving subject *is*" (1962, 97; emphasis added). He continues,

> To be consciousness or rather *to be an experience* is to hold inner communication with the world, the body and other people, to be with them instead of being beside them. . . . Let us then return to the "characteristics" of one's own body and resume the study of it where we left off. By doing so we shall trace the progress of modern psychology and thereby contrive along with it the return to experience. (97)

Exploring consciousness, it seems, has been the emphasis of *psychologizing* all along. Consciousness is the structure of our experience—it is how the world appears to each of us in a meaningful way. So let us take a moment to look at how consciousness can be a useful approach for understanding experience.

Two points are to be gleaned from the perceptual analyses supplied by Noë. He argues that you are not your brain and that consciousness can never be reduced to the brain. The brain is, however, an important part of consciousness, but this does not mean that we should look to the brain and nowhere else. Indeed, it is not enough to map out consciousness as a catalog of one-to-one "neuron-to-experience" correlations. Noë is not alone in this argument. Henri Ey shares a similar sentiment, adding that this doesn't mean we should stop asking about it:

> It is obvious to common sense, as it is to the most certain neuro-bio-psychological knowledge, that there is a relation between "consciousness" and the "brain." This, however, does not prevent certain thinkers from remaining closed off from this evidence, either by considering that "consciousness" does not exist (that it is a question of a superfluous concept or word) or by considering it to be a simple "function" (such as memory, intelligence, etc.). These negations of consciousness lead either to excluding it from the brain or to localizing it in one of its parts (the notion of "centers" of wakefulness). In both cases the problem of the relations between the brain and consciousness is distorted by the dualism that radically separates the brain and the mind or that juxtaposes in the cerebral space a function of consciousness as well as other functions having their seat in one or another part of the brain. (1978, xvii)

If consciousness is not located in the brain, then where must we look? Certainly *my* consciousness is limited to the boundaries of *my* body. Or is it? Throughout this book we have looked at our relationship to other things:

persons, stimuli, experience, and so on. Is it possible that consciousness extends into these things as well? Noë thinks so. He explains that consciousness extends beyond the boundaries of body:

> As our body schema changes, our relation to the world around us changes. How big a parking spot looks will be affected by the size of the vehicle you're driving; how steep a hill looks has been shown to vary, depending on the weight of the pack you are carrying. Indeed, it has been shown that the apparent size of the baseball varies in direct correspondence to the hitter's batting average. The better you are at hitting, the bigger the speeding balls you are trying to hit will seem! When you're slumping, the balls actually appear to shrink! (2009, 79)

Consciousness extends beyond the boundary of skin. Driving around and trying to park a new car is always difficult for a few weeks: it feels big and bulky or deceptively small. After you have driven it for a while, the front and rear bumpers become an extension of you. Indeed, after many months, you are able to squeeze your car into the smallest of spaces. This is why getting into a new car is awkward—because it has different dimensions from the one you have been occupying. The argument I am trying to make is that we experience the boundaries of ourselves outside of our body—we coordinate our cars as extensions of ourselves. This is why it takes some time practicing this.

Any sport that utilizes tools, instruments, or equipment will aptly demonstrate this as well—pick the one that works for you. In each example, consider how the body is incorporated into perception and where the sensory processes stop: handling a racquet used in tennis, racquetball, and badminton; catching a baseball bare-handed or with a glove; negotiating moguls with downhill skis, cross-country skis, or a snowboard; how much space does your body fill while playing table tennis? Tennis?

If the tendency for the body to absorb tools as extensions of itself is not yet apparent, consider making a minor change to any of the pieces of equipment mentioned. Decrease the tension on your tennis racquet by five pounds; raise the net by one inch; increase the grip size by a quarter of an inch. You will be met by an experience of the uncanny: the once-familiar tool will announce itself in its unfamiliarity (even though it still occupies the exact same physical space). Indeed, while in the midst of a heated volley, the tennis racquet becomes an extension of the singles player. Just like the height and speed of the player, the tennis racquet is a multiple of the amount of space a given player can cover on the court—it increases a player's court coverage. As soon as the racquet strings break, it becomes obtuse, unpredictable, and obstinate. For all other intents and purposes, the now-relieved tension should feel no different to the corpuscles on the palms of the player, but it nevertheless does; the change extends beyond the racquet strings. Suddenly her side of the court seems much larger—the area that a return may be successfully blocked back has been considerably reduced; the change extends beyond her body. And finally, the side opposite her seems much smaller and more difficult to hit and the player occupying it much more capable and intimidating; the change extends beyond her side of the court.

Consciousness cannot be reducible to the brain, but the brain *is* an important, even necessary component. Consciousness also cannot be reduced to the body, because it necessarily extends beyond the body and into the objects that we use. Its extension needn't even be limited to the things with which we are in contact. When somebody walks into the room, sometimes your affect changes: suddenly you become anxious, or excited, or upset. We find here that consciousness extends even into your social milieu. The more time you spend with someone, the more you pick up some of their mannerisms, habits, style of thinking, behavior, attitude, and so on.

Psychology is the study of consciousness: the complicated interconnection of body, mind, other persons, and world. By considering it in this manner, we remember that a simple explanation can never be sufficient for understanding our experience because experience is always more complicated and nuanced than this. We remember that experience is always personal and that, therefore, subjective data is equally as important as objective data: both are useful in better understanding persons and their experience—that is, psychology. And finally, we remember that a tremendous investment of our time and devoted attention is necessary for the careful consideration of our subject matter.

The consequence of practicing psychology in this way is the creation of a deeply meaningful, deeply insightful, and deeply personal study of persons. From this, we will more deeply understand ourselves and those we care about.

SUMMARY

This concluding chapter looked at consciousness. I argued that the entire book has been concerned with consciousness all along. Is consciousness a thing or a process? Your answer to this question will set you up for all sorts of assumptions regarding the psychology of a person.

We spent time looking at two theories of consciousness: the material theory assumes that consciousness is a thing that takes up time and space and can eventually be found (in the brain or stomach or some other part of the body). Along with this, one may reason that one's personality can be found in various bits and pieces of the nervous system or elsewhere. One could otherwise admit that consciousness is more complicated than this—existing, as it were, in the gaps between bits of matter and our experiences: that it is both embodied and the process of living. The latter is, of course, what we have been looking at all along.

PSYCHOLOGIZING IN ACTION

Washing the Dishes to Wash the Dishes

The Sutra of Mindfulness says, "When walking, the practitioner must be conscious that he is walking. When sitting, the practitioner must be conscious that he is sitting. When lying down, the practitioner must be conscious that he is lying down. . . . No matter what position one's body is in, the practitioner must be conscious of the position. Practicing thus, the practitioner lives in direct and constant mindfulness of the body" (7).

Thirty years ago, when I was still a novice at Tu Hieu Pagoda, washing the dishes was hardly a pleasant task. During the Season of Retreat when all the monks returned to the monastery, two novices had to do all the cooking and wash the dishes for sometimes well over one hundred monks. There was no soap. We had only ashes, rice husks, and coconut husks, and that was all. Cleaning such a high stack of bowls was a chore, especially during the winter when the water was freezing cold. Then you had to heat up a big pot of water before you could do any scrubbing. Nowadays one stands in a kitchen equipped with liquid soap, special scrubpads, and even running hot water which makes it all the more agreeable. It is easier to enjoy washing the dishes now. Anyone can wash them in a hurry, then sit down and enjoy a cup of tea afterwards. I can see a machine for washing clothes, although I wash my own things out by hand, but a dishwashing machine is going just a little too far!

While washing the dishes one should only be washing the dishes, which means that while washing the dishes one should be completely aware of the fact that one is washing the dishes. At first glance, that might seem a little silly: why put so much stress on a simple thing? But that's precisely the point. The fact that I am standing there and washing these bowls is a wondrous reality. I'm being completely myself, following my breath, conscious of my presence, and conscious of my thoughts and actions. There's no way I can be tossed around mindlessly like a bottle slapped here and there on the waves.

Source: Nhat Hanh 1975, 3–4.

Glossary

American Psychological Association (APA): The national professional organization for American psychologists.

anxiety: The body's autonomic response to a potentially catastrophic situation when the danger cannot be traced to the immediate environment.

applied psychology: The umbrella term for all areas of psychology that puts psychological research to work—in hospitals, schools, community organizations, and psychotherapy centers.

associationism: The assumption that there is a direct connection between two or more things. Associationism in learning is the knowledge that two ideas are connected, like "2 + 2" and "4," but with no understanding as to why. Associationism in the nervous system is the knowledge that a particular brain state is responsible for a particular thought or a behavior.

autonomic nervous system: A division of the central nervous system that regulates each of the unconscious processes that keep an organism alive such as heartbeat, breathing, digestion, and so on.

autonomy versus shame/doubt: The second of Erik Erikson's stages of psychosocial development, where a person struggles with the tension of understanding what she can and cannot do: she is proud of what she can do and ashamed of what she cannot.

banking methodology: Brazilian radical educator Paulo Freire's term for a poor quality of teaching, where the expert teacher fills the empty receptacles, students, with knowledge.

basic trust versus basic mistrust: The first of Erik Erikson's stages of psychosocial development, where a person struggles with the question of whether or not she belongs. Feelings of acceptance are important, particularly in the early stages of life.

behaviorism: The practice of psychology made famous by Ivan Pavlov, John Watson, and B. F. Skinner that begins and ends with behavior: everything is behavior, which means it can be seen, manipulated, and controlled.

biological psychology: The practice of psychology that emphasizes the role of the body, specifically the nervous system and brain.

blind spot: A blank spot in the visual field that corresponds to a section on the retina where there is a gap in rods and cones at the spot where the optic nerve leaves the eyeball.

classical conditioning: A form of behavioral modification where a previously neutral stimulus acquires the ability to elicit a behavior in an organism.

clinical psychology (applied): The practice of psychology that takes psychological research and applies it in the treatment and care of psychological disorders.

clinical psychology (experimental): Psychological research that is devoted to understanding the causes and testing the treatments of psychological disorders.

cognitive psychology: A branch of psychology that emphasizes the structure and content of thought processes in learning, speaking, reading, thinking, perceiving, and so on.

community psychology: An applied practice of psychology that designs, implements, develops, and evaluates community organizations.

conditioning: The learning or unlearning of behaviors through behavioral manipulation.

conscious (-ness): The behaviors, thoughts, and experiences of which one is aware and in which one is present.

continuous development: The recognition that development occurs in stages that do not have easily identifiable boundaries. While becoming a parent may have a definite starting date, it has usually begun many months (or even years) before and will continue many years after this date.

critical thinking: The kind of engaged thinking that recognizes that learning transforms the learner.

deficiency motivation: A form of motivation described by American psychologist Abraham Maslow, where a person believes that he lacks something and must find this in order to be made whole again. That is to say, the person is motivated by his deficiency.

developmental psychology: A psychological approach that focuses on the growth of a person's body, mind, relationships, cognition, sexuality, health, and so on.

discontinuous development: The recognition that development occurs in stages that can have easily identifiable boundaries. Retirement ushers in a new phase of late adulthood, and it can usually be expressed as the date at which one stopped one's normal routine of employment.

dissociate: The pathological and/or neurotic behavior wherein a person ceases to identify with himself or herself or his or her experience. Finding herself bored by a conversation, Janice dissociates and begins thinking about what she's doing that weekend; she continues to act like she's interested in the conversation but left it long ago.

ennervation: The role of the parasympathetic nervous system that leads to relaxation, digestion, rest, and other upbuilding mechanisms of the organism.

Erik Erikson's psychosocial stages of development: Basic trust versus basic mistrust; autonomy versus shame/doubt; initiative versus guilt; industry versus inferiority; identity versus role confusion; intimacy versus isolation; generativity versus stagnation; and ego integrity versus despair.

experimental psychology: The practice of psychology that carefully follows the axioms of the scientific method.

extrinsic motivation: Any motivation that comes from without an organism. It can come from the hope to impress another person or to satisfy someone's needs.

fear: The body's autonomic nervous system response to a potentially catastrophic situation where the danger can be traced to something immediate and present in the environment.

Gestalt psychology: The theory that perception occurs in wholes that are greater than the sum of parts. One does not see red waxy skin, a stem, and crunchy sweetness; these perceptions come together in the experience of an apple.

growth motivation: A form of motivation described by American psychologist Abraham Maslow, where a person's aim is self-actualization.

health psychology: An area of applied psychology that emphasizes health and well-being. Health psychologists often work very closely with physicians or in hospitals.

hierarchical: The vertical arrangement of people, groups, categories, or stages in terms of value or worth.

holism: The assumption that a person cannot be divided up in any way but must be taken as a whole person.

identification: The act of being aware of and in touch with one's behaviors, thoughts, and experiences. The opposite of dissociation.

identity versus role confusion: The fifth of Erik Erikson's psychosocial stages of development, where a person tries to distinguish her identity from the identities of those around her (e.g., her parents, friends, and mentors).

industry versus inferiority: The fourth of Erik Erikson's psychosocial stages of development, where a person learns what she does well and what she does poorly—deriving a great deal of satisfaction from doing something well and a sense of inadequacy when doing something poorly.

initiative versus guilt: The third of Erik Erikson's psychosocial stages of development that follows the cognitive development of imagination. In this stage, a person begins to imagine who or what she might be in the future, but along with this comes the ability to imagine what she could have done in the past. This can lead to the experience of guilt if there is a disparity between what she has done and what she wishes she had done.

intellectualist theory of consciousness: The theory that consciousness is entirely composed of thoughts.

intrinsic motivation: The motivation that comes from within an organism. Intrinsically motivated behaviors stem from a person's own desires, goals, and wishes.

introspection: The first documented method of psychological research that was practiced in the laboratories of Wilhelm Wundt and William James. Introspection is the process of describing the flow of consciousness in as detailed a manner as possible.

invigoration: The role of the sympathetic nervous system that initiates fight-or-flight responses in the organism.

materialist theory of consciousness: The theory that consciousness is entirely mediated or caused by brain states.

mechanism: The assumption that human behavior follows the rules of mechanical physics, where all causes and effects may be traced out along axes of time and space.

network of intentionalities: The relationship between past, present, and future that is always experienced in the present.

neural associationism: The assumption that a given brain state always corresponds to a given behavior or cognitive process with a one-to-one correspondence.

neuroplasticity: The capacity of the nervous system to change through experience.

normal: The assumption that the distribution of a sample or population follows a normal bell curve wherein the mean, median, and mode are identical.

objective knowledge: Knowledge whose verification is thought to occur through third-person means.

operant conditioning: The experimental manipulation of behavior through the systematic reinforcement of approximations of a given target behavior.

pathological: The consequences of the presence of a pathogen in an organism. A pathogen is anything that is a detriment to the flourishing of an organism. In clinical psychology, it is any behavior that does not fall within the normal distribution.

parasympathetic nervous system: The division of the autonomic nervous system that is responsible for the upbuilding mechanisms of an organism (rest, relaxation, digestion, and so on).

percept: How a stimulus appears to an observer.

perception: An individual's meaningful awareness and recognition of the world of experience (via sight, smell, hearing, tasting, and touching).

personality: The process of being a person with unique and individualized temperament, sociability, interests, and potential.

phenomenology: The systematic examination of the meaning of experience.

phenomenon: The experiential quality of an event.

positive psychology: The branch of psychology that is devoted to the right side of the normal distribution that focuses, for instance, on human flourishing, happiness, and quality of life.

positivism: The philosophical assumption that there is but a single world of scientific inquiry that scientists must carefully examine until everything has been discovered.

productive thinking: The term that Gestalt psychologist Max Wertheimer uses to describe the kind of learning where the learner participates in the process of problem solving.

prospection: Looking to the future from the vantage point of the present (experiencing the present upon the background of the future).

psychoanalysis: A school of psychology developed by Sigmund Freud that assumes that the meaning and significance of experience is rooted in the past.

psychologizing: Any practice of thinking like a psychologist. For this book, thinking like a psychologist is aimed at better understanding the experience of persons.

psychology: The systematically empirical study of human experience, including behavior and thoughts.

quality of life: A new dimension of medical wellness that emphasizes global life satisfaction and well-being.

recall: The ability to retrieve information from memory.

reproductive thinking: The term Gestalt psychologist Max Wertheimer uses to describe the style of learning wherein the learner simply repeats the knowledge that has been dispensed by the instructor.

response: This is *anything* an organism (or person) does that can be observed. It is particularly important to behavioral psychologists.

retrospection: Looking to the past from the vantage point of the present (experiencing the present upon the background of the past).

saccade: The unconscious procedure of eye movement; the rapid movements that the eyes take whenever they explore surroundings.

salutogenesis: The term that medical sociologist Aron Antonovsky uses to replace the typical medical-model term "pathogenesis." It describes healthful behavior or anything that helps an organism move toward health, well-being, and life satisfaction.

self-actualization: The term introduced by holistic biologist Kurt Goldstein to describe the natural processes of becoming an organism. It has been used by Maslow to describe the process of realizing one's ownmost potential.

self-concept actualization: This is the process of inventing a new personality (that is, a self-concept) for oneself and trying to approximate that as closely as possible. Self-concepts are typically shaped by moral strictures, social ideals, and efforts to impress others. Humanistic psychologists argue that this leads to psychological problems such as anxiety and depression.

sensation: The stimulation of any of the five senses of an organism that has been caused by an object in the environment.

sense of coherence: The quality in an organism that medical sociologist Aron Antonovsky argues is a best indicator of health, well-being, and recovery in a life-threatening situation. It includes comprehensibility, manageability, and meaningfulness.

social psychology: A branch of psychology that recognizes that persons are social beings. It examines the influence that a person's social context has on his or her behavior.

sports psychology: An area of applied psychology that focuses on an athlete's performance and well-being.

stimulus: *Anything* in the environment that produces a bodily or behavioral response.

stress: Any stimulus in the environment that exceeds an organism's ability to handle it. This leads to certain physiological breakdowns which, if allowed to recover, leads to the strengthening of the organism.

subjective knowledge: Knowledge that can be verified only through first-person experience.

sympathetic nervous system: The division of the autonomic nervous system responsible for organismic excitation, such as the fight, flight, and flee response.

two-factor theory of emotion: A theory positing that emotion is made up equally of physiological state and cognitive appraisal.

unconscious (-ness): The behaviors, thoughts, and experiences of which one is unaware and in which one is not present.

References

Allan, Robert, and Jeffrey Fisher, eds. 2011. *Heart and Mind: The Practice of Cardiac Psychology*. Washington, DC: American Psychological Association.

Antonovsky, Aron. 1987. *Unraveling the Mystery of Health: How People Manage Stress and Stay Well*. London: Jossey-Bass.

Baars, Bernard. 1986. *Cognitive Revolution in Psychology*. New York: Guilford.

Bach-y-Rita, Paul. 1967. "Sensory Plasticity: Applications to a Vision Substitution System." *Acta Neurologica Scandinavia* 43: 417–26.

———. 2005. "Emerging Concepts of Brain Function." *Journal of Integrative Neuoscience* 4 (2): 183–205.

Bendelow, Gillian. 2010. "The Mind/Body Problem in Contemporary Healthcare." In *Making Sense of Pain: Critical and Interdisciplinary Perspectives*, edited by Jane Fernandez, 21–30. Oxford: Inter-Disciplinary Press.

Bevan, William. 1991. "Contemporary Psychology: A Tour inside the Onion." *American Psychologist* 46 (5): 475–83.

Boss, Medard. 1963. *Psychoanalysis and Daseinsanalysis*. Translated by L. B. Lefebvre. New York: Basic.

Braidotti, Rosi. 2013. *The Posthuman*. Malden, MA: Polity.

Braud, William. 2001. "Experiencing Tears of Wonder-Joy: Seeing with the Heart's Eye." *Journal of Transpersonal Psychology* 33 (2): 99–111.

Bruner, Jerome S., and Leo Postman. 1949. "On the Perception of Incongruity: A Paradigm." *Journal of Personality* 18: 206–33.

Buber, Martin. 1958. *I and Thou*. New York: Scribner.

Canguilhem, Georges. 1991. *The Normal and the Pathological*. New York: Zone, 1991.

Chalmers, David. 1995. "Facing Up to the Problem of Consciousness." *Journal of Consciousness Studies* 2 (3): 200–219.

Cowley, Sue. 2010. *Getting the Buggers to Behave*. New York: Continuum.

Deresiewicz, William. 2014. *Excellent Sheep: The Miseducation of the American Elite and the Way to a Meaningful Life*. New York: Free Press.

DeRobertis, Eugene M. 2008. *Humanizing Child Development Theory: A Holistic Approach*. Lincoln, NE: iUniverse.

Dutton, Donald G., and Arthur P. Aron. 1974. "Some Evidence for Heightened Sexual Attraction under Conditions of High Anxiety." *Journal of Personality and Social Psychology* 30 (4): 510–17.

Erikson, Erik. 1990. *Identity and the Life-Cycle*. New York: Norton.

Erikson, Erik, and Joan Erikson. 1998. *The Life-Cycle Completed*. New York: Norton.

Ey, Henri. 1978. *Consciousness: A Phenomenological Study of Being Conscious and Becoming Conscious.* Translated by J. H. Flodstrom. Bloomington: Indiana University Press.

Flanagan, Owen. 2007. *The Really Hard Problem.* Cambridge, MA: MIT Press.

Frankl, Viktor. 2006. *Man's Search for Meaning.* Boston: Beacon.

Freire, Paulo. 2012a. *Education for Critical Consciousness.* New York: Continuum.

———. 2012b. *Pedagogy of the Oppressed.* Translated by M. B. Ramos. New York: Continuum.

Fromm, Erich. 1990. *The Sane Society.* New York: Henry Holt, 1990.

Gardner, Howard. 1983. "Artistic Intelligences." *Art Education* 36 (2): 47–49.

Gendlin, Eugene. 1978. *Focusing.* New York: Bantam.

Giorgi, Amedeo. 2009. *The Descriptive Phenomenological Method in Psychology: A Modified Husserlian Approach.* Pittsburgh: Duquesne University Press.

Goldstein, Kurt. 1966. *Human Nature in Light of Psychopathology.* New York: Schocken.

———. (1934) 1995. *The Organism: A Holistic Approach to Biology Derived from Pathological Data in Man.* New York: Zone.

Griggs, Richard A., and Montserrat C. Mitchell. 2002. "In Search of Introductory Psychology's Classic Core Vocabulary." *Teaching of Psychology* 29 (2): 144–47.

Grusin, Richard. 2015. *The Nonhuman Turn.* Minneapolis: Minnesota University Press.

Halling, Steen. 1975. "Implications of Emmanuel Levinas' *Totality and Infinity* for Therapy." In *Duquesne Studies in Phenomenological Psychology*, edited by A. Giorgi, C. T. Fischer, and E. L. Murray. Pittsburgh: Duquesne University Press.

Harlow, Harry F. 1958. "The Nature of Love." *American Psychologist* 13: 573–685.

Harper, Steven. 1995. "The Way of the Wilderness." In *Ecopsychology: Restoring the Earth, Healing the Mind*, edited by T. Roszak, M. E. Gomes, and A. D. Kanner, 183–200. San Francisco: Sierra Club.

Heidegger, Martin. 2008. *Being and Time.* Translated by J. Macquarie and E. Robinson. New York: Harper & Row.

Horney, Karen. 1950. *Neurosis and Human Growth.* New York: Norton.

Horwicz, Adolf. 1872. *Psychologische Analyzen auf Physiologischer Grundlage.* Halle: C. E. M. Pfeffer.

Husserl, Edmund. 1970. *The Crisis of European Sciences and Transcendental Phenomenology.* Translated by D. Carr. Evanston, IL: Northwestern University Press.

James, William. 2007. *Principles of Psychology.* 2 vols. New York: Cosimo Classics.

Kaelin, Eugene F. 1964. "Being in the Body." In *Sport and the Body: A Philosophical Symposium*, edited by E. W. Gerber, 165–74. Philadelphia: Lea and Febiger.

Kanizsa, Gaetano. 1979. *Organization in Vision.* New York: Praeger.

Keen, Ernest. 1982. *A Primer in Phenomenological Psychology.* Lanham, MD: University Press of America.

Kelly, Edward F., Emily W. Kelly, Adam Crabtree, Alan Gould, Michael Grosso, and Bruce Greyson. 2007. *Irreducible Mind: Toward a Psychology of the 21st Century.* Lanham, MD: Rowman & Littlefield.

Kierkegaard, Søren. 1989. *The Sickness unto Death.* New York: Penguin Classics.

Knowles, Malcolm. 1989. *Making of an Adult Educator.* San Francisco: Jossey-Bass.

Knowles, Richard T. 1986. *Human Development and Human Possibility: Erikson in the Light of Heidegger.* Lanham, MD: University Press of America.

Koch, Christof. 2012. *Consciousness: Confessions of a Romantic Reductionist.* Cambridge, MA: MIT Press.

Kohn, Alfie. 1993. *Punished by Rewards: The Trouble with Gold Stars, Incentive Plans, A's, Praise, and Other Bribes.* New York: Houghton Mifflin.

Kuhn, Thomas. 2012. *Structure of Scientific Revolutions.* Chicago: University of Chicago Press.

Laing, R. D. 1990. *The Divided Self: An Existential Study in Sanity and Madness.* New York: Penguin.

Lashley, Karl. 1930. "Basic Neural Mechanism in Behavior." *Psychological Review* 37: 1–24.

Lauwereyns, Jan. 2011. *The Anatomy of Bias: How Neural Circuits Weigh the Options.* Cambridge, MA: MIT Press.

Levinson, Daniel. 1986. *The Seasons of a Man's Life*. New York: Ballantine.
———. 1996. *The Seasons of a Woman's Life*. New York: Ballantine.
Lindeman, Eduard C. 1926. *The Meaning of Adult Education*. New York: New Republic.
Loftus, Elizabeth F., and J. C. Palmer. 1974. "Reconstruction of Automobile Destruction: An Example of the Interaction between Language and Memory." *Journal of Verbal Learning and Verbal Behavior* 13: 585–89.
Loftus, Elizabeth F., and John E. Pickrell. 1995. "The Formation of False Memories." *Psychiatric Annals* 2 (5): 720–25.
Maslow, Abraham H. 1966. *The Psychology of Science: A Reconnaissance*. New York: Gateway.
———. 1968. *Toward a Psychology of Being*. 2nd ed. New York: Van Nostrand.
May, Rollo. 1977. *The Meaning of Anxiety*. New York: Norton.
McGraw, K. O. 1978. "The Detrimental Effects of Rewards on Performance: A Literature Review and Prediction Model." In *The Hidden Costs of Reward: New Perspectives on the Psychology of Human Motivation*, edited by M. A. Lepper and D. Greene. Hillsdale, NJ: Erlbaum.
Merleau-Ponty, Maurice. (1945) 1962. *Phenomenology of Perception*. Translated by C. Smith. New York: Humanities Press.
———. 1968. *Visible and the Invisible*. Edited by Claude Lefort. Translated by Alphonso Lingis. Evanston, IL: Northwestern University Press.
———. 2008. *The World of Perception*. Translated by Oliver Davis. Abingdon, UK: Routledge Classics.
Moustakas, Clark. 1972. *The Alive and Growing Teacher*. New York: Ballantine.
Nhat Hanh, Thich. 1975. *The Miracle of Mindfulness: An Introduction to the Practice of Meditation*. Boston: Beacon.
Noë, Alva. 2009. *Out of Our Heads: Why You Are Not Your Brain, and Other Lessons from the Biology of Consciousness*. New York: Hill and Wang.
Perls, Fritz S. 1969. *Ego, Hunger, and Aggression*. New York: Random House.
———. 1972. *In and Out the Garbage Pail*. New York: Bantam.
———. 1974. *Gestalt Therapy Verbatim*. New York: Bantam.
Proust, Marcel. 1982. *Rememberance of Things Past*. Vol. 1: *Swann's Way* and *Within a Budding Grove*. Translated by C. K. S. Moncrieff and T. Kilmartin. New York: Vintage.
Rilke, Rainer Maria. 2002. *Letters on Cézanne*. Translated by Joel Agee. New York: North Point.
Rogers, Carl. 1961. *On Becoming a Person*. New York: Houghton Mifflin.
———. 1969. *Freedom to Learn*. Columbus, OH: Merrill.
———. 1980. *A Way of Being*. New York: Houghton Mifflin.
Satel, Sally, and Scott O. Lilienfeld. 2013. *Brainwashed: The Seductive Appeal of Mindless Neuroscience*. New York: Basic.
Schacter, Stanley, and Jerome Singer. 1962. "Cognitive, Social, and Physiological Determinants of Emotional State." *Psychological Review* 69: 379–99.
Seligman, Martin. 2006. *Learned Optimism: How to Change Your Mind and Your Life*. New York: Vintage.
Siegel, Daniel. 2009. "The Power of Mindsight." Presentation at TEDx Blue, New York, October 18.
———. 2012. *Pocket Guide to Interpersonal Neurobiology: An Integrative Handbook of the Mind*. New York: Norton.
Skinner, Burrhus F. 1955. "The Science of Learning and the Art of Teaching." In *Current Trends in Psychology and the Behavioral Sciences*, edited by John T. Wilson, C. S. Ford, B. F. Skinner, G. Bergmann, F. A. Beach, and K. W. Pribram, 38–58. Pittsburgh: University of Pittsburgh Press.
———. 1971. *Beyond Freedom and Dignity*. New York: Bantam.
Spring, Joel. 2011. *The American School: A Global Context from the Puritans to the Obama Era*. 8th ed. New York: McGraw Hill.
Stanovich, Keith. 2012. *How to Think Straight about Psychology*. 10th ed. Edinburgh: Pearson.

Toulmin, Stephen, and David E. Leary. 1985. "The Cult of Empiricism in Psychology, and Beyond." In *A Century of Psychology as a Science*, edited by Sigmund Koch and David Leary, 594–617. New York: McGraw-Hill.

Van den Berg, J. H. 1972. *Different Existence: Principles of Phenomenological Psychopathology*. Pittsburgh: Duquesne University Press.

Vaughan, E. D. 1977. "Misconceptions about Psychology among Introductory Psychology Students." *Teaching of Psychology* 4: 138–41.

Watanabe, Tsuneo. 2010. "Metascientific Foundations for Pluralism in Psychology." *New Ideas in Psychology* 28: 253–62.

Watson, John. (1930) 1962. *Behaviorism*. Rev. ed. Chicago: University of Chicago Press. Reprint, Chicago: University of Chicago Press.

Watson, John, and Rosalie Rayner. 1920. "Conditioned Emotional Responses." *Journal of Experimental Psychology* 3 (1): 1–14.

Weissberg, Robert. 2010. *Bad Students, Not Bad Schools*. Livingston, NJ: Transaction.

Wertheimer, Max. 1938. "Laws of Organization in Perceptual Forms." In *A Source Book of Gestalt Psychology*, edited and translated by W. Ellis, 71–88. London: Routledge and Kegan Paul. Available at *Classics in the History of Psychology*. http://psychclassics.yorku.ca/Wertheimer/Forms/forms.htm.

———. 1959. *Productive Thinking*. New York: Harper.

Wertz, Frederick J. 2011. "The Qualitative Revolution and Psychology: Science, Politics, and Ethics." *Humanistic Psychologist* 39 (2): 77–104.

Wertz, Frederick J., Kathy Charmaz, Linda M. McMullen, Ruthellen Josselson, Rosemarie Anderson, and Emalinda McSpadden. 2011. *Five Ways of Doing Qualitative Analysis: Phenomenological Psychology, Grounded Theory, Discourse Analysis, Narrative Research, and Intuitive Inquiry*. New York: Guilford.

Whitehead, Alfred N. 1957. *Aims of Education and Other Essays*. New York: Free Press.

Wittgenstein, Ludwig. 2001. *Tractatus Logico-philosophicus*. New York: Routledge Classics.

Wolfe, Cary. 2009. *What Is Posthumanism?* Minneapolis: Minnesota University Press.

Yalom, Irvin D. 1980. *Existential Psychotherapy*. New York: Basic.

Index

Lightning Source UK Ltd.
Milton Keynes UK
UKHW01f0709180618
324228UK00021B/1000/P